INTERNET MARKETING
START-to-FINISH

Catherine Juon, Dunrie Greiling & Catherine Buerkle

800 East 96th Street,
Indianapolis, Indiana 46240 USA

Internet Marketing Start to Finish

Copyright © 2012 by Que Publishing

ISBN-13: 978-0-7897-4789-1
ISBN-10: 0-7897-4789-8

Printed in the United States of America

First Printing: August 2011

Library of Congress Cataloging-in-Publication data is on file.

Trademarks

Warning and Disclaimer

Bulk Sales

Que Publishing offers excellent discounts on this book when ordered in quantity for bulk purchases or special sales. For more information, please contact

U.S. Corporate and Government Sales
1-800-382-3419
corpsales@pearsontechgroup.com

For sales outside the United States, please contact

International Sales
international@pearson.com

Associate Publisher
Mark Taub

Acquisitions Editor
Trina MacDonald

Development Editor
Sheri Cain

Technical Editors
Derek Overbey
Ted Prodromou

Managing Editor
Sandra Schroeder

Project Editor
Seth Kerney

Copy Editor
Keith Cline

Proofreader
Debbie Williams

Indexer
Erika Millen

Publishing Coordinator
Olivia Basegio

Interior Designer
Anne Jones

Cover Designer
Anne Jones

Page Layout
Trina Wurst

CONTENTS AT A GLANCE

Preface

I Building a Formula For Success

    1 Why Online Sales Matter   1

    2 What an Online Sales Engine Can Do   21

    3 Building a Metrics-Driven Practice   43

    4 Breaking Down Silos to Get the Metrics You Need   69

II Building the Engine

    5 The Audience Is Listening (What Will You Say?)   93

    6 Putting It All Together and Selling Online   117

    7 Making Websites That Work   147

    8 It's All About Visibility   177

III Running the Engine

    9 Running the Feedback Loop   217

    10 Special Considerations for International Organizations   239

    Appendix TropiCo's State of the Web Report   263

TABLE OF CONTENTS

I Building a Formula For Success

1 Why Online Sales Matter 1

  First Things First 2

    Internet Research Equals Internet Sales 2

    Advantages of Internet Marketing 3

  The Bird's Eye View 4

    Standard Practice 4

    Your Online Sales Engine 5

  Back to Basics: Business Strategy 101 7

    The Customer Is King 7

    Understanding the Buying Process 7

    Remove Organizational Silos 8

    Get the Most Bang for Your Buck 8

    Find Out What's Working 9

  Lessons We've Learned 9

    Keywords, Keywords, Keywords 9

    Paid Search Mismatches 10

    Get the Fundamentals Right First 11

    Bigger Is Better 11

    Content and Inlinks 12

    Websites Are for Spiders and People 12

    Small Business Safety 12

    Budget for Marketing the Website Itself 13

  Learn by Example 14

    B2C Example: Happy Puppy 14

    B2B Example: TropiCo 15

  Online Sales Engine Success Stories 15

    Case Study: Moving into New Global Markets 16

    Case Study: Manufacturing Company Improves Sales . . . 16

    Case Study: Large Childcare Provider Increases
      Web Conversions 17

    Case Study: Major Software Company Grows Sales 17

  Summary 19

2   What an Online Sales Engine Can Do **21**

What Is an Online Sales Engine? 22

Why Adopt the Online Sales Engine? 22

The Online Sales Engine Components 23

The Components Form a Process 25

Avoid "Dangerous Data" Nightmares 25

Case Study: Identifying Junk Leads 26

The Customer-Driven Process 26

1. Define Your Goals 27

2. Configure Tracking and Set Goals for Metrics 28

3. Conduct Research and Improve the User Experience ... 30

4. Sell Online 32

5. Manage Your Website 34

6. Increase Visibility with SEO and Paid Search 34

7. Revisit the Metrics 38

Close the Loop with Metrics 38

Maintain Your Analytics 39

The ROI-Driven Process 39

Summary 40

3   Building a Metrics-Driven Practice **43**

The New Era of Website Metrics 44

Which Metrics Matter Most? 44

Influencing Leads and Revenue 44

The Conversion Funnel 45

Lead-Generation Businesses 46

E-Commerce Businesses 47

Choosing a Contact Method 47

What to Measure 49

SEO Key Performance Indicators 50

Paid Search KPIs 53

Use Business Analysis to Define Your KPI
Benchmarks and Goals 55

When to Measure Matters 56

Integrating Web KPIs into BusinessDecision Making 58

Case Study: Landing Pages with Custom 800 Numbers ... 59

Web to Lead to CRM Analysis: Close That Loop! 60

The Impact of Internet Marketing on Sales 60

Case Study: Reviewing Customer Conversion Data
in Salesforce 62

Moving Data into Salesforce 63

KPI Reporting on Leads and Sales 64

Quantity Versus Quality 64

Projections for Future Gain Based onPast Performance 65

Summary 67

4   Breaking Down Silos to Get the Metrics You Need **69**

Do More Than Gather Data: Build a Team 70

Web Analytics: Types, Purpose, Popular Tools for Each 70

Logfile Versus Script-Based Analytics Tracking 71

Click Analytics 81

Call Tracking: Why It's Essential and How to Select
Granularity Needed 82

Measuring If the Phone Rings (Memory Doesn't Count) 82

Selecting the Granularity Needed 83

Lead Management: SFA/CRM Integration 84

CRM Products 84

CRM Basics 85

Next Steps for Follow-Up 86

Next Steps for Analysis: Quantifying "Assists"
Through Lead Attribution 88

A Case Study in Lead Management 90

Summary 91

5   The Audience Is Listening (What Will You Say?) **93**

Where Do You Start? 94

Start with the Tasks and Goals of Your Potential Audiences ... 94

Other Important Audiences 95

Listen to and Watch Your Audience 97

Develop Website Personas 100

Persona and Scenario Development Process 101

Sample Personas 102

Adapt Your Website to Your Personas' Needs 105

Next Steps: Gather More Feedback 105

Consider Their Path to Your Content 105

Case Study: Persona-Driven Redesign 107

Speak Your Audience's Language: The Real SEO 109

Do Your Keyword Research 109

Evaluate Your Keyphrases in the Context of the Entire
Word Market 110

Case Study: Word Market Focuses Tutor Time on the
Right Descriptors 113

Summary 114

6   Putting It All Together and Selling Online **117**

Designing Your Website 118

Incorporating Information Architecture Techniques 118

Experiment with an Unconventional User-Driven
Architecture: McKinley.com 119

The Information Architecture Process 120

Investigate and Inform Your Information Architecture .. 122

Develop a Website Skeleton or Wireframe 122

Test the Information Architecture 126

Graphic Design Comes Later 127

A Process Overview 127

Information Architecture Case Study 128

User Personas and Keyword Analysis 128

High-Level Information Architecture 128

Page Templates with Content Specified 131

How the Website Mission Can Affect Information
Architecture 133

Designing Your Landing Pages 133

Landing Page Basics 134

The Design Cycle 138

Getting More Granular: When Do You Need a New
Landing Page? 138

Long-Term Maintenance Is Critical 139

Optimizing Your Landing Pages 140

When to Optimize 141

Use Your User Research 142

How to Measure 143

You Have Data. Now What? 145

Summary 145

7   Making Websites That Work 147

Improving User Experience and Conversion Rates 148

The Basics: What to Fix Before Testing 149

Follow Web Conventions 149

On Key Pages: Form Optimization Basics 150

Template-Level: Automated Attention Analysis 151

On Every Page 152

Beyond Best Practices: User Research 155

Where Do Surveys Fit In? 155

Quantitative User Research: Form Analytics,
and A/B Testing 156

Qualitative User Analysis: Observations,
Usability Tests 158

UX Checklist 161

Website Planning and Maintenance 162

Plan for Graceful Failure 162

Website Maintenance Tasks 165

Planning a Website Refresh or Relaunch 168

Case Study: Poor SEO Execution Hurts 173

Summary 175

8   It's All About Visibility 177

Who Sees What and How 178

What Search Engine Spiders See 178

What Search Engine Visitors See 179

Writing Web Content for Users and Spiders:
On-Site Optimization 181

Page-Level SEO Best Practices 181

Page-Level SEO Guide: An Example 183

Case Study: Call It What It Is to Increase Findability 185

Special Considerations: Blogging for SEO Benefit 185

Blogging Best Practices 186

Get Out of Your Own Way: Make Sure Your
    Content Is Findable 187

    A Digression into the Guts of Web Code 188

    Watch Your Web Technologies 190

    Take Advantage of Universal Search: Tag Your Media
        Files with Target Keywords 190

    Have Fun with Widgets, but Avoid Putting Interesting
        and Relevant Content Inside Frames 192

    Don't Spread Yourself Too Thin: Consolidate Your
        Content Power on Your Main Domain 194

    Crawler Control: Speak to Your Spiders 194

Increase Your Findability via Link Building 200

    How to Approach Website Owners for Links 201

Increase Your Findability: Claim and Maintain Your
    Local Business Listings 202

    Monitoring, Responding to, and Encouraging
        Reviews Online 203

Advanced Visibility Strategies: Going Social 204

Extending Your Reach with Paid Search Advertising 205

    Search Engines as Paid Search Vendors 206

    Effective Paid Search Management 206

    Define Your Market 208

    Qualify Your Market with Specific Ad Copy 209

    Convert Your Visitors into Customers 211

    Revisit, Refine, and Refresh Your Campaigns 211

Advanced Visibility Strategies: Display Advertising 212

    The Best Ways to Target Display Ads 214

Summary 215

9 Running the Feedback Loop **217**

Revisiting the Project Goals 218

    Your Goals Will Change as Your Process Matures 218

Analyzing Across the Online Sales Engine 220

    Pulling Data from Various Silos 221

    Common Data Analysis Pitfalls 223

Proving ROI 226

    What to Consider When Calculating ROI 226

    When ROI Doesn't Matter 228

How to Set Projections for Future Performance 229

How to Set Projections for Future Performance 229

Boardroom-Ready Reporting 234

Provide Context for the Numbers 234

Boardroom Reporting Best Practices 236

Summary 237

10   Special Considerations for International Organizations ... 239

Going Global in the New World Order 240

The Return of the Silo Problem 240

Triage for International Disorientation 240

The Impact of Language, Culture, and Transparency 241

Working with Translators and Localization Experts 241

Case Study: Spidering to Keep All Localized Websites
Up-to-Date 246

Basic Mechanics for a Global Metrics-Driven Practice .. 246

Use a Single Website Analytics Program Globally 247

Set Your Web Analytics to Track Across Top-Level
Domains 247

Unify Your CRM or SFA Process 248

Talk to Each Other! 248

Basic Mechanics for Global Organic Search Visibility ... 250

Focus on the Correct Search Engine 250

Tune Your Social Strategy to the Right Channel 252

Mind Your Website Top-Level Domains 252

Basic Mechanics for Global Paid Search Configuration ... 253

Create Regional Campaigns 253

Set Geographic Targets 254

Use the Right Language 254

Working with Time Zones 256

Basic Mechanics for Global Usability 258

Before You Translate: Character Set Issues 258

Working with Forms 258

Working with Other Data 259

A Note for E-Commerce Websites 259

Making It Usable 260

Summary 262

Appendix TropiCo's State of the Web Report   **263**

Table of Contents 264

Executive Summary 264

  About Part I 264

  About Part II 265

  About Part III 265

Part I. The Year in Review: The Data 265

  General Traffic Trends 265

  Geographic Distribution 266

  Traffic Sources 267

  Quarterly Leads Trends 268

Part II. How It Happened 269

  Paid Search (Setup, Management, and Expansion) 270

  Search Engine Optimization 274

  Usability 275

  Strategy, Analysis, and Reporting 276

  Local Search 278

  Referral Media 279

Part III. Looking Forward to 2012 280

  Localize the Online User Experience 280

  Engagement: Move Online Strategy Toward Interactive Brand Experience 281

  Maintain Momentum from FY 2011 281

About the Authors

Catherine Juon is co-founder and Catalyst of Pure Visibility, passionately leading the charge for companies to grow via the Internet. Catherine traces her love of the Internet back to Poland, where in 1991 she began teaching at the University of Warsaw. There, she experienced the power of the Internet to transform international communication, from weeks to seconds, in a way we now take for granted.

Catherine believes a similar transformation is taking place in commerce—and dubbed the system of harnessing the power of the Internet for commerce Your Online Sales Engine. Based on the experience of helping companies from the corner store to global enterprises, Catherine and her company teach companies how to benefit from the web by sharing the foundations you'll learn in this book.

Dunrie Greiling is Pure Visibility's Director of Happiness and its lead Relationship Manager, responsible for national and global online sales engine engagements for Pure Visibility clients. Dunrie often draws on the hypothesis testing and data analysis skills she learned during her doctoral dissertation in Ecology and Evolutionary Biology at the University of Michigan and her undergraduate degree in that field from Princeton University.

She left academics in 2000 and has since managed software design, web design and development, and search marketing projects. She supplemented her lessons learned with training and certification as a Project Management Professional by the Project Management Institute.

Catherine Buerkle is an independent User Experience and Technical Communication Consultant currently living in Germany. She has extensive experience defining and writing interactive content for a broad array of industries and applications (both web based and offline).

Before moving to Germany and under her maiden name of Titta, Catherine founded and ran a technical communication and user-experience consulting practice that won several international and best-of-show awards. Based on both the wide variety of her consulting experiences and her extensive time spent in the IT world, she has become a strong user advocate and an evangelist for applying practical and sound methodologies.

Dedications

I dedicate this book to my family. To my husband, Dave Zerweck, and our children, Christian and Phillip, and the blessings you bring to my life. And to my parents, Jim and Pat; and in-laws, Herman and Sue, who taught me a great deal about entrepreneurship and so much more. Your faith in me and in the business is invaluable. Thank you.

—Catherine Juon

I dedicate this book to my mentor, Beverly Rathcke, 1945–2011. Your logical and scientific rigor and your editing prowess encouraged my growth as a thinker and a writer. Your friendship and the community of Ann Arbor gourmet potluck enthusiasts you fostered continue to enrich my life. Thank you.

—Dunrie Greiling

I dedicate this book to my family. First, to my very supportive husband, Martin, and our young children, Nicholas and Stephanie (who try to understand why Mommy has meetings and deadlines in different time zones instead of traditional work like other moms). And last but not least to my parents, Peter and Judy, who have always supported me with love, no matter what unusual turn my life has taken. Thank you.

—Catherine Buerkle

Acknowledgments

It is with deep gratitude that we thank the contributors to this book. In particular, we thank our clients and the Pure Visibility team, who have worked diligently together to test and prove what works (and sometimes, what didn't). Together, your collective questions and business challenges led us to develop Your Online Sales Engine to help guide businesses through the sometimes mystifying process of getting visible in the search engines—and turning that visibility into new business!

Special gratitude to the following people who helped this book come to life:

- Bo Burlingham of *Inc.* magazine, whose infectious enthusiasm for writing and for business inspired the sharing of our lessons learned in Internet marketing and online sales. Your encouragement was priceless, thank you!

- Bill Wagner of SRT Solutions for your more-than-just-an-introduction to our publisher. We were warmly welcomed by the Pearson team on our very first call. Thank you.

- The fabulous technical editors and crew at Pearson: Trina MacDonald, Olivia Basegio, and Sheri Cain—especially Trina! A crew of first-time book authors couldn't have asked for a more helpful and supportive team! We are amazed at the speed at which things came together on so many levels and appreciate all of your efforts.

- Great visual artists can take a concept (even a fuzzy one) and turn it into a picture that clarifies and adds to the final product. We're blessed to have assistance from visual interpreter Dave Brenner in some of the illustrations herein.

- Our industry reviewers, Drew Bennett, Ted Prodromou, Derek Overbey, and Erin Brennan, who spent countless hours combing through our thoughts and early drafts, commenting and encouraging us to bring out the best in the final draft.

- Andy King, for introducing us to the world of book publishing, and for partnering with us from the early days in our search marketing careers.

- And to the greater business community of Ann Arbor and southeast Michigan, which nurtures young businesses with a wonderful web of support and provides the intellectual hub that brings together the great minds that produce game-changing ideas!

We Want to Hear from You!

As the reader of this book, you are our most important critic and commentator. We value your opinion and want to know what we're doing right, what we could do better, what areas you'd like to see us publish in, and any other words of wisdom you're willing to pass our way.

As Editor in Chief for Que Publishing, I welcome your comments. You can email or write me directly to let me know what you did or didn't like about this book—as well as what we can do to make our books better.

Please note that I cannot help you with technical problems related to the topic of this book. We do have a User Services group, however, where I will forward specific technical questions related to the book.

When you write, please be sure to include this book's title and author as well as your name, email address, and phone number. I will carefully review your comments and share them with the author and editors who worked on the book.

Email: feedback@quepublishing.com

Mail: Greg Weigand
           Editor in Chief
           Que Publishing
           800 East 96th Street
           Indianapolis, IN 46240 USA

For more information about this book or another Que Publishing title, visit our website at www.quepublishing.com. Type the ISBN (excluding hyphens) or the title of a book in the Search field to find the page you're looking for.

PREFACE

Ever wonder how to improve the effectiveness of your website in attracting new prospects? Or how to create more online sales? You're in good company; those are questions we hear every day! The constant evolution of Internet marketing, along with its increasing complexity, makes it difficult for even seasoned marketing executives to know where to invest for the best results.

The good news is, like all else in life, the more the Internet changes, the more it stays the same. By focusing on a few basic concepts, and expanding around those, you can succeed in building an online presence to help grow your business.

How This Book Is Organized

As Figure P.1 shows, we organized this book to cover the primary areas of Internet marketing that combine to create what we call an online sales engine. The beauty of this iterative process is that the end game is a measurable, repeatable sales system you can rely on to generate revenue for your business.

Figure P.1 *The five main components of Your Online Sales Engine®.*

Chapter 2, "What an Online Sales Engine Can Do," describes in greater detail how this book is organized, chapter by chapter.

You can also look at the online sales engine in terms of the three parts of this book:

- **Part I: Building a Formula for Success**, which explains what the online sales engine is and helps you define your measurement criteria.

  Metrics That Matter

- **Part II: Building the Engine**, which covers the nuts and bolts such as improving the user experience, landing pages, search engine optimization (SEO), paid search, and so on

  Speak to Your Audience

  Websites That Work

  Make Your Message Visible

  Selling Online

- **Part III: Running the Engine**, which walks you through closing the feedback loop and analyzing your results, as well as international considerations.

  Metrics That Matter (revisited)

How to Use This Book

No special expertise is required to use this book, only a fundamental understanding of your business model. That said, there are a number of ways you could approach getting the most out of the information in this book.

More details about applying the methodology outlined in this book appear in Chapter 2.

If You Want to Go Step by Step

Admittedly, figuring out where to start improving your online marketing can be a bit of a chicken-or-egg situation. However, two things in particular stand out as we coach businesses through this system.

You'll need

- **To make your message visible** to get more visitors to your website

- **A website that works** to turn more of those visitors into customers

Getting Visible   Given that we started out in the SEO business, our tendency is to start with visibility. And for good reason: Unless you have invested heavily in branding or advertising, you're going to need visibility to get more customers. (And even if you have made those investments, building strong online visibility can create competitive advantage.)

There are many myths and misunderstanding about how visibility works, which we sort through for you in Chapter 8, "It's All About Visibility." We'll also describe the most popular methods for improving visibility and offer direction on which methods suit different types of businesses.

Improving Your Website   After you've improved visibility and started generating more traffic to your website, it's time to make sure as many of those prospects as possible flow through your website and turn into a sale or a lead for your sales team.

Surprisingly small changes to your website can make a big impact on your results, which we discuss in Chapter 7, "Making Websites That Work," and Chapter 5, "The Audience Is Listening (What Will You Say?)."

Measuring the Impact   Then, to understand the impact of your changes, you'll need to be measuring key indicators with an understanding of how to evaluate the data (how much traffic you need to make a statistically valid decision and so on).

We give you an overview of what to measure in Chapter 3, "Building a Metrics-Driven Practice," and help you collect the data you need in Chapter 4, "Breaking Down Silos to Get the Metrics You Need." Later, we assemble all the pieces in Chapter 9, "Running the Feedback Loop," where you learn how to take the data you've collected and turn it into recommendations on which you can act immediately.

For Help in Specific Areas

We deliberately designed this book so that chapters stand alone. Feel free to jump in at any point to get help with a specific area.

For Relative Newcomers to Internet Marketing

That said, the finer points of the book can be better absorbed if you read it through sequentially. Get your feet wet in Chapter 1, "Why Online Sales Matter," and Chapter 2, "What an Online Sales Engine Can Do," before moving on to the chapters that are relevant to your particular business situation and goal.

For Seasoned Marketers

If there's any one chapter that's likely to be of interest to more seasoned Internet marketers or analysts, we suggest Chapter 3, "Building a Metrics-Driven Practice," which should be followed by both Chapter 4, "Breaking Down Silos to Get the Metrics You Need," and Chapter 9, "Running the Feedback Loop."

In our experience, even some of the world's largest agencies aren't fully utilizing the awesome opportunities for measurement that the Internet creates. Chances are, no matter how long you've been marketing on the Internet or who is helping you with it, there are opportunities for improvement in measurement, ultimately leading to improvements in results!

Additional Resources

For additional information for those who want to dig deeper into certain subject areas after reading this book, here are some additional resources (mostly online). Feel free to pick and choose what works for you.

Books We Recommend

Most of these references are mentioned at different points in this book, and we found them all to be helpful:

- *Predictably Irrational, Revised and Expanded Edition: The Hidden Forces That Shape Our Decisions,* by Dan Ariely
- *Blogging to Drive Business: Create and Maintain Valuable Customer Connections,* by Eric Butow and Rebecca Bollwitt
- *The Inmates Are Running the Asylum: Why High Tech Products Drive Us Crazy and How to Restore the Sanity,* by Alan Cooper
- *Website Optimization: Speed, Search Engine & Conversion Rate Secrets,* by Andy King
- *Don't Make Me Think: A Common Sense Approach to Web Usability, Second Edition,* by Steve Krug
- *Information Architecture for the World Wide Web: Designing Large-Scale Web Sites, Third Edition,* by Peter Morville and Louis Rosenfeld
- *The Non-Designers Design Book, Third Edition,* by Robin Williams

The Pure Visibility Blog

Of course, we are always adding to related topics on our corporate blog, which you can find at blog.purevisibility.com.

Three entries from the Pure Visibility blog are good starting points:

- blog.purevisibility.com/2010/04/seo-and-writing-for-the-web/

- blog.purevisibility.com/2009/10/has-your-google-ranking-suddenly-changed-dont-panic/

- blog.purevisibility.com/2008/08/why-is_flash-hard-on-seo/

Other Industry Blogs

One of the main blogs we use to follow the search engine industry is www.searchengineland.com.

A couple of useful search engine optimization blogs are

- www.seomoz.org/blog

- www.bruceclay.com/webrank.htm

An interesting analytics blog is www.kaushik.net/avinash.

Several blogs on social media, as well as paid search and SEO, are also relevant:

- googlewebmastercentral.blogspot.com/

- adwords.blogspot.com/

- www.searchenginejournal.com/

Some blogs out there cover the different aspects of social media:

- www.socialmediatoday.com

- www.socialmediaclub.org

- www.mashable.com (also covers paid search, SEO, and IT news)

Free Resources

In this book, we mention several free resources available, largely from Google, that will help you get the most from your website investment. Most require signing up with the service. Some, such as Google Analytics, require deployment of some code on your website to initiate data collection:

- **Google AdWords Keyword Tool:** Gives you keyword suggestions supported by data on the number of searches. Provides information related to keywords you specify, or it begins by reviewing your website and suggesting keywords based on your website content. Covered in "Speak Your Audience's Language: the Real Search Engine Optimization" in Chapter 5.

  https://adwords.google.com/select/KeywordToolExternal

- **Google Analytics:** A free web analytics service that operates through a JavaScript snippet deployed on your website. It provides summary data on visits and visitor behavior on your website. Discussed in "Web Analytics: Types, Purpose, Popular Tools for Each" in Chapter 4.

  http://www.google.com/analytics/

- **Google Insights for Search:** A visualization of search popularity trends over time for a small number of keywords or keyphrases. You specify the keyphrases, a time period, and a geography, and then look at trends in popularity of these keyphrases graphed over time.

  www.google.com/insights/search

- **Google Places:** Google's directory for brick-and-mortar businesses combines mapped results with business information such as hours of operation and payment types accepted. It includes photographs, videos, and customer reviews. Covered in the most detail in "Increase your Findability: Claim and Maintain Your Local Business Listings" in Chapter 8.

  www.google.com/places

- **Google Webmaster Tools:** Gives you data on how Google sees your website, lets you submit your sitemap.xml and your robots.txt files to Google, and lets you see your page load times compared to other websites. Covered in the most detail in "Crawler Control: Speak to Your Spiders" in Chapter 8.

  https://www.google.com/webmasters/tools/home?hl=en

- **Google Website Optimizer:** A free website optimization service that allows you to test large or small differences in website pages. By deploying its JavaScript and setting up alternative pages, it randomizes which version is shown to visitors and collects data on outcomes for each version. Discussed in "How to Measure" in Chapter 6.

  www.google.com/websiteoptimizer

- **Yahoo! Web Analytics:** A free website analytics tool that operates through JavaScript deployed on your website. It summarizes data on visits to your website and includes some demographic information about visitors. Discussed in "Web Analytics: Types, Purpose, Popular Tools for Each" in Chapter 4.

  http://web.analytics.yahoo.com/

1

Why Online Sales Matter

Why are we here? Why do online sales matter?

For both business-to-consumer (B2C) and business-to-business (B2B) companies, the Internet is an increasingly important marketing and sales tool. Purchasers love it because it's an information-rich medium where they can conduct research and easily make comparisons. Marketers love it because online efforts are trackable and measurable, in real time.

First Things First

The Internet is transforming nearly every kind of business, from the obvious B2C e-commerce examples to a niche B2B business. Yet today, a lot of untapped opportunity remains.

This book helps you identify where you are in your Internet marketing process maturity and improve your marketing models both to increase your return on investment (ROI) and to boost sales.

Our goal is to give you tools that let you identify, track, and measure what works and what doesn't—effectively tying your Internet marketing efforts directly to your sales results. *Measurable, repeatable sales* is the ultimate goal we hope to help you reach.

Internet Research Equals Internet Sales

As consumers, we all intuitively know that more and more research and shopping is done online today than ever before. But it's not just the B2C space that benefits from Internet research and a quicker sale.

According to sources such as AMR International, Enquiro, and Marketing Sherpa, Internet research is now part of nearly every major B2B transaction, and investment in online marketing continues to grow.

In 2009, Google commissioned a study by Slack Barshinger on how small to medium-size businesses use the Internet, and found that 77% of the business owners used online search to find new business suppliers, and 99% of them reported that search engines are the most effective tool for finding business suppliers.

Moreover, the larger the size of the purchase, the more likely the buyer is to make extended research efforts online. Without an integrated online strategy, your prospective customers won't be able to find your website (but they'll likely find your competitor's).

More business decision makers use the Internet to conduct research for their B2B purchases because it's

- An incredibly robust research medium, allowing multiple browsers, tabs, and windows to be open simultaneously for quick comparisons.

- A rich source of information. For more-complex purchasing processes or higher-ticket items, people need more time and more information to come to a final decision. An information-rich website can set a good foundation for the sales team. In addition, people rely on the many potentially persuasive "unbiased" third-party reviews.

- Conveniently open 24 hours a day. This means the buying process can progress over a weekend, instead of having to wait until Monday to ask a question on a toll-free number.

- A fast and economic way for one-to-one communication. Email, online chat, and web-based video conferencing reduce communication costs substantially.

- Dynamic. With ever-changing search engine algorithms and emerging tools such as Google Instant, an Internet search conducted today can reveal better results than the same one run last month.

Advantages of Internet Marketing

Just as Internet research becomes an increasingly important tool during the purchasing process, more marketers are seeing the advantages, too. It's a win-win situation.

Marketing departments are investing more in online marketing today because it's

- Attractive to a significant segment of the demographics for most customer profiles. It can effectively reach your target customer.

- Faster and less expensive to conduct direct marketing campaigns (for example, an email campaign or online newsletter compared with traditional printing and direct-mail costs).

- More economic to communicate via email, online chat, and video conferencing than long distance phone calls or toll-free numbers offered by your company.

- Measurable, which means that successes are identifiable and repeatable.

- Set up for real-time results monitoring, and it can handle real-time tweaks and on-the-fly changes.

- Open 24-hours a day, which means that even potential customers with insomnia can be reached at some point during the buying process.

- Targeted, allowing you to pinpoint using geography, contextual relevance, and other useful parameters to reach a very specifically defined audience. (Online reviews are used more by expert Internet users or in niche product markets.)

- Continuously available, letting you give away whitepapers or free webinars to gather good sources of leads over time. Products with high price points and long sales cycles require many "touches" and follow-up with a potential customer.

- Cost-effective, in the long run. By adjusting your paid search campaigns to find which ads work best for different keywords, you reduce your ad spend and online efforts over time while maintaining or increasing the number of leads or purchases gained.

- Going social, as more people share information among peers on websites like Facebook and LinkedIn, for business purposes. A recommendation from a friend or peer can go a long way toward closing a sale.

The Bird's Eye View

Most companies today have immature connections (at best) between their marketing and sales departments. With this book, you'll start to break down this silo mentality and get the different groups really talking and working together.

Which marketing efforts generated more leads? Which efforts generated better *quality* leads, thus enabling the sales team to close more sales? Which efforts cost more than others, particularly when compared to the actual sales they generated?

Metrics are at the heart of answering these questions, and metrics are what you use to assess your various marketing efforts, including search engine optimization, paid search campaigns, contact forms completed, and how many times the phone rings, too.

To get to the level where you have measurement tools in place—and can use them over time to measure results—requires a certain level of process maturity. Don't be annoyed if you're simply not there yet; that's what we'll do together using the tools in this book.

Standard Practice

It is not unusual for a company today to be fairly inexperienced when it comes to search engine optimization, paid search campaigns, or both.

Perhaps the company's been running campaigns for awhile but never ran the numbers to see which ads work better than others. Or maybe a business knows its products, and therefore what keywords should be woven into the website text, but never really approached it methodically. Perhaps they've never done a competitive analysis for multiple keywords and keyphrases in several keyword themes, which could identify new keyword opportunities.

We're not surprised. We see this all the time. But a desire to reach the next level of process maturity is the key—that's how we get new clients in the door, and that's why curious people like you have bought this book. You're hungry for more information and want to know how to squeeze more from every marketing dollar spent.

You're at the right place.

Your Online Sales Engine

Wrangling a website into something that generates measurable, repeatable results for your business requires blending together many different areas of expertise *and* building bridges to share information across departments. We call this process creating Your Online Sales Engine.

This book gives you a working knowledge of online sales components so that you can engage competently with your technical and marketing colleagues in a less-stressful environment while producing the most effective final product.

The online sales engine components are

- Speaking to your audience, analyzing keywords, and developing user personas
- Getting visible with organic and paid search
- Making websites that work, either from scratch or through improving what you have in place already
- Selling online, including landing page design and conversion rate improvement
- Reviewing metrics that matter, and revising the other online sales engine components based on sound business analysis

Chapter 2, "What an Online Sales Engine Can Do," covers what the online sales engine is composed of in more detail.

The Heart of It All: Metrics

To say that we are big believers in gathering and applying metrics is not really quite right... *evangelists* is a better term. You can't make sound business decisions without knowing what's really going on between your website and its visitors. And you can't know what's going on unless you have good data and even better analytic practices.

Paid Search and Organic Search

Digging into search engine optimization (SEO, or organic search) and paid search (pay-per-click [PPC]) work is just the beginning when you get an online sales engine up and running at your company.

WHAT WE MEAN

The term *paid search* refers to the paid ads on the search engine results pages. Some people prefer the term *pay per click* (PPC), which is the paid search term in this book.

Just an aside for advanced folks: There is some experimenting within the industry with a pay-per-acquisition model, which we say falls inside the paid search term definition, although it could not be described as PPC. As of this writing, none of the major search engines have identified a pay-per-acquisition that works well.

We also use the term *search engine optimization* (SEO) throughout this book, which is the process of optimizing organic search (some people prefer the term *natural search*, which is synonymous with *organic search*).

Although we often refer to Google throughout this book (and show Google tools in most screen captures), other search engines (such as Yahoo!, MSN, and Bing) also deserve attention. Google, however, is the number one search engine in all but five countries worldwide. Google also has a good set of Internet marketing tools available for professionals, which also happen to be free.

For example, Figure 1.1 shows that the bulk of the websites listed on the page come from organic search listings. The three websites at the top, highlighted with a shaded background, and the ones along the sidebar on the right under the map, are the paid search advertisements on the page. The organic listings include Google Places links (the ones with the "map pins" next to them).

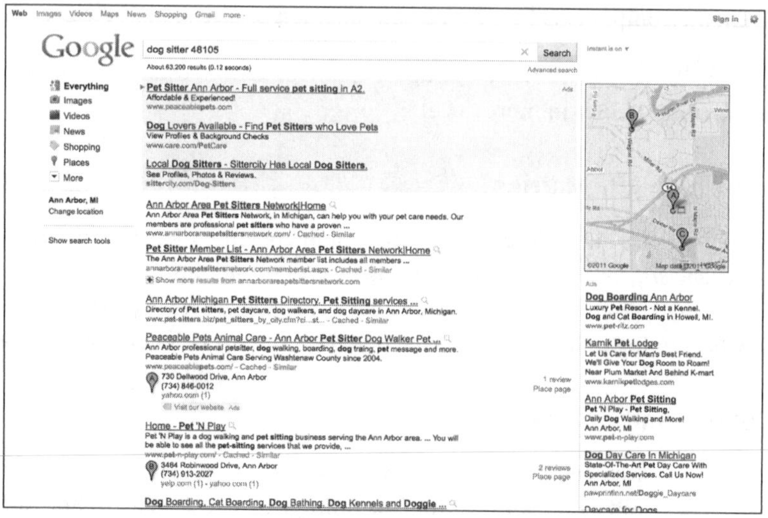

Figure 1.1 *The mixture of paid and organic search listings for "dog sitter 48105."*

Other Sales Engine Components

We also take a look at how your website's information architecture can better meet the needs of your website visitors (and better meet your business needs, as well). Other things that impact leads and sales include usability and user-experience design techniques, landing page design, and keyword analysis.

The entire Internet marketing package (everything mentioned so far) needs to be measured. You need to define which data you want to track and how, track it, and then analyze it to see what works (and what doesn't).

That is how to apply the online sales engine in your business to get tangible results.

Back to Basics: Business Strategy 101

Before we move forward and get your website and marketing and sales processes ahead of your competition, let's revisit a few basic business strategies to keep in mind.

The Customer Is King

In our view, the customer comes first. Period. Don't fall into the trap of designing your home page based on the most beautiful design from your favorite agency. Avoid prominently promoting a whitepaper on your website (written by a C*XX* at your company) if the download form is not converting enough leads.

How do you get out of these sticky political situations? With reliable user data. Do your user homework up front, track results, and you'll be able to talk your way out of any poor design decision. After all, the website is for customers and potential customers. If it's not reaching them or converting them or working for them, it needs to change. Fast.

We introduce you to some new tools and concepts that will get you there, such as user personas, usability techniques, and even how to redesign landing pages to benefit users and increase conversion rates. The user (that is, website visitor) is your primary focus.

Understanding the Buying Process

Website visitors interested in your products or services can be "mapped" to a place in the buying process. Provide different kinds of pages on your website to address different stages of the buying process, as shown in Figure 1.2.

By addressing the needs of your website visitors who are at different stages of the buying process, you can also support the sales process.

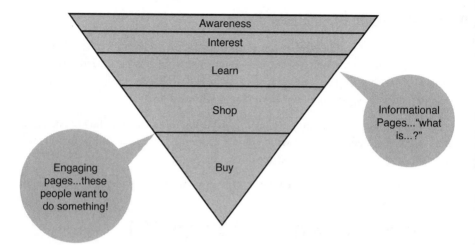

Figure 1.2 *Different buying process stages require different kinds of information from your website.*

Remove Organizational Silos

Getting your marketing, sales, and website teams to work with each other, share data, integrate their workflow, and coordinate efforts as a team could be your biggest challenge. With everyone sharing the goal to obtain the results we outline in this book, you'll be able to coordinate efforts across organizational silos with less resistance.

What results are we talking about? Essentially, being able to track closed sales back to specific marketing efforts, thereby identifying which marketing efforts bring in more and better-qualified leads than others. Well worth the effort, in our opinion.

Get the Most Bang for Your Buck

Should you code your own content management system (CMS) or customer relationship manager system (CRM)? We have seen this done, but we typically don't advise that you take this approach.

There's no need to reinvent the wheel or spend all your time under the hood of your website; it's best to use state-of-the-art components instead. Many good tools are available, such as software as a service (such as Salesforce.com) or free open source implementations (such as SugarCRM and CMS systems WordPress or Drupal).

You'll be able to spend your energy perfecting the parts of your website that your visitors will see and interact with. This will take all your creativity and cleverness, so save that for the good stuff, instead of reinventing the wheel.

Find Out What's Working

Discover what works, and abandon what doesn't. Be ruthless and cut a favorite (or fun) program if it's not giving you leads or sales. Save the funds (preferably as soon as possible!) and initiate new programs that you already know are doing better, thus improving the bottom line overall.

How do you find out what works? You guessed it: with metrics. Set them up, track them, and analyze them. Measuring which efforts drive more online sales or more conversions or more downloads (whatever your specific goal) lets you identify what's working and what isn't.

Lessons We've Learned

We delve into the nitty-gritty details of paid search, organic search, usability, conversion metrics, and more in subsequent chapters. This section, however, goes over some of the more common problems that stand out for many companies, as lessons already learned.

Keywords, Keywords, Keywords

The "keyword" issue is one that's nearly universal. Companies have one idea about what their keywords are, but after an initial conversation come away with a completely different concept of what their keywords *really* are, in the eyes of their potential customers.

Sometimes, the keywords that a company initially identifies are not bad, but simply need to be relegated to secondary status in favor of other more commonly used primary keywords. The point is that people use terms for your products and services that may be more everyday words than how you internally label and market your products or services.

Table 1.1 illustrates this concept better than a long-winded explanation. Some of these are real industry examples, some are imaginary (but realistic), but they all illustrate the point.

Table 1.1 List of Initially Proposed Keywords and Improved Keywords

Proposed Keywords	Improved Keywords
For a fast food company: creamy dreamy drink	Milkshake
For a real estate company: property	Home, house
For a rat-killing product: rodenticide	Rat killer, rat poison
For a security construction company: bullet-resistant divider	Bulletproof wall

Table 1.1 Continued

Proposed Keywords	Improved Keywords
For a clothing company: outerwear	Coat, jacket
For a leather goods company: handbag	Purse, pocketbook
For a clothing company: polar fleece pullover	Sweatshirt
For a dogcare company: doggie daycare	Dogsitter
For a daycare company: childcare, education	Daycare, preschool
For an automotive parts company: battery maintainer	Battery charger
For a software services company: user's guide	User manual

Sometimes, the business management isn't sophisticated enough to make these keyword mistakes. We often hear things like "my customers can find me if they search my brand name." But what about the potential customer who's never heard about you? Don't you want to capture them, too?

Or worse, what if you have a famous name within your business name, such as Blackbird Shoes or Cayenne Footwear. Perhaps there's a big pro sports team named the Blackbirds, or the hottest new Hollywood actor's last name is Cayenne. You're lost in the shuffle... and even customers who *do* know your business name can't find you online.

You need to put yourself in the shoes of someone who has never heard of your business, and then get visible on those search terms. The point is this: *Choose keywords that generate both interest and revenue.*

Paid Search Mismatches

It takes a couple of minutes to set up a new paid search advertising account, and a lot of effort after that to optimize it and your website so you're making money instead of spending it.

One of the major issues can be that keywords for ad campaigns are mismatched to actual search keywords.

For example, do a search on something like "pink snow boots" and click some of the paid advertisements. You'll go to websites of retailers, often major national ones, but won't necessarily find your pink snow boots. You might find snow boots (none of them pink) or pink leather boots.

Or maybe you're looking for a new suede coat, so you enter "women's suede coat" in your favorite search engine, only to find advertisers linking to women's down coats, or even men's coats, which is clearly off the mark.

With paid search, you can define rather narrowly exactly what the campaign will be, for which keywords your ad will appear, and which pages you'll link to on your website.

If you have this type of mismatch, you're

- Not getting a sale from the ad

- Paying for the keyword mismatch

- Potentially negatively impacting your brand due to the mismatch, because of frustrated website visitors

It's a lose-lose-lose situation, and one that can be fixed easily. Our general rule of thumb is to use broad matches for keywords and website pages on organic search, and narrow the focus for both landing pages and advertising keywords. Focused is better!

Get the Fundamentals Right First

We talk a lot about tactics throughout the book that could be thought of as "eating your vegetables," basic fundamentals that will get you very far.

Yes, we know that there are many exciting things out there today, like working with social media, but we don't focus on those areas too much, even though they're "hot." We know that where most businesses are today is still at the stage of getting qualified people to visit your website (and converting them to sales). (When these basics are taken care of, feel free to move on to other Internet marketing tactics, such as social media.)

The tools and techniques in this book help you to transform your business and grow your business online. We believe that combining these fundamentals in this way creates a unique competitive advantage. Simply apply these "eat your veggies" basics in the way we propose and you'll find that you are light years ahead and can really get some traction.

Then, at *that* point, you can play around with social media and do more "fun" things along those lines.

Bigger *Is* Better

It's true, when it comes to phone numbers, calls to action, and Buy Now buttons on either landing pages or regular website pages, bigger is better. In fact, you can very rarely make it too big.

You can find more information about good landing page design in Chapter 6, "Putting It All Together and Selling Online," in the section "Designing Landing Pages."

Content and Inlinks

Everything in the world of search engines, algorithms, and visibility changes constantly, with two exceptions. The more pages of content you have, the more opportunity you have to rank in Google or other search engines. Using a tool like WordPress or another content management system makes it easy to keep adding fresh content. Do it.

The second constant is inlinks (links from other websites to your website's content). How many other people are listing your website, and how reputable are they? The search engine algorithms factor this in when they judge your website and calculate its ranking.

It might be boring, but you really have to do it. It works... so work on your content and inlinks regularly. Yes, it takes time and patience, but these fundamentals can ensure that you make enough money in the long run to make it worthwhile. (When it comes to an ROI analysis for content and inlink effort, you need to be in it for the long haul.)

Websites Are for Spiders and People

Another thing that's often overlooked is that websites need to be designed and developed for two main audiences: people and the search engine spider programs that analyze your website. Design for spiders and people with every step you take.

For example, create a Sitemap page for people to see how your website is organized at a glance, but create a separate sitemap.xml file on your server for the spiders to read and understand your internal website structure.

Figure 1.3 shows just one of many tools that Google makes available for webmasters to improve their website's ability to be read by the spiders.

Small Business Safety

A word to the wise, particularly if you are a small business and don't have an IT department continuously checking your back door for hackers: Use a tool such as WordPress to manage your website content or blog.

WordPress (www.wordpress.org) is free, but has a large community of both developers and users. You won't get in the situation where the person who's helping you with your website goes off and gets a full-time job, leaving you high and dry. Customizable themes and templates are easy to configure and can save you thousands of dollars over time.

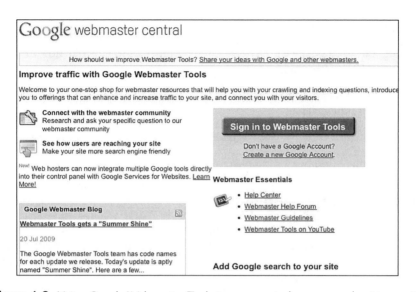

Figure 1.3 *Using Google Webmaster Tools is one way to learn more about improving your website for spiders.*

What's more, many CMSs are susceptible to hackers. WordPress is too, of course, especially if you don't keep up with the latest version that corrects a newly discovered security flaw. With a large development community, however, it's less susceptible.

It's not fun if you're working with a subcontractor to maintain your website and they get hacked. You're left hanging with a hacked website only to discover that the work required to repair it is considered out of scope.

Budget for Marketing the Website Itself

A common pitfall is that a "website budget" is earmarked solely for design and development, with little to no funding left for marketing the website itself. Leave enough money (for example, half or more of your budget) to actually promote the website.

Try to avoid overspending on the website itself. Many small businesses find that no one is coming to their new website and they have no budget to fix it. If you consider this issue up front and budget for it, you should be in good shape.

Learn by Example

Throughout this book, we use two fictitious companies to illustrate how to implement certain elements to improve your website and its marketing:

- **Happy Puppy**, a small service-based business that sells puppy- and dog-training classes

- **TropiCo**, a large conglomerate in the tropical fruit reselling business

Let's meet them both with a couple of quick Internet marketing scenarios.

B2C Example: Happy Puppy

The two small business owners running Happy Puppy are struggling with starting a paid search campaign from scratch. They're savvy enough to have created a keyword-rich website, but have focused on their preferred cutesy terms (*doggie daycare* instead of *dogsitter*, for example).

They found out about Google's Keyword Tool, and after playing around with it identified several keywords that were more likely to get results from people looking for their training classes and services.

Some of the discoveries, as shown in Figure 1.4, included that people were likely to search for specific training problems, such as crate training, housebreaking, or handling problem behaviors like chewing or pulling on a leash.

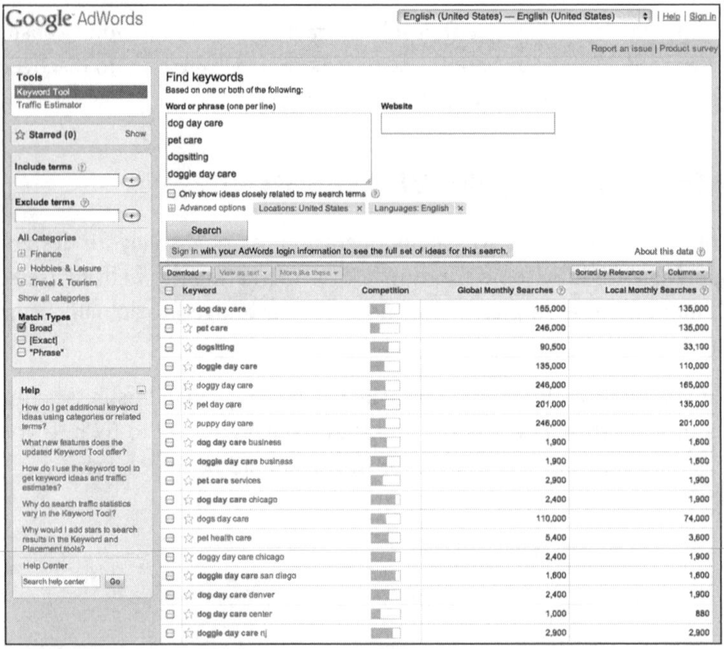

Figure 1.4 *Working through potential new keywords for the Happy Puppy website.*

This prompted them to turn back to their website and rework their existing content to use terms like *dogsitter* and include dog behavior problems for their daycare and training services pages.

They also decided to start a blog, where they could include posts targeting specific training for different behaviors, keeping the website relevant and fresh. They even decided to rename some of their training classes, before moving forward with their new paid search advertising campaign.

B2B Example: TropiCo

A recent review of their weblog data revealed that the new landing page graphic design launched last month actually slightly reduced their response rate. The question is, why?

After conducting an informal usability test with a handful of prospective website visitors, they quickly saw that people accessing their landing pages (after clicking their paid search ad) were carefully reviewing the content on the page. Yet, in doing so, they were scrolling down, and the call to action, which was located in the new page header, was scrolling away as well.

A-ha! People in the test were going directly into their main website to look for more information, instead of just picking up the phone or contacting the company online to place an order. No wonder the online lead conversions were dwindling instead of improving.

After a quick fix to the new landing page template, the prominent call to action within the page copy started to pay off, and they slowly saw an increase in their conversion rates.

Tip

Refer to the Appendix in this book for a detailed report for our fictional TropiCo company. This insightful "state of the web" report was prepared for their board of directors by the Internet marketing team at year end. It covers data and progress for the year in review, explains how it happened, and has a section looking forward to the following year.

Online Sales Engine Success Stories

We also quote several case studies throughout this book, which are from real life and relate directly to the subject of each chapter. Let's wrap up this chapter by looking at a few case studies of companies that have applied the online sales engine to improve their bottom lines.

Case Study: Moving into New Global Markets

One high-tech company, spun out of a major research university, develops high-performance cell-analysis systems at a fraction of the cost of competitors. This new start-up company needed to break into an existing and highly competitive market: life-science research equipment.

They needed to build a U.S. presence and break into the international community for their market. The strategy entailed SEO and ongoing paid search in the United States, South America, Europe, and the Asia-Pacific region.

Landing page testing and analysis was part of the package, ensuring that the target market for each country found just what they needed, when they needed it. Advanced strategies with Google Analytics were applied, to measure progress in new geographic markets. The company adapted this same data to inform offline marketing decisions and new target areas.

By applying the online sales engine metrics tools, they are able to follow their online traffic all the way into their CRM system. This way, they know which efforts have the biggest payoff in each country.

After working on these efforts for 2 years, they saw their cost per lead decrease by 64% and their conversion rate more than double. The results from their online lead tracking combined with in-depth website analysis is guiding their Internet marketing strategy for the coming year.

Case Study: Manufacturing Company Improves Sales

A manufacturer and installation service company for custom security systems needed to expand its reach and drive new sales. The new website just wasn't pulling in the target number or quality of leads they were hoping to garner, despite aggressive marketing efforts.

The strategy to drive more traffic involved focusing on the Google AdWords account to help the company realize return for its advertising expenses. The advertising funds weren't being spent as wisely as they could have been. The AdWords account was reorganized to focus on the keywords that would deliver the best leads back to the company. Expensive keywords that weren't entirely relevant to the business were eliminated, making advertising an effective driver of sales leads.

The impact of online advertising was further increased by more effective landing pages. Many savvy marketers miss the importance of a landing page that delivers, in a compelling way, the exact information a person is seeking when clicking an ad.

The website copy was also improved, adding keyword-rich text throughout, to improve search engine visibility. The effort also included redesigning the company's website and appropriately indexing the website with Google, to support organic search results.

The end effect was that the organic search rankings improved dramatically. More important, they began driving sales for the first time from their website, achieving just under $2 million in online sales by the end of their first full year with the new strategy.

This translated to nearly $20 in sales for every $1 spent on advertising. The following year, continuing optimizations allowed for an additional 40% increase in revenue with only a 30% increase in advertising spend.

Case Study: Large Childcare Provider Increases Web Conversions

A large provider of early education and care services to children between 6 weeks and 12 years of age wanted to leverage the web to deliver new business leads in a slow economy. With multiple brands, more than 1,100 schools (corporate and franchise) serving over 100,000 children in the United States and internationally, the company was using its brand websites as the primary point of contact to communicate both with prospects and existing customers.

Initial efforts after the initial website launch involved website analytics, paid search, and SEO, although the company was unsatisfied with the outcome of those efforts. They wanted to improve both their online presence and marketing efficiency.

Paid search improvements were tackled first; website-based lead generation was the primary measure of success for the project. A costly website redesign was avoided by identifying ways to rearrange and edit existing website content for increased effectiveness. Paid search was also integrated more fully into existing online marketing efforts, as part of a comprehensive online strategy.

Conversion rates were improved by applying usability improvements. These came from directly assessing website visitor behavior and interviewing both users and the sales team. Paid search campaigns were moved beyond just Google to Yahoo! and MSN, and the conversion rates improved by creating geotargeted landing pages.

The result from these usability, landing page, and paid search campaign changes was that the cost per conversion steadily declined in all three paid search programs and conversion rates increased overall by 35% over a 2-year period. In addition, advertising costs were reduced by 5% for a competitive keyword marketplace.

Case Study: Major Software Company Grows Sales

One of the world's leading organizations in optimizing application performance, this computer industry leader provides software, experts, and best practices to ensure applications work well and deliver business value. Supporting 46 of the top 50 Fortune 500 companies, and 12 of the top 20 most visited U.S. websites, the diversity of their products, services, and target audiences demands a measured, integrated visibility strategy.

Their initial goal was to appear on "page one" for search engine results listings and paid search results. They also were posing great questions among themselves, such as "How can we build upon and improve our existing online marketing efforts?"

Many strategic online elements were already in place: a successful website, analytics tools, a paid search program, and a talented team poised to implement a profitable visibility strategy. A plan focusing on earning the top spots in online search for multiple languages emerged. Additional objectives included elevating specific company solutions and reinforcing an international presence.

Three key components drove the success of their new online marketing initiative:

- **A review of the infrastructure for search engine optimization:** Search engine visibility improved significantly for nonbranded terms through implementation of a structured strategy for URL taxonomies, page redirection, page design, link building, and more.

  With numerous complex websites within the corporate global network, evaluating and leveraging existing content is key, as both the organization and its websites continue to grow.

- **Integrating online lead tracking into their CRM system:** Integrating search marketing activities with lead source tracking now links how customers are finding the company online and the effectiveness of their online marketing activities in converting online interest into sales.

- **Paid search arbitrage:** Building on existing successful paid search campaigns, the next level adds depth using a word market strategy and provides a strategy for the aggressive optimization of individual campaign elements, particularly landing page optimization.

  You learn more about the word market in the section "Speak Your Audience's Language: The Real Search Engine Optimization" in Chapter 5, "The Audience Is Listening (What Will You Say?)."

The company has deepened their level of expertise in the area of search marketing. In addition to investing in online marketing efforts, they are now getting a return on those efforts through metrics: tracking, analyzing, and measuring data. Their newly created online sales engine uses the web to drive and convert customers.

Summary

We see a lot of companies that have their Internet marketing initiatives (such as paid search and organic search) well underway, but still have room for improvement. But how and where to improve?

The heart of getting real traction out of your Internet marketing program is to tie marketing and sales data together, with metrics. Track what you're doing, track the impact, and track the resulting sales. You'll learn more about what works, or doesn't, for your company.

In addition, take these lessons learned to heart:

- The customer is king, and is your top priority when making website management decisions.

- Be aware of the buying process, and address the needs of your website visitors accordingly.

- Work to break down those organizational silos; get marketing, sales, and website teams talking with one another.

- Don't reinvent the wheel, use off-the-shelf software and spend your energy and money elsewhere on your website projects.

- Find out what's working and abandon what isn't.

- Reevaluate your keywords in the eyes of your potential customers, not your marketing copywriter or product development manager.

- Check for mismatches in paid search campaigns between ads and actual search keywords.

- Get the basic fundamentals right, before jumping into an exciting new area (like social media).

- To create a good call to action on a landing page or elsewhere in your website, bigger really is better.

- Work on adding and improving your website content and continuing to recruit new inlinks to your website as much as possible; they will both make a big impact in the long run.

- At every step, design your website for both search engine spiders (crawlers) and people.

- Small businesses should take a few extra precautions to discourage website hacking.

- Add money to the website budget to market the website itself, not just to design and build it.

2

What an Online Sales Engine Can Do

National and global businesses are moving beyond the basics of paid search advertising and keyword optimization to develop and enhance their Internet marketing programs. All of these organizations are met with an incredible optimization challenge, however, after they've successfully tackled the basics. The online marketing world is full of very specific, tactical approaches for using Twitter, social media, whiz-bang paid search accounts, advanced SEO, and the next great thing coming down the road.

To build true competitive advantage in today's online marketplace requires going beyond these tactical approaches to address your entire customer-acquisition process—from the first ad click to the final purchase which may occur hours, months, or even years later. Adopting Your Online Sales Engine can help you turn a handful of individual tactics into a strategic advantage.

What Is an Online Sales Engine?

Addressing the entire customer acquisition process requires bridging fields of expertise that have often existed within silos (marketing, sales, operations). It also forces tough conversations about goals and trade-offs on a scale that companies may have never needed to broach before. Each division, distributor, or department can no longer do their own thing when Google flattens the world and puts companies both large and small all on equal footing in one marketplace.

An "online sales engine" provides the missing road map to maximizing online sales, as your business and marketing decisions will be based on accurate data. This book guides you through the initial strategic decisions, shows you how integrating various disciplines can measurably improve your results over time, and teaches you how to track back through the data to determine the point of online contact to inform your future Internet marketing purchasing decisions.

Why Adopt the Online Sales Engine?

Treating your online presence as an online sales engine ultimately enables you to increase sales, whether you have an e-commerce website or use your website to generate leads. An online sales engine combines sound strategy, effective promotion, as well as accurate and complete data about the effectiveness of your efforts. Armed with this system, you will be able to make sound strategic decisions and get ahead of your competition.

With an iterative, measurable, and repeatable approach to Internet marketing, the marketing team can learn *which* online strategies bring *results*; at the same time the sales team benefits from better-qualified leads; while the whole company gains through increased sales.

The new paradigm of web-based business and the ability to measure the effectiveness of advertising and the progression of a prospect through the *entire* buying process means that marketers are no longer tied to "Return on Objective" (ROO). Instead of tracking project goals and whether or not they were met, marketers today can directly measure their efforts in terms of impact on the top line.

The goal of any company who chooses to adopt this online sales engine should be to generate measurable, repeatable sales. Adoption involves several iterations of strategic analysis, project execution, measurement and analysis, on each online sales engine component in turn, as shown in Figure 2.1.

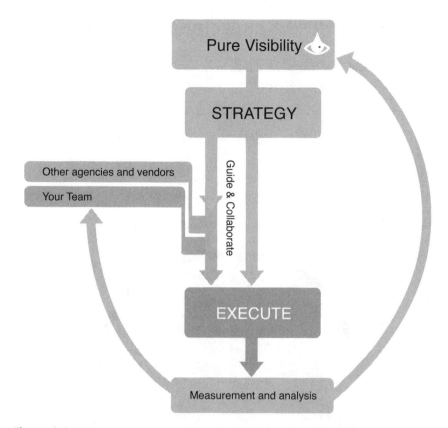

Figure 2.1 *Measurement and analysis drive each iteration of the adoption cycle.*

The core concept behind the online sales engine is that social media, search engine optimization, paid search campaigns and user experience improvements are merely tactical components of the same iterative Internet marketing process. To optimize the process you need to track back to the original point of contact for each new customer. Metrics are a crucial component.

We want to give you the tools to develop a more cohesive and concerted approach to broader corporate Internet marketing programs. This helps you to move away from independent island-like projects, corporate silo thinking, and haphazard internal efforts with no metrics to back them up.

The Online Sales Engine Components

The pieces and parts of this online sales engine begin to form one of two different processes when you adopt the engine at your company.

The online sales engine components are

- Speaking to your audience, analyzing keywords and developing user personas

- Making websites that work, either from scratch or through improving what you have in place already

- Getting visible with organic and paid search

- Selling online, including landing page design and conversion rate improvement

- Reviewing metrics that matter, and revising the other online sales engine components based on sound business analysis

The essential components of the online sales engine are shown in Figure 2.2.

Figure 2.2 *The basic online sales engine components.*

The chapters in this book describe the practical application of adopting each of the online sales engine components at your company. Table 2.1 lists the chapter where each component is discussed in detail.

Table 2.1   Where to Find the Online Sales Engine Components in This Book

Online Sales Engine Component	Chapter(s) in This Book
Speaking to your audience, analyzing keywords, and developing user personas.	Chapter 5, "The Audience Is Listening (What Will You Say?)."

Online Sales Engine Component	Chapter(s) in This Book
Making websites that work, or deploying an improved website.	Chapter 7, "Making Websites that Work."
Making your message visible with organic and paid search.	Chapter 8, "It's All About Visibility."
Selling online, including landing page design and conversion rate improvement.	Chapter 6, "Putting It All Together and Selling Online."
Working with metrics that matter, and revising the other online sales engine components based on sound business analysis.	Chapter 3, "Building a Metrics-Driven Practice," Chapter 4, "Breaking Down Silos to Get the Metrics You Need" and Chapter 9, "Running the Feedback Loop."

The Components Form a Process

The methodology to apply each of the components is a little trickier to codify. There are actually two ways you can adopt the components of an online sales engine:

- **Customer-driven**, which ensures that you start with defining your market and audience analysis activities first.

- **ROI-driven**, which ensures that you start saving money in paid search sooner and using those funds to drive implementation of additional components.

The structure of this book follows the customer-driven process, as each chapter looks at a different component (or aspect) of the online sales engine in a logical order, but you are welcome to apply the ROI-driven process if it makes more sense for your business situation.

Avoid "Dangerous Data" Nightmares

The major difference between this online sales engine and traditional media planning approaches is that metrics are at the heart of the process. While data analysis and traditional marketing sometimes seem worlds apart, a well-executed Internet marketing approach brings them together, gaining a strategic advantage.

Internet marketing, by its very nature, provides greater trackability over traditional marketing methods. A concerted, thoughtful approach will deliver results, over time.

But sometimes, having and acting on a little bit of data is more dangerous than having no data at all. Without the full picture, you can think that something is working, when in fact it's not. You could be optimizing your marketing efforts on the wrong elements altogether.

We're trying to avoid the nightmare where we have an incomplete picture of a company's marketing data and we actually turn off an ad or ad group that appears to be underperforming (perhaps it's not driving contact forms being filled out). It seems logical... but then the phone stops ringing, because that ad group instead was driving phone calls that no one had any way of knowing about!

The last thing any of us wants to do is to inadvertently make the phone **stop** ringing! Implement an online sales engine at your company, with a complete picture of your data, and you avoid these dangerous data nightmare scenarios.

Case Study: Identifying Junk Leads

Attendance On Demand, Inc., a company that has developed several employee time and labor tracking solutions, tracks their sales leads acquired from landing pages directly into their Customer Relationship Management (CRM) software.

One employee at Attendance on Demand, Inc., nicknamed "Sherlock," decided to do a bit of follow-up on the leads her team was producing. Because they had captured the search terms along with their lead information, they discovered that some of the paid search terms they *thought* were a good source of well-priced leads were a good source of junk leads.

"Sherlock" discovered this by simply calling the leads in the database, discovering that most people searching for "fair labor standards act" or "FLSA" and "family medical leave act" or "FMLA" who signed up for their whitepaper on how to use Attendance on Demand Inc.'s services to comply with the law, were actually disgruntled folks looking to sue their employer, instead of the executives looking to automate their system to ensure fairness and compliance.

Now they are no longer transferring these poor quality leads into their CRM. They are also giving away the whitepaper for the FLSA and FLMA search terms, instead of putting it behind a contact form. Simply using the phone and a bit of tracking removed poor quality leads from the system, allowing the sales team to focus on leads that might become sales.

The Customer-Driven Process

The "logical" way to think about the online sales engine adoption process is to start at the beginning, with your business goals, setting up metrics to track, and identifying who your website visitors really are. The rest of the customer-driven methodology works through improving and optimizing various aspects of your website, then reviewing the metrics that you decided to track up front.

The specific phases of the customer-driven online sales engine process are

1. Define your goals.

2. Configure tracking and set goals for metrics.

3. Conduct research and improve the user experience.

4. Sell online.

5. Manage your website.

6. Increase visibility with search engine optimization and paid search.

7. Revisit the metrics.

This book is organized based on the customer-driven method of adopting the strategy and tactics of the online sales engine. The chapters relate to specific process phases, as shown in Table 2.2.

Table 2.2   Relating Each Phase of the Customer-Driven Process to Chapters in This Book

Process Phrase	Chapter(s) in This Book
1. Define your goals.	Chapter 1, "Why Online Sales Matter."
2. Configure tracking and set goals for metrics.	Chapter 3, "Building a Metrics-Driven Practice," and Chapter 4, "Breaking Down Silos to Get the Metrics You Need."
3. Conduct research and improve the user experience.	Chapter 5, "The Audience Is Listening (What Will You Say?)."
4. Sell online.	Chapter 6, "Putting It All Together and Selling Online."
5. Manage your website.	Chapter 7, "Making Websites That Work."
6. Increase visibility with search engine optimization and paid search.	Chapter 8, "It's All About Visibility."
7. Revisit the metrics.	Chapter 9, "Running the Feedback Loop."

1. Define Your Goals

What defines success for your website? Is it improved quality of leads, or simply more leads in general, or increased profitability for products sold directly from the website? Perhaps you are looking to educate and inform potential customers as well, or need to impart specific information to them during the buying process.

How you define success for your website will impact your business, of course. But it will also inform the strategic decisions you'll make while adopting the online sales engine as an overarching process for your Internet marketing. Website goals are discussed in Chapter 1, "Why Online Sales Matter."

2. Configure Tracking and Set Goals for Metrics

Let's say it again: What defines success for your business? What part of that can you measure on your website? That defines what you'll need to track.

To configure tracking and metrics for your website, you need to

- Choose a contact method.
- Determine what to measure.
- Define the Key Performance Indicators (KPIs).
- Choose your basis for comparison.
- Begin to close the loop.
- Work with analytics tools.
- Don't forget the phone.

Choose a Contact Method

The telephone or an online contact form... which do you prefer? Perhaps both, or even live chat? The pros and cons of choosing each method (and why you should avoid using only a simple email link) are discussed in "Choosing a Contact Method" in Chapter 3, "Building a Metrics-Driven Practice."

Determine What to Measure

Look at each Internet marketing channel and determine what you need to measure, track, and analyze, over time. Every business needs to optimize both paid search (pay-per-click [PPC]) campaigns and search engine optimization (SEO) campaigns, to identify which keywords generate more interest and convert more visitors into customers.

You'll find more information in the "What to Measure" section in Chapter 3, "Building a Metrics-Driven Practice."

Define the Key Performance Indicators

Now, dig a little deeper and pinpoint exactly which primary and secondary Key Performance Indicators (KPIs) you want to measure for SEO, and do the same for paid search. Defining KPIs helps you measure the success of your marketing activities (either SEO or paid search).

You're spending money to get visitors through these means, so you should track carefully here (no one wants to overspend!). While this does take some effort up front, the payoff is that you can analyze exactly which elements of your online marketing efforts work better than others, down the road.

Detailed information on SEO and paid search KPIs appears in "SEO Key Performance Indicators" and "Paid Search Key Performance Indicators" in Chapter 3, "Building a Metrics-Driven Practice."

Choose Your Basis for Comparison

What do you want to compare these KPIs against? Do you want to report trends before and after a website update? Or would you rather focus on comparing the data week over week, month over month, or year over year?

Consider your sales cycle and the seasonality of your business, to determine when you should take the measurements.

Follow the advice in the "Use Business Analysis to Define Your KPI Benchmarks and Goals" section, as well as the "When to Measure Matters" section, both found in Chapter 3, "Building a Metrics-Driven Practice."

Begin to Close the Loop

Now you know what you want to measure and when, so you need to capture the data and get it where you need it: into your Customer Relationship Management (CRM) software. From there, your sales team can work with the leads and record ongoing customer interactions. Over time, you'll be able to "close the loop," identifying which marketing channels for specific keywords or campaigns delivered better sales results.

But that analysis can't take place unless you bridge the gap between your website data and your CRM... and get your sales team on board to enter data about each lead as they work with potential customers, for analysis down the road.

See "Integrating Web KPI into Business Decision-Making" and "Web to Lead to CRM Analysis: Close that Loop!", both in Chapter 3, "Building a Metrics-Driven Practice." There is also additional information in "Lead Management: SFA/CRM Integration," in Chapter 4, "Breaking Down Silos to Get the Metrics You Need."

Work with Analytics Tools

Now's the time to get your feet wet in terms of analyzing the existing data hiding in your website. Start using web analytics tools (such as Google Analytics, Urchin, Yahoo! Web Analytics, Omniture SiteCatalyst, and others) and look under the hood. Choose between logfile analysis or script-based analytics tracking, and set up your analysis tools.

This is your starting point for comparison purposes; you can start to identify which Internet marketing channels are pulling in more leads and customers than others. But what you don't know at this point is what the quality of those leads is. For that, you'll have to wait for your sales cycle to close more sales and then analyze the data from your CRM software in conjunction with the web analytics tools.

At this point, you'll start to learn who is coming to your website, what they engaged with while there, and what actions they took.

For more information, look at "Web Analytics: Types, Purpose, Popular Tools for Each" in Chapter 4, "Breaking Down Silos to Get the Metrics You Need."

Don't Forget the Phone

Your campaigns might spur a telephone call rather than a specific action on your website. If you value phone leads, make sure you are also tracking your telephone calls from your Internet marketing!

This can be as simple as getting an 800 number and using it exclusively as the call-to-action phone number throughout your website, or getting more granular and using multiple toll-free 800 numbers for different campaigns. You can even get to the level of individual keywords, assigning a different phone number for each.

You need to count calls before, during, and after marketing campaigns, and use your CRM system to provide a place for your sales group to log phone calls. These same tools can provide you with dashboards to measure the call volume.

Find more details about integrating telephone data with website data in "Call Tracking: Why It's Essential and How to Select the Granularity Needed," in Chapter 4, "Breaking Down Silos to Get the Metrics You Need."

3. Conduct Research and Improve the User Experience

The next few steps involve taking a look at your potential customers, and other members of the population looking at your website (such as job candidates, investors, etc.), to get to know them better. The research outcomes help you to define a better user experience for your website visitors.

To conduct research and improve the user experience for your website, you need to

- Define your audience.

- Develop website personas.

- Conduct user research.

- Conduct keyword research.

Define Your Audience

What are the goals of people visiting your website? Obviously a potential customer is looking for information on your product or service to evaluate making a purchase. But other people might be looking for a job with your company, or checking on an order, or any number of other tasks.

You can use several audience analysis tools to define the people visiting your website, many of which are outlined in "Start With the Tasks and Goals of Your Potential Audiences" in Chapter 5, "The Audience Is Listening (What Will You Say?)."

Develop Website Personas

Now that you've identified who's coming to your website and why, you're ready to develop website personas for each type of website visitor. The details and some sample website personas are available in "Develop Website Personas" in Chapter 5, "The Audience Is Listening (What Will You Say?)."

Conduct User Research

There are several ways to gather more feedback about your website, and that's the focus of the next step in the process. Choose one or more usability research methods to apply, and focus on the user personas that are most important for your website (a potential customer, for example).

Additional details are in "Adapt Your Website to Your Persona's Needs" in Chapter 5, "The Audience Is Listening (What Will You Say?)."

Conduct Keyword Research

One of the important considerations is to evaluate how they are getting to the content on your website. Look at all possible paths that people might use to get to your website content. Paths include everything from organic (natural) search to landing pages accessed via a paid search ad campaign.

Most of these online paths involve keywords or key phrases that a potential website visitor uses to reach your website. You need to do some keyword research to ensure that you are reflecting your target audience's language in your online marketing. You'll need to conduct what we refer to as a word market analysis to identify your target keywords.

Some companies also periodically use the Google Insights for Search tools (see Figure 2.3) to identify keyword trends, or use Google's Keyword tools (see Figure 2.4) to look at keyword volume.

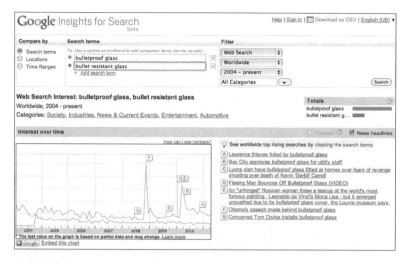

Figure 2.3 *Google Insights for Search tool, with an example keyphrase.*

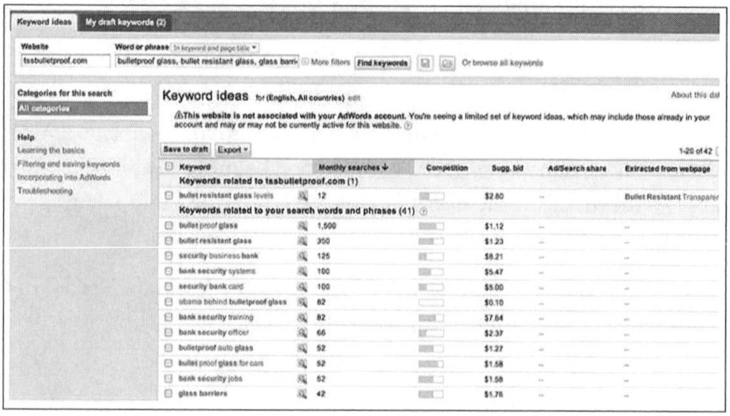

Figure 2.4 *Google Keywords tool, showing potential keyword ideas.*

Take a look at the additional information in "Speak Your Audience's Language: The Real Search Engine Optimization" in Chapter 5, "The Audience Is Listening (What Will You Say?)."

4. Sell Online

The next phase in the process is to work on the aspects of actually selling online. In a website (or website update) project, you'll need to optimize the user experience of the complete website. A critical but often overlooked aspect of most websites today is the landing pages that are part of a paid search campaign.

To sell online, you need to

- Design (or redesign) your website.

- Optimize landing pages.

Design (or Redesign) Your Website

Now that you have deeper insight into your website visitors and their needs, you can use the personas and user research to define a new information architecture for your website. You'll develop a website skeleton and define other paths people will use to get to your content.

Additional information architecture techniques help you to develop more detailed scenarios (using your user personas again) for each of the different goals you identified for your website visitors. The goal here is to avoid organizing the content of your website around your company's internal structure; the content should reflect how your potential customers think about your products and services, instead.

When you've built multiple scenarios, you'll need to reconcile the overlap between them, and create a content map. This content map is often simply a whiteboard with sticky notes that you've been working with to get to the page detail level. Feel free to identify new pages for your website, you can never have too much content!

Finally, you'll define the navigation structure, rough out the page layout, and begin working with a graphic designer to get the look and feel right for the functional elements you've identified.

The section "Designing Your Website" in Chapter 6, "Putting It All Together and Selling Online" describes all of these information architecture tools in detail.

Optimize Landing Pages

Do not overlook the landing pages that people use to access your website (typically through a paid search campaign or email marketing). Although separate from your main website, these are critically important paths into your website and directly affect your conversion rate.

One of the most important aspects of a landing page is the call to action. Make sure it's not in the page header that scrolls out of sight when someone reads the content further down the page. It should be clear and prominent (and perhaps a bit reminiscent of a late night infomercial). For a good call to action, bigger is better.

The section "Designing Your Landing Pages" in Chapter 6, "Putting It All Together and Selling Online" provides additional best practices for landing page design, examples, and granularity. It's also important to look at "Optimizing Your Landing Pages" in Chapter 6, "Putting It All Together and Selling Online" to ensure that you improve your conversion rate over time.

5. Manage Your Website

A critical component in the online sales engine is the project management piece, which covers everything from annual planning to specific deployment checklists and quality control.

To manage your website, you need to

- Conduct additional research.

- Maintain your website.

Conduct Additional Research

Now that you have a design to work with, even if it's just a paper prototype, it's time to do some additional testing. This step ensures that you both improve the user experience and optimize conversion rates (with tools such as A/B testing to compare the impact of two similar designs, for example). Apply both qualitative and quantitative research tools, if at all possible, to assemble a more complete picture.

See "Beyond Best Practices - User Research" in Chapter 7, "Making Websites That Work" for details on quantitative and qualitative usability and conversion rate test methods.

Maintain Your Website

We all know that a website is not a short-term or one-time project. After you've redesigned, analyzed, tested, and deployed your website, it's time to take a step back and make a maintenance plan. There are several website maintenance tasks that fall under annual, quarterly, monthly and weekly or daily planning and implementation.

Many search engine optimization tasks need to be addressed when planning a website update, as well as some often overlooked elements, such as handling 301 page redirects and 404 error pages.

More information can be found in "Website Planning and Maintenance" and "Planning a Website Refresh or Relaunch" in Chapter 7, "Making Websites That Work."

6. Increase Visibility with SEO and Paid Search

Next you'll need to monitor what is happening with your organic search and paid search campaigns. Update both using data from your web analytics tools over time, refining your keywords for both, as you go.

Don't forget that you are improving your website content for two main groups: website visitors, of course, but also the search engine spider (or crawler) programs as well. Optimize your pages, titles, and HTML tags to improve your search engine rankings. Improving your page content to more closely match your customer's search keywords also ensures that your potential customers will find your content more compelling as well.

Organic search and paid search advertising complement each other. Neither is free, even though you don't have to pay for organic visitors by the click, you do need to invest in website infrastructure and content to get organic visitors to find you at all. Some companies overlook the importance of location in their findability; don't forget to claim your listing in Google Places as well to boost organic search placement.

Figure 2.5 illustrates how you might target paid search campaign and search engine optimization (SEO) projects on different groups of key phrases.

Because the number of key phrases you can target with SEO is proportional to the size of your website, websites can target fewer terms with SEO than with paid search. Because it is a smaller list, organic search targets are typically more general search terms than paid search targets, but yield a higher number of searches per term.

Paid search keyword targets, by comparison, can be very specific terms, but individually lower volume.

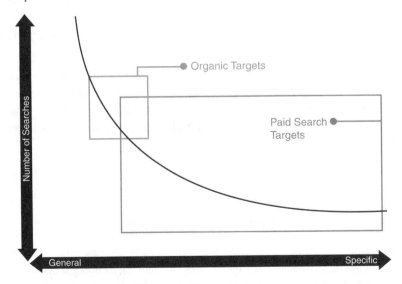

Figure 2.5 *Paid search campaign optimization tends to focus on more specific words than organic search optimization.*

Theoretically, using this approach, you can target your SEO and paid search efforts to complement each other, but keep your eye on the market and don't target too narrowly. Continue at least some advertising where your competition advertises... you don't want a qualified prospect to click on a competitor's ad because yours is no longer there.

Increase Findability with SEO

Search engine optimization (SEO), sometimes referred to as organic search, is the process of making a website more visible to people who use search engines such as Google, Yahoo!, or Bing to find what they need.

Because half of all Americans use search engines on a daily basis (according to the Pew Internet & American Life Project www.pewinternet.org/PPF/r/258/report_display.asp), optimizing for organic search can have a huge impact on your overall traffic.

Search engine spiders crawl websites across the Internet to identify which websites to display in response to a search query. They then assess the content and display the websites that have content matching the words used in the search.

At a tactical level, SEO involves making sure that your website is properly configured to allow these crawlers to find your content and easily identify its theme (explored in Chapter 8, "It's All About Visibility"). The core of SEO is the website content. Search engine spiders (or crawlers) consider what words you use, where they are positioned, and whether or not they match the keywords that people actually use when searching.

Google, Yahoo!, and Bing then determine the rank of a website based on their assessment of how relevant it is to the particular goals of the person executing the search. The goal of SEO is to improve that rank, by making sure that your themes and keywords can be readily identified by both website visitors and the search engine spiders.

Details on improving organic search ranking can be found in almost all of Chapter 8, "It's All About Visibility."

Extend Your Reach with Paid Search Advertising

Just as organic search ranking needs to be improved to increase your ranking with search engine results pages, your paid search advertising campaigns also rely on constant tweaking over time to gain incremental improvements.

You'll need to define your market, which involves targeting the right audience, identifying keywords and ad groups (based on keyword themes), and setting the campaign's region and time period. Working with a paid search advertising campaign also means that you need to qualify your market with specific ad copy, convert visitors into customers, and continuously revisit and refine your campaigns.

All of this is discussed in greater detail in "Extending Your Reach with Pay-Per-Click Advertising" in Chapter 8, "It's All About Visibility." You'll also want to consider landing page optimization tactics presented in "Designing your Landing Pages" in Chapter 6, "Putting It All Together and Selling Online."

Apply Advanced Visibility Strategies

While the number one method that people use to find a website is search (and within that realm, Google is the number one search engine), experts predict that sharing, not searching, is the wave of the future. That means that social media and other advanced visibility strategies will take on more importance in the near future. You need to devote a portion of your time, energy, and budget to managing a social media presence (alongside your SEO and paid search efforts) for your company.

GOING SOCIAL

Extending your website's reach into social media means that you should consider marketing your company (both directly and indirectly) on some of these social media websites:

- Facebook
- Google+
- YouTube
- Twitter
- LinkedIn
- Tumblr
- Flickr
- Formspring.me
- MySpace

Don't overlook niche social media websites for connecting more directly with your customers. For example, a yarn importer should be active on www.ravelry.com, a knitting and crocheting community.

Figure 2.6 shows a variety of social media tools, which should be considered when enhancing your online presence.

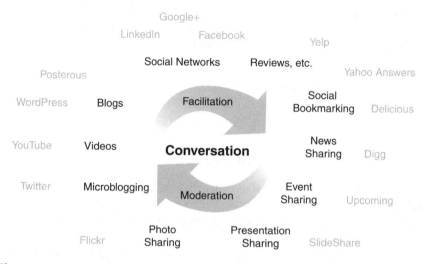

Figure 2.6 *A sample of current social media websites.*

Another advanced visibility strategy to consider pursuing is online display advertising, or banner (or pop-up) ads. While paid search ads are typically text-only ads, display ads are often animated or include media files. A display advertisement is meant to get you seen on a specific website. A paid search ad is meant to invite someone to take an action, such as clicking and visiting your website.

Both social media and display advertising are discussed in Chapter 8, "It's All About Visibility," in the sections "Advanced Visibility Strategies: Going Social" and "Advanced Visibility Strategies: Display Advertising."

7. Revisit the Metrics

Change your focus on which metrics and key performance indicators (KPIs) you measure, over time. Make changes to your website content and paid search accounts based on website visitor data.

Close the Loop with Metrics

The very last step, the gold mine actually, of the online sales engine, is where you have gathered enough data through multiple sales cycles over time (all captured in your web analytics tools as well as your customer relationship management software) to "close the loop." (To stretch this gold mine metaphor, you get a pot of gold at the end of the rainbow, when you close the loop.)

Now you can generate customer acquisition reports in your CRM system and analyze the reports in conjunction with your search marketing plan. You can identify the most valuable paid search and organic search keywords for your business. Then look at both the quality and quantity of lead conversions. Measure your results, and tweak your website content, marketing, and advertising campaigns based on those results.

Finally, you'll run the ROI numbers and calculate future projections based on past performance. Then adjust your marketing plan accordingly, armed with the new information.

Additional details on applying metrics to close the loop can be found in Chapter 9, "Running the Feedback Loop."

Maintain Your Analytics

Like anything, your web metrics are subject to entropy, or "creeping" disorder. So make sure you include regular tracking inspections in your website maintenance! Do this to avoid loss of valuable data through incomplete tracking or loss of connection between your business systems.

The ROI-Driven Process

In this version of the online search engine methodology, you'll use savings from your paid search campaign to drive the rest of the engine. Revenue is generated from improvements in this area early on, helping you see an early return on your investment.

After applying paid search campaign improvements, you move into the search engine optimization and keyword analysis areas, and then move on to improving the landing pages.

The final step in the ROI-driven model is to return to the beginning, which is audience analysis and improving the usability of your website. This important work often tends to bog a team down as it can be very time-consuming.

You might opt for this ROI-driven version of the online sales engine methodology to ensure that your company can get traction early on in the engine adoption process and get team buy-in for larger and more fundamental efforts.

The basic steps in the ROI-driven implementation process are

1. Configure tracking and set goals for metrics.

2. Improve the paid search advertising campaign:

   • "Weed out" underperforming keyphrases, ad copy, and landing pages (be careful if you only have data from web forms though, you might "optimize" and turn off phone calls or the seemingly underperforming group that lands large contracts).

   • Expand on good performers. Invest more of your budget here, constantly test and improve your ad copy, landing pages, and key phrases.

   • Focus on better calls to action and targeted usability updates to garner incremental increases in landing page conversion rates.

   • Lather, rinse, repeat.

3. Optimize the website for organic search.

4. Revisit the metrics.

5. Continue to implement the online sales engine by revisiting other components you skipped (such as audience analysis and usability) and make continuous improvements to your website.

Summary

Social media, paid search, SEO, and user experience improvements are the tactical components in an iterative Internet marketing process. Metrics tracking the improvements and results help you optimize this process.

There are two ways to implement the online sales engine:

• **Customer-driven**, which ensures that you start with defining your market and audience analysis activities first.

• **ROI-driven**, which ensures that you start saving money in paid search sooner and using those funds to drive implementation of additional components.

The specific phases of the customer-driven online sales engine process are

1. Define your goals.

2. Configure tracking and set goals for metrics.

3. Conduct research and improve the user experience.

4. Sell online.

5. Manage your website.

6. Increase visibility with search engine optimization and paid search.

7. Revisit the metrics.

The basic steps in the ROI-driven implementation process are

1. Configure tracking and set goals for metrics.

2. Improve the paid search advertising campaign.

3. Optimize the website for organic search.

4. Revisit the metrics.

5. Continue to implement the online sales engine by revisiting other components you skipped (such as audience analysis and usability) and make continuous improvements to your website.

Are you ready? Then, let's move ahead to the next chapters and dive into the details of each online sales engine component.

3

Building a Metrics-Driven Practice

Static online brochures used as company websites lose leads and sales to websites that make and maintain direct connections to customers. A company's website is the key connection between a business and its customers, driving bottom-line results.

The challenges of today's economy accelerate this trend. Savvy business leaders demand a new level of accountability. Chief marketing officers (CMOs) and marketing managers are rapidly shifting advertising spend online because it is more trackable (and because people are moving away from traditional media in favor of online media).

They're also investing in tools such as Google Analytics, social media, and customer relationship management (CRM) systems (such as Salesforce) to improve accountability and to make better connections with customers.

If the goal is to use your website to connect to customers, how do you do it? Your business decision-making processes need to be better informed about what's happening on your website. Website metrics hold the key to business success, teaching you which online marketing tactics work better than others to generate new leads and convert them into customers. These metrics, and how you can start to track them, are the focus of this chapter.

The New Era of Website Metrics

Web analytics offers a dizzying set of possible metrics to review and master. Web dashboards serve up values and trends for visits, page views, pages/visit, bounce rates, time on site, the proportion of new or returning visitors, and information about the source of visitors. (Do they come from search engines? Paid search advertising? Banner advertising? Referrals from other websites?)

These same tools track average click-to-conversion time, average number of clicks to conversion, average impressions to conversion, visitor loyalty, browser capabilities, new versus returning visitors, and so on. They count and summarize information about what your visitors do on your website, including where they start on your website, where they leave it, and where they spend the most time.

In addition, companies with e-commerce websites may review browse-to-buy ratios, revenue, revenue-to-expense ratios, average order value, visits, or days to purchase, and the performance of particular categories of products.

These measures might seem to contradict each other sometimes. For example, a successful website might have a high bounce rate. By focusing on words that result in sales, website traffic may drop while sales increase, strengthening your return on investment (ROI).

It's easy to drown in all this data, to suffer from "analysis paralysis" and hesitate to act. So, it's critical to drill down to the fundamental goals of the website and select a handful of the right metrics to monitor. These are your Key Performance Indicators (KPIs).

Which Metrics Matter Most?

For lead-generation websites, such as the PupMed example we use throughout this book, the critical measurement is new leads, whether it is email, contact form submissions, or phone calls.

Yet a huge number of leads that your sales team must wade through is not necessarily a good thing if many are unqualified. So *qualified leads* is a better metric, and the connection must be made from leads to sales.

For e-commerce websites, such as the TropiCo example elsewhere in this book, the critical measurement is of course revenue, or more accurately put, *profitability*.

Influencing Leads and Revenue

Because website outcomes such as leads and sales result from several factors, however, monitoring the influence of a few more things on leads and sales can unlock the means to increasing them.

Start with old-fashioned sales techniques. What can turn a website visitor into a prospect or lead? What turns your prospect into a customer? Some transactions depend on price, others on quality or trust, most on a combination of these factors.

Think of your business in terms of "data hinges." What are those data points that open the door and turn a random visitor into a potential customer? Is it a phone call to your sales staff or an online inquiry? Which search engine keywords result in more customers than others? Dig deep to get the answers. If you don't know, rework your website to tell you!

For example, try to evaluate which type of prospect results more often in a sale: a website visitor or a caller on the phone. Typically, a website will have contact form submissions and phone calls scattered equally throughout the website. But perhaps in reality, phone calls convert far better into sales.

Why might that be? Maybe there are unique product options that can be better explained and highlighted on the phone, resulting in an immediate sale. If that's the case, then downplay the contact form and highlight the phone number throughout the website, instead.

The Conversion Funnel

You can think of turning a random website visitor into a potential customer as a conversion process, using a funnel metaphor.

A website visitor who came from a paid search advertisement or organic search typically ends on a custom landing page where a specific call to action is defined.

The prospect either

- Takes the call to action (calls your company or completes an online form), or

- Uses the navigation on the landing page to move elsewhere on your website first, to learn more

Figure 3.1 shows the prospect conversion funnel for both offline (left) and online (right) methods. The left side shows the traditional (pre-Internet) sales process, which is pushing information at the prospect and involves regular communications such as ads, direct mail, phone calls, and so on to get them to the final purchasing decision.

By contrast, the right side of Figure 3.1 shows how a website affects people at different stages of the buying process, each is probably using different search terms at different stages. As Internet marketers, it's our job to make sure that the website is visible on keywords used at *all* stages of the buying process and that we are sending prospects to content that's appropriate for their current stage in the process.

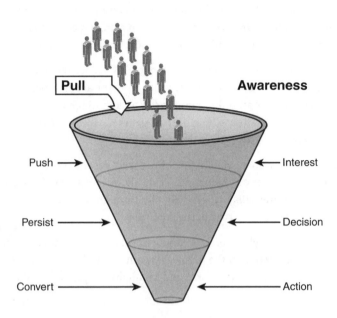

Figure 3.1 *How awareness and website content work together to funnel and convert leads.*

🔍 *Tip*

> Of course, the content of the website itself is a consideration. If your copy isn't converting prospects into customers, isn't prompting them with the right call to action, or is difficult to use, all the website visitor data in the world won't help you. These issues are addressed in Part II, "Building the Engine."

Lead-Generation Businesses

Many (non e-commerce) businesses need to generate leads, but lead generation is only the beginning of the sales process. The next step is typically for the leads to be collected, prioritized, and then handled online or offline (via telephone) by a sales professional.

The sales team identifies the prospect's needs from the data provided by the website visitor and discusses the company product or service line, crafting the conversation just for that prospect.

E-Commerce Businesses

If you're selling products directly online, the online contact form or live chat most likely is the best way for visitors to pose a question (get an answer) and become a customer.

Don't underestimate the use of the phone for an e-commerce website, though. Many businesses with corporate clients still sell heavily using a telephone-based sales team. This is because either their website can't handle purchase orders or corporate credit card limits can't accommodate high-end purchases.

Ultimately, you are the best judge of how your business works with its customers. But you can still identify and test which contact methods result in more new customers over other methods.

Choosing a Contact Method

For both lead generation and e-commerce businesses, the type of contact method defined in the calls to action on your website has a great impact on tracking marketing metrics.

Using Mailto Links

Many lead-generation websites rely on a link to an email as a call to action, something like "Have questions or want to learn more? Contact Sales-Team@Example.com for more details."

Tracking links to emails (called *mailto* links because that is the Hypertext Markup Language [HTML] code for this type of link) is imperfect. Mailto links launch a separate program (such as Microsoft Outlook) from where the email is sent (or not). The only way to track this using your website analytics tool is to track how often the link is clicked, but a better measure is how often the email is *sent*. This second metric is unavailable from a mailto link. In addition, although your sales team can count the number of email messages they receive, critical information that would be available within web analytics about the website visit would not be associated with the email.

Although there are other email-only options to tracking this, such as including specific or dynamic email addresses for your particular level of desired granularity, these methods are generally weaker than using an online contact form.

Another such email option is to create a specific paid search-only email address to see how many visitors arrive at each landing page (and how many click the link or send an email to that address). This does require additional work to input the total number of emails into your CRM system. In addition, this form of tracking is weaker than using a contact form as other important associated analytics data is not included.

Using an Online Contact Form

A better option is to use an online contact form as a call to action on your website. Online contact forms with thank you pages are more trackable than mailto links. Your website analytics tool can be set up to watch and count the number of thank you pages that are shown and connect this information with how visitors who viewed contact pages came to your website.

However, sometimes online contact forms are not configured with a separate thank you page, having tracking problems similar to mailto links. For example, you can count how often the form was viewed, and maybe even count how often the Submit button was clicked, but ideally you send folks to a separate thank you form to accurately count how many users made it to the end of the funnel.

In addition, the thank you page is an opportunity to continue the conversation immediately with your prospects, set their expectations in terms of the swiftness and nature of your sales teams' response, and offer custom information based on their interest in a whitepaper, a request for quote, or whatever tempted them to share their contact information in the first place!

Whether a contact form is an appropriate first contact depends on your audience and their preferences. To many, contact forms feel cold and impersonal (not to mention one sided). Yet contact forms are useful for people who are surfing for personal items on company time. Given the web analytics patterns for business-to-consumer (B2C) websites, this seems to be a typical occurrence!

Contact forms are also useful for shy people who would prefer an impersonal start to the inquiry and those who are surfing outside of business hours and have difficulty dictating contact information via a voicemail, which includes those for whom your language is a second language or anyone with a name or email address that is difficult to spell.

On the plus side, your contact form is open 24 hours a day, 7 days a week. Your sales staff probably does like to sleep, occasionally.

Using Telephone Contact

Many other people would like to reach out via phone, to get a few questions answered and know more before sharing their email address or phone number. So, it's also important to offer a telephone contact option, and critical to track it.

Phone tracking can be done at several levels of granularity. See the section "Integrating Web KPIs into Business Decision Making," later in this chapter.

Using Live Chat

Another popular option is to offer live chat. This has been shown to be popular with folks who need an answer to a question about your product or service but cannot make a phone call. (Again, think of those people surfing for personal items while at work.)

Live chat can be expensive, but can provide a more real-time interactive way to engage visitors before they look elsewhere to solve their problem.

Consider the Contact Method Carefully

You need to think carefully about what, how, and when you want a potential prospect to respond to your website copy, and how that potential prospect might want to contact you.

It very well may *not* be the current way that the call to action is set up on your website.

What to Measure

You might want to review your website performance as a whole, looking at total traffic and total leads driven by the entire website. Yet we find it more informative to break things out by Internet marketing channel because the patterns tend to vary based on the different channels.

We usually analyze these Internet marketing channels (sometimes referred to as a medium):

- Natural search (also known as organic search). Improvements come through concerted search engine optimization (SEO) activities.

- Paid search (or pay-per-click [PPC]) marketing.

- Referring websites (can include web-based email programs). These incoming inlinks may come from social websites (such as Facebook, LinkedIn, or Twitter), conventional link building, or from online PR activities. You can read about some related metrics in the "Secondary SEO Metrics" section, later in this chapter.

- Direct visitors (who arrive via a bookmark or link in an email). These may come from offline marketing, typing in a link seen on a billboard, or may be someone who already knows you or works for you. We do not spend much time on this channel.

- Custom-defined channels (can include email, banner ads).

Whichever core type of business you have, both lead-generation and e-commerce companies need to optimize search engine keywords using both natural and paid search advertising keyphrases.

You're optimizing not just to drive more traffic to your website, but to identify *which keywords convert more visitors into customers* and which keywords are the most cost-effective at doing so. That is your ultimate goal, the bottom line in SEO and paid search metrics.

To measure that, you need to put many elements in place:

- Start a program of keyword-rich content generation as part of your website maintenance plan.

- Build inlinks through a link building or link exchange program to improve SEO.

- Begin or continue a paid search advertising campaign.

- Build landing pages (discussed in detail in Chapter 6, "Putting It All Together and Selling Online").

After these elements are in place, you can watch as your plans unfold and your traffic and leads grow. Some answers will emerge quickly. For instance, paid search may have higher volumes and provide quicker feedback than SEO, which takes care and patience. However, the data you will get from your SEO initiatives is critically important.

In the end, you need to gather this data over time for it to have any impact on your future business decisions.

Don't be surprised if the seeds you sow today aren't harvested for 2 more years. (This is particularly true regarding SEO data you're gathering, less so for paid search.) But the fruits of this effort will be worth it if you can pinpoint exactly which search engine phrases generate more customers for different products or services and be able to quantify that precisely. Armed with this new information, you can make sound business decisions regarding paid online advertising, among other things.

SEO Key Performance Indicators

Your SEO key performance indicators (KPIs) should describe the expected progress of SEO at the level of traffic and leads, as well as some of the intermediate stages, such as changes in web rank and increase in keyphrase visibility.

The categories of activity that you should track and review are

- Changes in on-site outcomes
- Changes in keyphrase rank
- Secondary metrics, based on your business situation

In addition, you need to conduct a competitive comparison against known online competition.

On-Site Metrics

The primary on-site activities that matter are visits and leads or sales, but to analyze this you look at these specific metrics:

- **Organic visits/month:** Total number of organic visits per month.
- **Nonbranded organic visits/month:** Number of organic visits that do not include a brand name.
- **Organic conversions/month:** Conversions and conversion rates (the proportions of raw counts) from each type of organic visit per month. You should expect your branded terms to have higher conversion rates, because potential customers close to a buying decision tend to use them.
- **Revenue from organic conversions:** If you are running an e-commerce business.
- **Number of keyphrases:** Total organic keyphrases for which the website is found.
- **Category coverage:** Percentage of targeted keyphrases that are in the top 20 search results.

For each of these metrics, higher counts and higher rates are good and show progress in your SEO visibility.

Off-Site Metrics: Keyphrase Rank

You also need to measure changes in things off your website, such as your rank in search engines over time. Be careful about Googling yourself constantly and writing down your rank. This does not give you accurate information.

Google shows organic results based on your geographic location and your past search and clickthrough history, so the results you see are not "universal" and might not even be common.

Instead, you should invest in a service such as Advanced Web Ranking, Yield Software, SEO Clarity, or SEM Rush to monitor the rankings for you. You'll need to start monitoring the changes in keyphrase rank over time.

One way is to create an extensive table that shows the detailed drilldown of the competitive comparison, using the keyphrases of interest. Show the change in rank for each keyphrase, by competitor as well as the degree of change.

For more on the SEO word market, see the section "Evaluate Your Keyphrases in the Context of the Entire Word Market" in Chapter 5, "The Audience Is Listening (What Will You Say?)."

Secondary SEO Metrics

There are a number of other potential metrics, including the following:

- Increase in count of entrance pages
- Number of inlinks you have versus your competitors
- Number of inlinks built
- Visits and conversions from referring websites
- Visits and conversions from elements such as images, videos, news, and local searches
- Social mentions or online reviews

Some of these secondary metrics are appropriate for certain business situations, but not for others. When you should include each metric is further explained in Table 3.1.

Table 3.1 Applications for Secondary SEO KPI Metrics

Secondary Metric	Useful When You Need To
Increase in entrance pages count	Evaluate whether changes your technical team has made to expose content previously hidden are working. Have search engine crawlers surfaced more of your website to searchers? Evaluate whether new content you are creating is attracting new visitors to the website. Note: Google Analytics uses the term *landing pages* in its user interface. We use the term entrance pages here, to distinguish it from paid search landing pages.
Number of inlinks	Evaluate SEO ranking. Inlinks are a leading indicator for other, more important SEO metrics such as your ranking. Counting links and assessing their relative quality is a part of planning a link-building program. Yahoo Site Explorer provides inlink counts for free, while SEO Spyglass provides a counting and quality-evaluation service for a license fee.

Secondary Metric	Useful When You Need To
Number of inlinks built	Assess the velocity and impact of your link-building program or an online PR initiative.
Visits and conversions from referring websites	Evaluate the investment of any "pay to play" websites where you have purchased listings. Evaluate the impact on your link-building program. Assess the direct influence of thought leaders who mention you. Note: Referring websites have indirect effects on your SEO rank (see the section "Link Building Fundamentals" in Chapter 7, "Making Websites That Work"), so it is more than just visits and conversions that are important to consider for these activities.
Visits and conversions coming from images, videos, news, shopping results, and/or local searches	Evaluate the impact of programs to increase your visibility through images, videos, news releases, product feeds, and local information, respectively.
Social mentions or reviews (measuring the number and tone of comments)	Evaluate the perception of your brand and which online conversations you need to join. Social media websites are typically only indirectly useful for SEO, because many of the links to your website from social websites are "no follow" links. Yet, these conversations influence your current and prospective customers and cannot be ignored.

Review these secondary SEO KPI metrics as possible ones to track.

Learn more about how to improve your website's performance on these metrics in the "Get Out of Your Own Way: Make Sure Your Content Is Findable" and "Advanced Visibility Strategies: Going Social" sections in Chapter 8, "It's All About Visibility."

Paid Search KPIs

Your paid search KPI should monitor your paid search performance at the level of traffic, costs, and leads or sales.

The categories of activity that you should track and review are

- Changes in traffic and on-site outcomes
- Secondary metrics, based on your business situation

Measuring Paid Search Traffic and On-Site Outcomes

The critical measures are traffic, leads or sales, and costs. These are interrelated and shouldn't be considered in isolation.

You could drive lots of cheap traffic on words irrelevant to your business and gain no sales. Or, you could invest in a handful of keyphrases that do not drive high traffic but push users through the conversion funnel.

To analyze this, you look at these specific metrics:

- **Paid search (or PPC) visits/month:** Total number of paid search visitors per month.

- **Nonbranded paid search visits/month:** Number of paid search visits that do not include a brand name.

- **Paid search conversions/month:** Conversions and conversion rates (the proportions of raw counts) from each type of paid search visit per month. You should expect your branded terms to have higher conversion rates, because potential customers close to a buying decision tend to use them.

- **Cost per lead or cost per sale:** Both overall and by keyphrase, splitting out branded and nonbranded phrases. This metric is the cost per click times the average conversion rate of a click. So, cost per lead is more informative about the entire process than cost per click.

- **Average rank of your keyphrases:** This shows where your ads show within the sponsored listings on the search engine results page.

- **Quality score:** Provided for each keyword by Google AdWords, it is a measure that includes weighting for your clickthrough rates and the match of your landing page to the search term, among other things.

- **Revenue:** Value of online orders from paid search.

- **Revenue-to-expense ratio:** The ratio of revenue to expenses (paid search spend and any management or infrastructure costs related to paid search).

Those accustomed to reviewing paid search metrics may notice the absence of clickthrough rate (CTR). We do look at this, but its interpretation is more nuanced. Sometimes low is good if your ad copy qualifies visitors well, sometimes high is good if you want to maximize traffic. Because you do not pay for visitors who do not click, it is not a primary metric.

Because paid search visitors do cost you money for each click, higher is not necessarily better for visits (although higher is better for conversion counts and rates). The cost per lead or cost per sale should be as low as possible.

Secondary Paid Search Metrics

Depending on your business situation, you can review a number of other potential metrics, including the following:

- **Number of keyphrases** (The total paid search keyphrases for which the website is found)

- **Number of ad copy variations** (The number being tested)

- **Number of landing pages in use**

- **Conversion rate by landing page**

Table 3.2 Applications for Secondary Paid Search KPI Metrics

Secondary Metric	Useful When You Need To
Number of keyphrases (perhaps grouped for reporting to different business units)	Assess the coverage of your paid search ad buy. Larger is not necessarily better if omitted keyphrases produced low-quality leads or no leads at all.
Number of ad copy variations being tested	Quickly review a measure of whether your team is taking an exploratory, hypothesis-driven approach to your paid search program.
Number of landing pages in use	See a quick view of the diversity of pages you are using. Higher is not necessarily better, but testing landing pages is key to online success.
Conversion rate by landing page	Evaluate whether your landing pages are working to turn website visitors to leads or sales.

Review these secondary paid search KPI metrics as possible ones to track.

Learn more on how to optimize based on these primary and secondary metrics in the "Effective Paid Search Management" section in Chapter 8.

Use Business Analysis to Define Your KPI Benchmarks and Goals

The website KPIs mentioned earlier should be generally useful and are standard reports available within common web analytics and paid search management platforms. But, what do you use as a basis for comparison?

Do you report trends before and after a change in your web infrastructure? Do you focus week over week, month over month, year over year?

When you design your KPIs, you may want to consider the following:

- **Seasonality** in your business determines what values to use as benchmarks.

  - In a highly seasonal business, such education, real estate, or retail, considering metrics month over month will cause a fair bit of spin. If August is a peak month and September is a valley, comparing month over month trends is less useful than looking at the same time the previous year.

- If day of week matters, and it typically does, then aligning your year-over-year comparisons to capture the same number of weekdays will also matter; otherwise, you'll see differences in metrics that might be due to April of 2012 having a different number of weekend days than April of 2011.

- **Length of your sales cycle** determines how soon you get to measure leads.

  - Unpack the decision process of your prospect; what do they need when? Use this understanding to focus on waypoints in a long cycle. For instance, metrics such as time on site may indicate engagement with your website's content that might be a leading indicator for a sale in the future.

  - In addition, some pages on your website (say a pricing page) may have information critical to folks later in the sales cycle, and so measuring engagement with those pages may be valuable.

Many people start with just recording the data and then move to creating specific goals and timelines for improving performance after an adequate baseline has been created.

The best baseline is a year of tracking data before starting to measure change, because web behavior for lead-generation and e-commerce websites is very seasonal. Year-over-year comparisons are a staple for decision making.

When to Measure Matters

It is important to consider which call-to-action contact options are available at what times and when your prospects might want to contact you. The time of day, day of the week, or season often affects the contact method of choice for your prospects.

Traffic patterns and high periods vary among businesses. Some of the differences are by category. For instance, business-to-business (B2B) websites sometimes have stronger weekday/weekend patterns than business-to-consumer (B2C) websites.

Web analytics shows activity and conversion peaks. For instance, a B2C company might see higher web traffic during weekdays, and fewer conversions but higher web conversion rates on weekends because on weekends the web is the best way to make contact (as in Figure 3.2).

You might think that a B2B lead-generation company may see little to no traffic on weekends, but there is typically some, although not as much as on weekdays (see Figure 3.3).

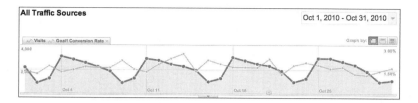

Figure 3.2 *An example B2C lead-generation website showing a strong weekly dip in traffic but an increase in conversion rate on weekends.*

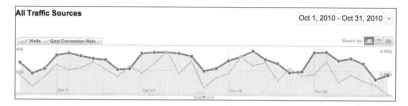

Figure 3.3 *An example B2B lead-generation website showing a weak weekly dip in traffic and conversion rates on weekends.*

As shown in Figure 3.4, the B2C e-commerce website example does not show as marked a weekday/weekend pattern as shown in Figure 3.5 for a B2B e-commerce company. B2B e-commerce websites have weekday traffic and conversion rates higher than weekend traffic and conversion rates, but with nontrivial weekend activity.

Instead, the B2C website shows stronger seasonal pattern, with a dip around Christmas as the holiday shopping frenzy in the United States subsided.

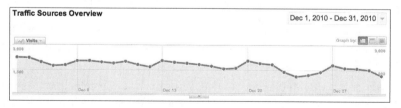

Figure 3.4 *A traffic and conversion rate pattern example from an e-commerce B2C website showing seasonal patterns (decline around Christmas) but without strong week-day/weekend patterns.*

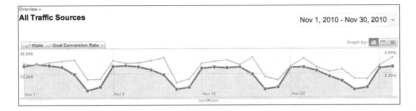

Figure 3.5 *A traffic and conversion rate pattern example from an e-commerce B2B website showing strong weekday/weekend patterns.*

These figures are merely examples, and experience with your own website and your prospects is the best guide.

Integrating Web KPIs into Business Decision Making

Now that you've identified which KPIs you want to track, you need to rework your internal business processes and website calls to action to gather that data. The goal is to integrate tracking these metrics into your existing online strategy.

Do you want prospects to contact you via an online form, "like" you on Facebook, or pick up the phone? Customize the call to action on each website page as it applies to your goal and target audience.

HERE'S A GREAT PHONE TIP

Did you know that discount toll-free 800 numbers are now commonplace for some businesses? Charges vary, based on number of minutes used per month or can be monthly flat rates.

If you use call forwarding on the line, you can route the calls to your sales team's incoming land lines. Just make sure you track which number was used on an incoming call so that you can identify that it came from your website, a specific page, or even from a specific medium.

For different options, see the section "Call Tracking: Why It's Essential and Selecting the Granularity Needed," in Chapter 4, "Breaking Down Silos to Get the Metrics You Need."

If you haven't implemented any customized call to action methods just for your website, you aren't able to dig into the sales data from your website.

If you're buying online advertising, you need to use a tool such as AdWords Conversion Tracking to begin gathering data about which ads are working better for you than others. (If you're not even doing that, you're essentially flying blind and might as well be buying print advertising.)

Case Study: Landing Pages with Custom 800 Numbers

We recently worked with a manufacturer of bullet-resistant devices (building construction items such as doors, counters, and transaction windows). Although the company had a website, it wasn't generating either the number of leads or the quality of leads they were looking for.

After reorganizing their Google AdWords account to focus on the keywords that would deliver better leads, we focused on crafting effective landing pages for those keywords. We initially went with a simple strategy for the toll-free (800) telephone numbers: one 800 number for all paid search landing pages, and a second 800 number for the rest of the website.

This company's business is complex and detail oriented, so prospects usually need to talk with a sales representative about the particulars of their project before placing an order.

Consequently, paid search drives a lot of qualified phone calls. Without a separate dedicated paid search 800 number, the company was making changes to their marketing efforts based on incomplete data. If a particular campaign drove an increase in calls but not website contact form leads, that success would have been impossible to recognize. The client risked misinterpreting the results of their efforts.

Furthermore, the missing data meant it took longer to evaluate the success or failure of any marketing experiment. With only half the data, it took twice as long to understand whether a trend was statistically significant or just a random variation.

After the 800 number tracking was in place, the company was able to make more informed decisions and make them faster. They were able to turn confidently away from underperforming campaigns and reallocate the budget to new marketing trials.

They quickly evaluated the results of these new pilot programs and moved the successful efforts into their regular advertising program. These tactics resulted in 27% year-over-year growth in online leads and a more than 30% year-over-year growth in sales revenue.

The plan is for later versions to get more granular, adding additional 800 numbers to tease out the organic, direct, and referral traffic and analyze the bottom-line results better (by attaching traffic source data to each lead to better understand the direct effects of marketing efforts on sales and revenue).

Web to Lead to CRM Analysis: Close That Loop!

If you're committed to converting your website into a competitive advantage for your company that drives new sales growth, you need to gather data. Data that lets you act at a strategic level to adjust your online marketing plan over time.

Your Internet marketing strategy needs to drive qualified new prospects to your website and then work to steadily improve the rate at which these prospects become customers. You'll improve this conversion rate by gathering and analyzing website visitor data, on a regular basis, to inform your sales and marketing teams about prospect conversion.

If your sales team is working within an existing CRM system, the right choice is to add new data to the existing process rather than reinvent it. If your sales team works without a CRM, hurry up and get one!

WHAT DOES *CLOSE THE LOOP* MEAN?

The phrase *close the loop* is somewhat related to the field of attribution modeling, which strives to find data correlating to business results. We're talking about it here in terms of digging deep for the data that connects the dots between your online marketing efforts and actual sales that result from them.

The Impact of Internet Marketing on Sales

To give yourself a full picture of the impact of your Internet marketing efforts on your sales process, start using this tracking methodology:

1. Capture the keywords that people use (both organic search and paid search) to find your website.

2. Bring the data about website visitors and their keywords into your CRM system.

3. Make sure your sales group indicates that each lead was converted into a customer within your CRM system, making the data ready for reporting.

4. Generate customer acquisition reports using your CRM system. Analyze the reports in conjunction with your search marketing plan to identify the most valuable paid search and organic search keywords for your business.

Close the loop between sales and marketing by capturing and analyzing the sources of your leads and sales over time to improve ROI.

To do this, capture website visitor and conversion data over time and display it in a CRM, and then use it to refine marketing activities. Figure 3.6 shows an overview of this process.

Figure 3.6 *Closing the loop between sales, marketing, and the website.*

Let's look at the first two steps of the "close the loop" tracking process in greater detail.

Step 1: Capture the Source of Each Lead

Web analytics provides data in aggregate on keyphrases that convert visitors into leads or sales. This is usually enough for e-commerce businesses, unless they want to aggregate information on repeat purchases.

For lead-generation businesses, however, there's another step in the process. The information on the source of the lead needs to persist as the lead is nurtured from a prospect through the sale.

Several lead-attribution systems are available, and Pure Visibility offers one of our own. For our tool, we often customize the data we collect based on specific business or company drivers, but we always gather the following:

- The referring URL of the website that brought the prospect to your website, which identifies the search engine and so forth

- The keywords or keyphrases used to find the website

- The initial page viewed in your website, which is often a landing page

- The website page where the call to action was initiated

- The type of marketing referral, such as paid search, referrer, organic search, or direct link

In addition, we recommend that you store the data for a website visitor's initial visit without overwriting it with data about subsequent visits. You want to track how the prospect initially found you so that you can improve the online marketing channels that bring more (and better qualified) prospects to your website.

Step 2: Move the Lead Data into Your CRM

One of the leading CRM applications today is Salesforce, but it shouldn't matter which CRM your company uses; any database system can handle a batch script to upload the website data you've culled on a regular basis.

You might need to adjust your business processes to better handle or route requests for information or follow-up phone calls that come specifically from your website.

Figure 3.6 illustrates how to close the loop and work iteratively, over time, for best results. Getting data into your CRM is just the first step. You need to analyze the data after you've been gathering it over time, to determine which search engine keywords (or online ads) produce higher conversion rates than others.

This iterative process of closing the loop from marketing to lead to sales ultimately improves your ROI as you gain insight and focus your efforts based on website conversion data.

Case Study: Reviewing Customer Conversion Data in Salesforce

One of our clients is a manufacturer of research laboratory equipment, accessories, and consumables. Because of the complexity of the sales process and the need to educate their prospective customer, they needed to measure the effectiveness of many marketing campaigns (PR, email blasts, banner ads, organic search, and paid search).

The landing page contact form data is captured using JavaScript and moved into their Salesforce application. The company had to make a few changes to integrate the website data about prospects into their sales process.

This particular company wanted to track not just landing pages and contact forms but also what type of information was being requested by each new prospect.

Over time, this data can reflect which whitepaper, newsletter, product demonstration, or search keyword triggered the prospect to initially contact the company, which materials supported the final sale, and in what order.

Moving Data into Salesforce

The basic steps in the process are as follows:

1. Include code that handles capturing the data on every website page.

2. In Salesforce, create fields to accept the lead source data with a new lead, and create the mappings so this data flows between the website and Salesforce as a lead evolves into a contact or opportunity.

3. Adjust your website's lead contact form to hand the lead source data to your CRM, by applying the data entered into the form.

You can customize the fields in the website script and in your Salesforce form to track data such as specific email campaigns or responses to traditional advertising media, as well. You'll probably want to customize the script to capture the referring web page URL, the search engine and keywords entered, and perhaps the link type (organic search, paid search), along with the contact information. For instance, a lead that comes through a search engine might have the following fields attached:

Search Engine: Google.com

Keyphrase: Atlanta Puppy Supplies

Link Type: Paid search

Or

Search Engine: Bing.com

Keyphrase: Best Smoothies in Fort Lauderdale

Link Type: Organic search

KPI Reporting on Leads and Sales

After you move the data from your website into your CRM system, you have to wait for the sales cycle to close. Make sure that your sales team knows to close the loop when they make a sale, by going into the CRM system and changing a prospect into a customer.

Over time, when many sales have been closed, you'll have a statistically significant amount of data that can be analyzed. That's when you run a set of opportunity conversion reports, or customer-acquisition reports, and begin to analyze which online methods have generated more new customers over others and the costs associated with each.

Sometimes with long sales cycles and multiple touchpoints, it is not leads generated but leads influenced that provides the important information.

Quantity Versus Quality

After you run the reports, the analysis should examine both the quantity and quality of lead conversions.

Which set of search engine keywords would you choose to invest in again?

- The keywords that generated 200 prospects over a month's time but only resulted in 3 closed sales

- The keywords that generated only 20 prospects but resulted in 10 closed sales

Although the answer may appear obvious, it might actually be an "it depends" situation, where with a few minor adjustments to your website copy you can improve the conversion rate on the landing page that's capturing 200 prospects per month... and surpass the second set of keywords in closed sales.

And what if the first product costs $2,000 and the second one $50? Again, it depends. You need to dig a little deeper instead of analyzing the numbers at first glance.

Closing the loop helps to quantify which online marketing method improves advertising spend over another. Ideally, during the reporting and analysis phase, you'll be able to see which marketing efforts introduce new customers to your company, which channels influence the prospect, and which channels help to close the transaction.

A WORD OF CAUTION

Make sure the persons analyzing this data in Salesforce (whoever is closing the loop) has some statistical analysis experience. It's extremely dangerous to make business decisions based on a "trend" with a sample size of, say, three. A statistical analyst instinctively knows this, whereas someone from your marketing or sales team might not.

Google Analytics is a powerful statistical analysis tool but does require some training and some thoughtfulness to apply it properly. The same goes for Google AdWords, where you can conduct A/B testing with different website page versions using Website Optimizer. Approach both with caution.

The bottom line is that any time you are crunching data, you're also making some underlying assumptions. The catch is that when the assumptions are faulty, the data analysis is, too.

Projections for Future Gain Based on Past Performance

ROI for your website is a large topic, as it encompasses so many things: the initial investment in design work and coding to implement the website, the costs of hosting and maintaining the website, the costs of content generation, the costs of paid search advertising, of link building for SEO, of online PR, and more.

It might seem easier to break things into smaller pieces for analysis, yet so much is interconnected. You need to work out whether calculating the ROI for paid search activities includes only the ad spend budget, or that plus management fees if managed externally, or that plus time for internal support, or all the preceding plus a share in the basic website maintenance costs.

It is easy to calculate over the wrong investment sum. Get agreement on this before moving forward!

When you do have a sense of the investment, work through the exercise in Table 3.3. This table summarizes the basic method to calculate the value proposition for online lead or sales generation.

Working through it, you will figure out the maximum you are willing to pay for a lead through paid search or SEO activities. You can then use this value to gauge whether new investments will be fruitful.

Table 3.3 Basic ROI Calculation Method

Index	Item	Calculated By or Taken From
1	Value of a lead. ($)	= 2 x 3
2	Proportion of leads that become sales. (%)	Your sales records (CRM).
3	Average value of a sale (can be individual or lifetime value of a customer). ($)	Your sales records (CRM).
4	Average margin from a sale. (%) The revenue after you make and ship the product or perform the service.	Your financial team, 10% is a starting point if you don't have a figure.
5	How much of your margin you are willing to spend to get the lead. (%)	Strive to do better than breaking even. A good starting point is 4% to 5%.
6	Maximum you should pay for a lead. ($)	= 1 x 4 x 5

Now that you know target investment for leads, you can calculate what you might be willing to pay for a click in paid search (see Table 3.4) or a visitor via SEO (see Table 3.5).

Table 3.4 is essentially extra rows for Table 3.3 that work through the investment for paid search advertising. Table 3.5 holds the rows for calculating projected ROI for an SEO initiative.

Table 3.4 Paid Search Calculation

Index	Item	Calculated By or Taken From
7	Average cost per click ($)	Your paid search management dashboard, although this is under your control and you may back into this by multiplying 1 x 5 x 8 or dividing 9/10.
8	Conversion rate from visitor to lead (for lead generation websites) or visitor to buyer (for e-commerce websites)	Average for paid search visitors, from your web lead (%) analytics, typically less than 5%.
9	Ad spend ($)	Your investment, although you could create projections by modeling the impact of this.
10	Clicks	Your paid search management dashboard, although this is under your control and you may back into a larger budget from a small sample by multiplying 7 x 9.

Table 3.5 SEO Calculation

Index	Item	Calculated By or Taken From
11	Cost of proposed infrastructure or content initiative	Business decisions
12	Increase in organic visits per month	Projected increase in organic traffic due to proposed initiative in line 7
13	Conversion rate from visitor to lead (%)	Average for organic visitors, from your web analytics, typically less than 5%
14	Duration over which to calculate the gain (months)	Business decisions
15	Projected revenue from improvement	$= 12 \times 14 \times 13 \times 1$
16	Break-even point	When $11 = 12 \times 14 \times 13 \times 6$

Summary

Does your website speak to customers? Are you improving your website with each addition? Or are you annoying your visitors with unnecessary Flash widgets and frustrating their attempts to purchase from you?

You won't know unless you set up your website for measurement and then watch the numbers for trends. Measure your performance ruthlessly!

The KPIs for your website should flow directly from the KPIs for your business. This process will help you focus on the right set of metrics and help you track and improve them.

To get started with Internet marketing metrics for your website and company

- Decide how you want website visitors to respond to your call to action.
- Identify your key performance indicators:
  - Primary and secondary KPIs for SEO.
  - Primary and secondary KPIs for paid search.
  - Use business analysis to define your KPI measures and goals.
  - Determine when you want to measure.
  - Integrate the website KPIs into your central business decision-making process.

- Close the loop between your website, lead generation, and CRM system:

  - Capture the keywords that people use to find your website (organic and paid searches).

  - Bring the website visitor and keyword data into your CRM system.

  - Ensure that the sales team indicates when a lead is converted to a customer within your CRM system.

- Generate customer acquisition reports in your CRM system and analyze the reports with your search marketing plan.

- Identify the most valuable paid search and organic search keywords for your business. Look at both the quality and quantity of lead conversions.

- Run the ROI numbers; calculate future projections based on past performance. Adjust your marketing plan accordingly, armed with the new information.

4

Breaking Down Silos to Get the Metrics You Need

Making informed decisions about marketing activities requires information about which marketing activities are turning into leads and sales. Of course, many activities contribute toward leads and sales, so untangling the influences is an involved process.

This information is owned by many groups, from IT through marketing and sales. It takes an interdisciplinary perspective to collect and interpret data. It's a rare organization in which the marketing department already has great data about which of their efforts influences sales and revenue.

Precisely because this is so rare, we believe connecting the dots between your online marketing efforts and sales builds incredible competitive advantage. We walk you through which information is critical to building a feedback loop and why so that you can unlock the key to more sales!

Do More Than Gather Data: Build a Team

We're going to get into the nitty-gritty of the setup and configuration of all sorts of tools and systems to track your data, to connect the dots between marketing and sales. But, proper setup and reporting is just the beginning. Data capture is not understanding; reporting is not analysis.

A customer relationship management (CRM) system does not replace talented salespeople following a consistent process, but it can support them and ease communications between team members. After the initial setup and configuration, only about 20% of your metrics process should be spent generating reports. The other 80% should be analysis and reflection.

A truly comprehensive web analytics program usually requires the participation of multiple groups within the business. The most common obstacle to successful analytics is not technology (as most businesses predict) but rather cross-team integration.

Web Analytics: Types, Purpose, Popular Tools for Each

Now that you've defined your goals and decided which key performance indicators (KPIs) you will measure as part of your metrics-driven marketing practice, it's time to make sure your website is capturing the information you need for decision making.

Knowing how your website will help your business leads to defining which actions you want visitors to take on your website. This describes which actions you need to watch carefully, and should point out key reports you should monitor and key attributes of the website you should emphasize.

Several tools are available to watch your website and its constituent pages and gather aggregate and individual-level data on website visitors and usage patterns. We start with tools suited to websites and pages, logfile and web analytics programs, and then move to page-level and element-level monitoring programs, such as form analytics.

Don't fall into the perfectionist/data quality trap. Web analysts and business users alike, online and at conferences, are known to trade arguments against web analytics programs on the accuracy of data collected, citing numerous technical reasons that prevent tracking.

However, web statistics are still by far the most measurable and accurate source of marketing data available! So, data that is pretty good is much better for decision making in the absence of data.

Logfile Versus Script-Based Analytics Tracking

There are a couple methods to gather data on what your website visitors do on your website: through server logfiles, which record every file request and visit; and through script-based tracking, available through web analytics software services such as Google Analytics, Yahoo! Web Analytics, Adobe SiteCatalyst (formerly Omniture), and others.

One of the main differences between logfile analysis and script-based web analytics programs is the type of data they can gather and the relative ease of access and reporting.

Logfile Analysis: Deep, Less Accessible

Web server logfiles record the files requested by each visitor to the website. Essentially, the web server "logs" every request, including information such as the file requested, the date, and whether the request was successful.

Because the logfiles record data regardless of whether the visitor has cookies enabled, data on visits by search engine spiders is recorded in logfiles, and not recorded in analytics programs. Logfiles usually require a request to the IT team to pull the files from the web server and then IT team time for the analysis.

Logfiles can be more or less information rich, depending on the server's configuration. The extended log format described in Table 4.1 captures critical information, such as referring URL and user agent (whether it is a spider, a human visitor, or so on).

To get the most out of your logfiles, make sure you have the extended format recording. This data is small enough to store, and not retrievable retrospectively; grab the data while you can, you never know when or why you'll need it!

Table 4.1 W3C Extended Logfile Format

Field	Description
Date	The date when the activity occurred.
Time	The time, in coordinated Universal Time (UTC), at which the activity occurred.
Time Taken	Duration of time to complete the transaction, in seconds.
Bytes	Size of information transferred, in bytes.
Cached	Indicates whether the cache was used, with 0 indicating no cache access.
Client IP Address	The IP address of the client that made the request.
User Name	The name of the authenticated user who accessed the server. In the case of an anonymous user, this field contains a hyphen.

Table 4.1 Continued

Field	Description
Server IP Address	The IP address of the web server.
Server Port	The server port number on the web server.
Method	The requested action, for example GET.
URI Stem	The target of the action, for example Default.htm.
URI Query	The query, if any, that the client was trying to perform. A universal resource identifier (URI) query is necessary only for dynamic pages.
HTTP Status	The Hypertext Transfer Protocol (HTTP) status code.
User Agent	The browser type that the client used.
Protocol Status	The substatus error code.

Sample Logfile   The following is a sample logfile:

```
#Version: 1.0
#Date: 20101119
#Fields: date time cs-method cs-uri
20101119 00:19:15 GET /index.html
20101119 01:57:45 GET /products/index.html
20101119 02:32:12 GET /index.html
20101119 02:32:19 GET /images/image.jpg
```

An upside of logfiles is their completeness; a downside is their format. They are a big long text file recording server transactions.

Imagine staring at the green screen of characters that flowed across the screen in the *Matrix* movies. For those of us without the ability to stare into streams of text data and recognize repeating patterns or without programming skills, logfiles remain difficult to access and use.

Some tools can be used to review and report on logfile data, such as Sawmill, but they are trickier to use and configure than the premade dashboards ready-to-go in web analytics data.

Another difference is timeliness of the data. Logfiles provide a great way to retrospectively review large quantities of web data. Yet, logfile analysis tends to be something done at some frequency (annually, quarterly, monthly), but typically is not done on a daily basis. Although web analytics programs tend to have a several-hour lag, and so by definition are not "real time," they do provide ongoing reporting on an almost-immediate basis.

Web Analytics: Information Rich Dashboard

Web analytics programs, such as Google Analytics, Urchin, Yahoo! Web Analytics, Omniture SiteCatalyst, and others, provide a wealth of data about visitor behavior on your website. They typically do this through running scripts on pages of the website and storing cookies on the visitor's computer. These cookies are how they distinguish whether the visitor is a new or a returning one, and which page views are part of the same session on the website.

Data on visitors who have cookies disabled, and this includes many kinds of robots and search engine spiders, does not get captured in script-based analytics programs. This information is captured by logfiles.

Google Analytics is widespread and well priced (for example, free after the installation and configuration labor) and is what we use on our website and recommend our clients use. It is the main software and dashboard we reference throughout this book, although many of its features and reports are available within other web analytics packages.

Website analytics packages

- Enable you to set and track specific business goals
- Allow you to compare present data directly to past
- Give you deep demographic insight into users
- Compare website effectiveness by locale
- Visualize funnels
- Show how users maneuver through your website
- Integrate fully with other Internet marketing campaigns, such as AdWords
- Customize your view of data
- Overlay important statistics on the page
- Set up automated report emails and alerts
- Let you export report data
- Allow you to customize access to accounts by user
- Allow you to set intermediate website goals

They do not show you

- Real-time statistics
- Data that corresponds exactly to server data

Who's Out There? Define Your Visitors   Web analytics lets you see and monitor trends in the real-world attributes of your visitors such as their location, their primary language, whether they are new to your website or a returning visitor, and what operating system, browser, and screen dimensions they're using.

Analytics cannot tell you anything about the people who are not visiting your website, but you can examine who is coming and check whether you are capturing the right audience.

Metrics tracked about visitors include number of visits, number of unique visitors, location, language, and whether the visitor is new or a returning visitor. Some analytics programs get a little deeper with some basic demographic information.

For instance, Yahoo! Web Analytics does include some demographic data about your visitors, including gender, age, and Yahoo!-specific selections such as interest groups and Yahoo! pages frequented by your visitors (see Figure 4.1). They know this demographic information because some people have shared this kind of data with Yahoo! already and opted in that it can be shared in an aggregate way with users of Yahoo! products, such as its Web Analytics.

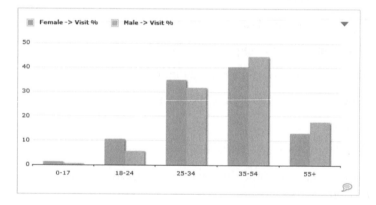

Figure 4.1 *Age and gender report from Yahoo! Web Analytics.*

Use the data about your website visitors to assess whether you're reaching your target customers. Are they from the locations (see Figure 4.2) and languages (see Figure 4.3) you expect? Do the demographics match your goals? If not, you might need to adjust the marketing you're doing to reach folks not yet included in your website visitors.

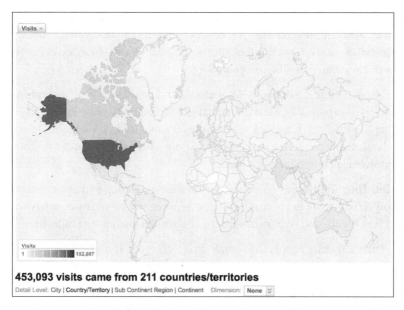

Figure 4.2 *Map overlay showing locations of website visitors.*

	Language		Visits ↓	Pages/Visit	Avg. Time on Site	% New Visits	Bounce Rate
1.	en-us		373,073	2.33	00:00:46	94.51%	54.51%
2.	ja		2,708	3.78	00:03:31	70.61%	46.20%
3.	de		2,549	3.05	00:02:27	79.13%	50.49%
4.	fr		2,160	3.44	00:02:46	78.94%	46.48%
5.	zh-cn		1,698	3.44	00:03:37	73.85%	42.82%
6.	en		1,456	1.85	00:01:14	80.63%	68.89%
7.	en-gb		1,226	2.64	00:02:19	74.80%	48.86%
8.	es		1,027	3.23	00:02:50	78.09%	49.66%
9.	pt-br		1,012	2.86	00:02:50	81.23%	47.04%
10.	ko		966	2.47	00:01:20	41.10%	70.39%

Figure 4.3 *List of languages of website visitors.*

You might possibly find the inverse is true, that folks you didn't anticipate serving are using your website and even becoming leads or making purchases. Use the information in your web analytics to challenge your current definition of a target customer.

For instance, your web analytics may reveal demand for services and demand for translated content in new countries and languages. You might need to fill in more details about the target customer through outreach and interviews, but analytics can give you a place to start.

You can test whether your website is loading and displaying correctly to most of your visitors. Analytics provides you with a ranking of the screen sizes, browser versions, and operating systems used to view your website. You can review how your website looks under all combinations of these criteria to make sure your website is accessible and useful for popular combinations.

If you do not have all of the requisite hardware and software for seeing your website under all the common conditions seen in your web analytics, you can use a service like CrossBrowserTesting.com that shows you how your website looks on each hardware/software combination you choose.

If you've been building out content to attract and retain new visitors, you might want to track progress by measuring changes in Visitor Loyalty, Recency, Length, and Depth of Visit. Yet, a quick visit that results in a lead or a sale should still be considered a successful one, so be careful about assumptions about these statistics in complete isolation from your goals.

How Did They Get Here?   Much of the data for managing and optimizing your campaigns will come to you in the Traffic Sources area of your web analytics dashboard (see Figure 4.4). We track sources or channels such as the following:

- **Direct Traffic:** People who come directly to your website via a bookmark.

- **Paid Search:** People who come to your website through clicking a sponsored search link on a search engine page or on another website that features contextual advertising through AdWords or MSN/Yahoo!

- **Organic Search:** People who come to your website through clicking a natural search result.

- **Referral Sites:** Other websites that send visitors to your website not included in other categories.

- **Banner Ads:** Incoming links from banner ads can be tagged to be distinguished in your web analytics.

- **Email Marketing:** Incoming links from email campaigns can be tagged to be distinguished in your web analytics.

- **Paid Directories:** Paid directories such as online yellow pages.

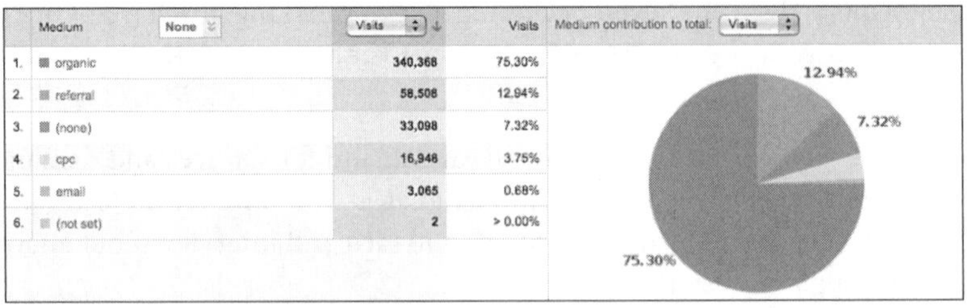

Figure 4.4 *Visits by marketing channel: (none) is direct visitors, cpc is paid search.*

For the paid and organic search sources, you can dig deeper into the paid and organic keywords that are driving traffic to your website. In addition, you can link Google Analytics to your AdWords account to provide deeper cross-dashboard reporting.

The questions you can answer with data in the traffic dashboard allow you to qualify and better understand your audience. You can see how they're reaching your website and the keywords they used to find you, which gives a clear indication of their intention and goal. You might find surprising things in your keyword lists, and change your search engine optimization (SEO), paid search, or referral strategies based on traffic source data.

For instance, you might notice you have high visibility on surprising terms. At one point, one of the authors noticed she got a lot of organic traffic on a surprising term to her blog, and it turned out she had misspelled the word and ranked high for the misspelling. Apparently, other people also misspelled the term similarly and so found her in searches. She didn't want to appear on the misspelling (although sometimes that's advantageous), so in this case, she used information about organic traffic to correct an on-page typo!

You can also look at the balance of incoming traffic channels and how they perform relative to each other. This may show you which initiatives are paying off, and which attract interest but result in few leads or sales.

This relative contribution to lead or sale generation may allow you to make decisions on relative budget allocation (but see the section on lead attribution later in this chapter before doing anything drastic). For instance, if you are getting qualified leads at a good price through paid search advertising, you may consider shifting budget from a less-well-performing email campaign.

Your list of referring websites may turn up some great performers that could do even better with a little investment of time to build a relationship or build out your content on their website.

Analyze your visitor's expectations by examining search terms. Do the search terms you see surprise you? Do they match the major themes on your website? Are any relevant terms proving ineffective in conversion rates? Are these terms specific enough? Are there keyword variations that are vital to your website focus that are not showing up?

And then, use your findings as input to SEO and paid search optimization. You can insert valuable terms into your page copy, `<meta>` tags, page titles, and URLs whenever possible. Then, delete ineffective keywords from your paid search campaigns, and add valuable words unique to organic search.

ADVANCED TRAFFIC CONFIGURATION: TAGGING INCOMING LINKS

To provide insight across online marketing efforts, tag all marketing inlinks to the website in a way that can be captured by the web analytics program in use. What follows are descriptions of tags we find particularly useful: Campaign Name, Medium, Source, and Content tags, each of which is discussed here.

These recommendations can be used in conjunction with the link building tool provided by Google (www.google.com/support/googleanalytics/bin/answer.py?answer=55578):

- **Campaign Name (utm_campaign):** The marketing-level effort that takes place across delivery media (i.e., a mainframe campaign message that is delivered via radio, magazine, and booth expo).

- **Medium (utm_medium):** The type of delivery channel, such as a magazine, radio, or search engine. Common Medium tags are "organic," cpc, referral and (none). In addition to these, socialmedia, email and pressrelease will be useful. Others, such as article, directory, partner, etc., could also be considered, depending on their importance, frequency of use, and the level of detail (and complexity) you're comfortable with.

- **Source (utm_source):** The specific place where the visitor originated. So, in the medium magazine, the sources could be *The Economist* or *Time*. In the medium organic, the sources could be Bing or Google. In the medium socialmedia, the sources could be Twitter, Facebook, or LinkedIn among many others.

- **Content (utm_content):** Lastly, you may want to include a unique identifier associated with certain efforts, such as the release date of an email or press release.

When tagging incoming links, you might trick the search engines into thinking there are extra copies of your pages available. For example, a web crawler could find a page through an untagged link, and then find it again through a link with Analytics tags appended to the URL, like this:

www.example.com/mypage.html

www.example.com/mypage.html?utm_source=globenewswire&utm_medium=pressrelease&utm_content=july2011&utm_campaign=getreadyfor2012

Although these two URLs return the same page, the search engine might view them as separate, thereby "diluting" the organic strength of the page. This issue is already addressed to some degree by maintaining a complete and accurate sitemap.xml file to guide the web crawlers, but it doesn't hurt to take the following precaution.

To avoid this duplication, employ the canonical <link> tag (<link rel="canonical" href="INSERT-CANONICAL-URL-HERE"/>) in the <head> section of the page being linked to, to tell web crawlers to ignore the analytics parameters, and index *only* the canonical URL (in the case above, the shorter one!). This extra tagging will help address potential duplicate content concerns.

What Did They Engage With on My Website?   You can approach your web analytics data by focusing on content performance, using data on pages viewed, navigation patterns, exit pages, and bounces to identify and address usability issues with specific pages or sections within the website. You can delve into which pages are working to convert visitors to leads and which are not.

Additional insights can be gleaned from reviewing on-site search logs (where you can see what your visitors were searching for in their own words). This data can be pulled into your web analytics program quite easily by configuring your on-site search to follow the conventions needed for tracking by your web analytics program.

You can also track events, such as counting the number of times a video was played on a website.

What Actions Did They Take?   Translate your website goals into measurable attributes, and then make sure your analytics program measures them! Within web analytics programs, you can set up specific pages as goals and monitor goal funnels, the paths to these goals.

By monitoring goals and measuring progress toward them, you can drill into conversion rates and abandonment points. Many tracking pitfalls in goal setup are covered in the section "Choosing a Contact Method" in Chapter 3, "Building a Metrics-Driven Practice."

On a lead-generation website, an important path is from website contents to the contact or request a quote form, and then completing the form. Figure 4.5 shows a typical drop off of only a small proportion of people who search for the website and view the contact form, actually electing to fill it out.

For an e-commerce website, examining the path from viewing a product page to checking out is critical! Figure 4.6 shows the path from shopping basket to sale for an e-commerce website. In these cases, the biggest drop-off is from filling the basket to buying its contents. We all understand this, because shopping baskets are often used to hold items under consideration.

Watching these metrics gives clues into the broken places on your website, within your shopping cart, or in your request for quote process.

Figure 4.5 *Sample lead-generation conversion funnel.*

Figure 4.6 *The funnel from shopping basket to confirmed sale.*

Take a Hybrid Approach to Get the Best of Both Worlds

Each method has its own strengths.

You might choose to review logfile data when

- You need to analyze the website's performance for a prior period.

- You have server space to keep the logfiles going back in time.

- You have specific ideas for how you want to mine the data and want full control over how you segment it.

- You are comfortable programming.

Web analytics dashboards are best when

- Multiple people in your company, organization, and so on will need to analyze the data, each with different needs.

- You have limited time to spend analyzing the data.

- You want the data for the present onward (no past analysis).

- You prefer to use a web interface whenever you can.

When a visitor interacts with a website, both the web server and the visitor's browser track information about the session. So, you can record data in logfiles and have a script-based web analytics program running concurrently.

We recommend this combination, analytics for common use, and logfiles to dig more deeply into questions less easily addressed in web analytics (such as average load times and information about individual visits, such as clickpaths through the website).

Click Analytics

Specialized scripts are available to fill in where web analytics has less resolution, such as the mechanics of an individual page. Vendors such as CrazyEgg and ClickTale provide scripts that watch behavior on individual pages, summarizing aggregate click or mouse movement patterns.

ClickTale also has form analytics to identify which form fields stymie visitors. UserFly goes further by providing visualization and playback of an individual visitor's interaction with one or several pages on the website. These additional tools let you drill into parts of your website and can help you diagnose and fix issues you turn up with web analytics or logfile analysis.

Call Tracking: Why It's Essential and How to Select Granularity Needed

Just as you need to capture web form data and connect it to marketing initiatives, if your business lives by the phone ringing, you need to ensure your phone calls get tracked with the same rigor. Make sure you know whether phone inquiries are up or down, where those phone calls originate, and whether the phone calls are from qualified or unqualified prospects.

Fewer calls from qualified prospects is better than more, worse calls, though too many qualified calls is a great problem to have. Make sure you're logging the data you need to pick these trends out.

Business-to-business (B2B) lead-generation websites and B2B and business-to-consumer (B2C) e-commerce websites can use custom tracking phone numbers to identify the source of each call.

Measuring If the Phone Rings (Memory Doesn't Count)

Are your marketing initiatives driving phone calls? Hard to tell if you aren't counting calls before, during, and after marketing campaigns. CRM systems can provide your customer contact team a place to log phone calls and provide you with dashboards to measure the call volume.

Companies that live by their phone calls may engage with call centers to handle incoming calls professionally and predictably, and these contact management companies will provide standard call count and other metrics for analysis.

It could be as simple as a shared spreadsheet where you tally the number of phone calls and the number of qualified callers. You might engage with a company such as RingCentral that gives you a virtual call center that routes calls to your land lines and provides you with reporting summarizing call count, call length, and other attributes. Or, it could be as automated as a shared dashboard populated by web analytics, phone tracking data, and call center daily reporting.

It is obvious to many that call tracking is the next frontier of metrics-driven advertising on the Internet. New players are emerging, and existing powerhouses are adding new features to support call tracking. One new player is Mongoose Metrics. An existing powerhouse, Google, is also offering solutions.

Google AdWords features "click to call" phone numbers in paid search ads that will be tallied along with clicks and lead conversions in your AdWords dashboard. Plus you can track calls from Google Places listings (discussed in more detail in the "Increase Your Findability via Local Search and Link Building" section in Chapter 8 "It's All About Visibility").

We're happy to say that call analytics are getting deeper and more integrated with existing dashboards, and by the time you are reading this, the call-tracking services available to you will be even better than they are at the time of this writing.

Interpreting trends in your call data gets easier once you have more than a year of data by which to gauge seasonal trends. Maybe calls always crash right before the Fourth of July in the United States, or maybe they go up.

In addition, staffing to provide quality customer service is expensive. So, you need to verify that the calls you are receiving are ones you want! You cannot do this without tracking the number of calls, their sources, and the outcomes.

Selecting the Granularity Needed

Table 4.2 illustrates different ways that you can use to set up custom toll-free phone lines to track your website prospects or customers. Depending on the complexity of your sales process and your business's needs, you can apply the most basic solution, an extremely complex custom solution, or something in between.

Table 4.2 Custom Call to Action Methods, from Simple to Complex

Level of Complexity	What It Entails
Basic (web versus nonweb calls)	A separate toll-free 800 number just for the website, identifying website prospects from offline prospects.
Medium (landing pages versus website)	Multiple email addresses and toll-free numbers for different paid search landing pages (each with its own phone number).
Complex (identify callers by market channel)	Dynamically insert 800 numbers using JavaScript for each marketing channel directing traffic to the website, using a tool from Mongoose Metrics or Who's Calling. Costs depend on your call volume as well as the number of phone numbers required.
Very complex (identify callers by keyphrase)	Dynamically insert 800 numbers using a JavaScript for each person that lands on each page, using a tool from Mongoose Metrics or Who's Calling, that provides custom phone numbers letting you see calls resulting from individual keyphrases. This approach increases your paid search fund by about 10%, so you need to have a solid business reason to justify this level of granularity.

WHEN CALLING GETS COMPLEX

You might wonder how to handle all of this additional data tracking when you've also got a call center to manage in your business model. One client of ours outsources initial follow-up on web form inquiries and fields all incoming calls from marketing activities to a call center. We exchange data with the center daily. They pull our daily web counts into their daily reporting. Our website data helps them project staffing needs as well.

Lead Management: SFA/CRM Integration

Get ready for some acronyms....

Sales force automation (SFA) and customer relationship management (CRM) systems provide shared contact logging and lead tracking for sales and customer contact staff. They provide the functionality behind a call center knowing you called 24 hours previously and can provide status on your request even if you are talking to a different agent.

CRM systems are used for

- **Communication:** In all directions and across different disciplines. They allow tech support people insight into the history of an account, and give the sales team insight into the activities or issues that have come up. When used well, they can reduce phone/email clutter for individual team members and make information easier to locate for all.

- **Reporting:** Data can be analyzed to review individual leads in detail and to show pipeline health and leading indicators for revenue forecasts.

- **Common format:** CRM systems provide common format across all global regions and sales managers, crucial for international organizations.

- **Accountability:** CRM systems share status on opportunities and spotlight any information gaps.

CRM Products

A commonly used SFA/CRM system is Salesforce.com. This is the CRM we use ourselves and that we tend to see our clients use. Its use and gaining buy-in on its use is a book unto itself. *Salesforce.com: Secrets of Success*, by David Taber, from Prentice Hall, provides a comprehensive reference and how-to guide to the political and technical dimensions of implementing Salesforce.com.

Beyond Salesforce.com, there are many SFA/CRM systems that range from streamlined services for small businesses to more feature-rich services for enterprise clients. On the small business end, 37Signals's Highrise and KarmaCRM provide contact and task management.

For enterprise situations, NetSuite, Plex (a Pure Visibility client), Applicor, and SAP include back-office functions such as accounting and enterprise resource management (ERP).

Marketing automation is another category that includes CRM. So, a leads database might be included in your marketing automation software, such as Marketo, Eloqua, or SilverPop. And these systems may be layered on top of each other, with a marketing automation system CRM holding leads until they are nurtured to a state where they belong within the sales team's CRM.

We will not recommend any vendor (no vendor is suitable for all situations), and likely the market will mature in the time between this writing and your reading. Nor will we advocate for CRM sitting within or outside of your ERP or marketing automation system. We're agnostic, as long as the integration is in place to get the reporting you need.

CRM Basics

The CRM is designed to support your marketing and sales process. Just like web analytics or logfiles won't give you a web strategy, neither will CRM data give you a sales strategy or a sales process.

What it will do, if you provide it with the right inputs, is help your team identify which marketing channels, and perhaps which tactics within these channels, are providing you quality leads, letting you refine your activities to gain more of the good leads that turn into sales and fewer of the ones that waste your team's time in follow-up and quotes that do not produce revenue.

We recommend that you plan your marketing and sales process to include tracking such as you can find within marketing automation software, which you can create within a standalone system or purchase out of the box. For our purposes, we focus on how to track your Internet marketing campaigns through from a lead to a sale. Leads from your website should flow into your CRM and data on sales should percolate back into marketing for informed decision making.

Sounds easy, right?

Required Input: Web Form Lead Data

CRM systems can integrate with your website so that web form submissions flow directly (without needing any rekeying) into the system by which your company is already tracking and monitoring leads and follow-up activities. This should be relatively straightforward; most CRM systems enable you to receive data from your web forms as part of their basic offering.

Required Input: Phone Inquiry Data

For many businesses, the website may generate as many as two to three times the phone inquiries than it does web leads. Without capturing data from phone inquiries in your CRM, and without capturing the marketing channel data with the phone inquiry, you might be leaving as much as 66% to 75% of your lead data "on the table" untracked. Call data is every bit as important as web form data and deserves the same treatment.

Required Input: Marketing Channel Data

CRM basic templates should require lead and contact records to include information about whether your lead originated as a phone call or a web form completion, and maybe even which web form/offer or which phone number. Get beyond the basics to capture the original source of the web visit or phone call.

Do this for web leads by capturing information about how the visitor came to your website and including it with the user-entered data during a website form submission. Do this for phone calls by custom phone numbers. Did they call from the website? A refer-a-friend email?

The short version of how this is done for website form submissions is through tracking parameters attached to the URL links used for different marketing activities. These tracking parameters can be stored in a cookie or otherwise maintained as the visitor peruses the website and then be submitted at the same time as the web form.

Next Steps for Follow-Up

What happens once the web or phone lead data hits your database, from a process perspective, is the interesting part. Ideally, as visitors return to your website or call again for additional information, perhaps signing up for a whitepaper or webinar, their additional activities should be added to or merged with their original contact details.

This lets your team develop an understanding of which marketing channels drive which types of on-site behavior and which resources on the website prime prospects' interest and which support late-stage inquiries.

Whatever your process, whether you have your call center follow up on web form leads with a callback within 11 minutes or you commit to getting back to a visitor by email within 24 or 48 hours or within the month via Pony Express courier... the follow-up activities and contact with your prospect should be logged within your CRM.

Lead Scoring

If you're in the enviable situation of being buried in leads and having to sort through to prioritize follow-up activities, you might turn to lead scoring. Your sales team probably is already doing this, either by gut or using a more overt method.

You can use your CRM to automate lead scoring based on attributes of the lead itself such as whether the business is on a target customer list or has revenues above a certain threshold, and based on on-site behavior (number of whitepapers down-loaded, attendance at a webinar) you have identified as good signals of a warm prospect.

Lead Nurturing

Marketing does not stop after you have gained someone's contact information. That's just the start of a relationship. People need more time, more information, and a deeper connection with your company to make a purchase.

To grow a relationship over time, consider lead-nurturing activities such as the following:

- Email autoresponder mini-courses.

- Ongoing email marketing newsletters.

- Invitations to local events.

- Invitations to online demos or webinars.

- Initiating and maintaining a relationship with prospects via social media services like LinkedIn, Facebook, or Twitter, depending on what is suitable for your industry or outreach team.

- Maintaining prospects' interest through publishing new and relevant information in the form of a blog on your website or in a forum that attracts your prospects.

- Keeping your company top of mind to people who have already visited your website or expressed interest through remarketing. AdWords and other paid search and display ad vendors offer remarketing programs, where you can show targeted ads to people who have already visited your website or performed a specific action on your website (such as filled out a contact form or downloaded a whitepaper).

Next Steps for Analysis: Quantifying "Assists" Through Lead Attribution

You've got data. Now what? What if your analysis turns up that the only sales are coming from searches on your trademark and then you justify a decision to end all banner advertising and paid search on nontrademark terms? Well... you might decide that based on the data, and you might accidentally throttle your sales pipeline and eliminate all incoming leads on trademark queries.

You see, it might be the generalized queries that stimulate the relationships that turn into sales via trademark search terms only after a few months of lead nurturing and exploration.

At its best, lead attribution takes into account different information needs along a complex sales cycle. At its worst, it can be used to prop up underperforming marketing initiatives by claiming they are "assisting" the better performers.

Only a thoughtful hypothesis-driven strategy can separate the alternatives.

Last Click

The basic scenario just described might result in a last-click attribution model, where the last action the user took before a sale would receive the "credit" for the sale. Suppose, for instance, that someone is shopping for winter boots and searches on the term "snow boots" or "winter boots" coming up with some general options browsing through a bunch of e-commerce websites.

In the search shown in Figure 4.7, the person might click a few paid search ads, review the visually prominent product search listings, and maybe browse a few favorite online shoe stores like Zappos or outdoor stores like REI.

Then, after deciding on a particular pair of Sorels, and knowing they'll get a good price and a good return policy at Zappos, they might go back to Zappos.com via typing the web address into the browser address bar, navigate to the boots, and the credit for the sale might go to a direct visit.

This scenario omits the history and ignores the fact that the person remembered they liked Zappos at all because they saw it in organic or sponsored search results before making the purchasing decision.

While purchasing a pair of shoes is a B2C example, we also see this happening in B2B situations. Before making a final decision on a large B2B purchase, the person invests a lot of time researching products: clicking both ads and organic search listings. The buyer might attend a webinar, download whitepapers, or watch product demos online.

Figure 4.7 *Google results page for "winter boots."*

When a final decision is made, the buyer often just clicks an ad with the company's brand name instead of typing the company's URL in his or her browser. This last click on the ad gets credit for the final sale.

First Click

An alternative to last-click scenarios is to give 100% of the credit for the sale to the first click. If the buyer ends up buying at Zappos, regardless of the medium that facilitated the visit that produced the sale, the first trip to Zappos would get credit for the sale.

In this scenario, perhaps the first visit sets a cookie on the person's computer capturing the search terms (if it was search) and the medium used to find the website. This cookie might then be cleared when the purchase is made, or it might persist for a long time, giving credit for the winter boots purchase to the search done for baby booties for a baby shower in some other season.

Limitations of this scenario are that the first click might be in a different browser on the same computer or a different device altogether (think work computer, home computer, smartphone, tablet computer... the list goes on), so your data may be imperfect, but even imperfect first-click attribution might provide better insight into leading influencers than last-click attribution.

Hybrid Approach: Count Assists!

In a lead-generation environment, the search and the decision might be drawn out over time, and there might be several website conversion events that support a sale. It would still be possible to give only the last click credit for the sale, or only the first click credit, but of course that's more clearly an oversimplification than in the two e-commerce examples just discussed.

You might weight the contributions of all touchpoints along the sales cycle, from the first web form submission to download of a whitepaper, through the webinar sign-ups, and then on to the request a quote form submissions that results in a proposal and contract.

But, how to take into account offline media? You might weight the contributions of all "in market" advertising that could possibly have supported the contact. So, a form submission during a month when you're also doing a direct mail piece, a billboard, and a promotion with an industry thought leader might give partial credit to the medium that produced the contact form submission, an assist to the billboard, the thought leader promo, and the direct mail piece.

As you can imagine, the possibilities are endless. And, it might be possible to construct a model that does not reflect the reality of your lead generation but instead reflects a political reality inside your organization. This is the dark side of lead attribution.

Our recommendation? Start simple. Test through adding and eliminating online and offline visibility and monitoring the results. If your sales cycle is long, you might want to run concurrent tests in different geographies (billboards in Tucson, direct mail in Detroit, banners in New York) to evaluate contributions of different activities.

A Case Study in Lead Management

In February 2010, an IT services provider installed scripts to capture online marketing data when a visitor submits a web form through their website. This particular system is "first in;" that is, it identifies the sources that the visitor used to reach the website the first time, even if the visitor submits the form after subsequent visits. This allows a clear link between the earliest introduction of visitors and their ultimate decision to reach out.

The default out-of-the-box values for any submission are

- **Referrer URL:** The full URL of the referrer source
- **Search terms:** The keyphrases used to find the website

- **Landing page:** The first page reached on the website

- **Marketing type:** Referrer, organic search, paid search, or direct

Between June 1 and December 31, 2010, there were 2,490 total leads via web forms. Reviewing leads by source showed that website contacts were much more likely to be promoted to opportunities than leads from other sources, which included purchased contact lists. In the second half of the year, about 7% of all new leads came from the website, but about 14% of the opportunities in the same time period were attributed to website sources.

In addition, we found that form leads from Referrer traffic turned into opportunities well. This underscored the value of having domain experts and industry commentators discuss the company's products and services online, particularly in ways that get the attention of target customers.

The analysis provided a list of industry websites and press release websites that had referred visitors who turned into leads and opportunities, a great list to prioritize for further activities and perhaps some cross-promotions.

Summary

Build a process to get the metrics you need to make informed decisions. To do so, you must to start or deepen your company's commitment to web analytics and lead management through call tracking and CRM.

Few individuals have the skills and breadth of experience to aggregate and analyze this information. You need to build a team that spans marketing, sales, and customer service to tie together the rich data that has previously been the province of each department. Those who participate will be rewarded with a richer perspective on your company's activities and the outcome of each.

To establish a mindset for analytics success and track and manage your leads:

- Establish an analytics process.

- Decide how much time you can devote to analysis (and resulting action items) within a given period (week, month, and so on).

- Stick to this schedule, moving through a incremental sequence for improvement:

  - Move through the three major steps in the process (defining visitors, qualifying visitors, and turning visitors into visitors of value) alternately, analyzing the appropriate reports for each on a regular basis, then making changes.

- Reporting is not analysis. Only about 20% of your analytics process should be generating reports. The other 80% should be analysis.

- Use the reports as a jumping off point for action items. Always experiment and test to ensure a "democracy" of ideas, where no idea is favored over another without a good reason.

- Adopt a shared system for tracking lead and customer contacts, such as a CRM system like Salesforce:

  Automate the capture of critical marketing data along with contact name, address, and telephone information through web form integration and custom phone numbers.

- Nurture your leads through email marketing, social media, and providing relevant and useful information through blogs, whitepapers, and events.

- Consider how multiple touches may contribute to a lead or a sale, and develop a lead-attribution weight that considers "assists."

5

The Audience Is Listening (What Will You Say?)

A mistake many websites make is that they are really written for the company rather than for the company's potential customers or clients. Perhaps that is because making a website involves so many different roles both inside and outside the company (marketing team, sales team, IT/infrastructure, creative folks, some of whom may be external vendors).

Getting agreement from that long list of players exhausts the energy of the project and leaves little room to get a customer involved, much less the number of them that would be required to get a good cross-section of their potential intentions, desires, wishes, and needs. Too often, a website's information architecture reflects the organization of the company instead of the needs of the website's target audience. Let's put an end to this!

Where Do You Start?

How you get started depends on your goal for the website. If it's a personal blog meant for you to express yourself, start with what's on your mind. It's all about you. If it's a website for an organization with a mission, such as a nonprofit food bank serving a particular town or a global pharmaceutical company looking to cure a particular form of cancer, the place to start is outside your organization.

Start with the people you are trying to reach with the website. To make a connection with them, your website has to be all about what *they* need, which is related to (but not the same as) everything about you or your organization. A great place to start is to list the groups you are trying to reach, understand their goals, and lastly move to the language they use to describe what they need.

Your plan should include building a website and writing web copy to show your customer how your product or service will solve their problem. This chapter covers audience analysis, persona development, and choosing the right words so that your audience recognizes you understand them and so they can find you using search engines.

Start with the Tasks and Goals of Your Potential Audiences

Your audience is the group of people whom your website serves. It is often composed of several types of folks, a mixture of people you have not met (potential customers) and those you know well (such as current employees).

Potential customers coming to your website at different stages in the sales cycle have different information needs. Those in the information search stage are looking for more general information about the problem they're trying to solve, whereas those in evaluation of alternatives may be looking for different vendors who offer specific solutions to their problem.

So, to continue the puppy-training example, information searchers are looking for ways to solve particular issues (puppies that jump up, puppies that don't listen, or puppies that growl at certain family members). Other website visitors in the evaluation of alternatives section are more solution focused; they know they need puppy training, and they are seeking to determine the pros and cons of different puppy training programs and vendors, such as cost and location.

Table 5.1 describes the goals and tasks of potential customers, organized by the stages of the sales cycle.

Table 5.1 Goals and Tasks of Potential Customers, Ordered from Early to Late in the Sales

Sales Cycle Category	Goal	Tasks They Might Perform on Your Website
Need recognition	Articulate what will help them solve a particular problem.	Off the website.
Information Search	Research the problem itself, see what others have done in their situation. Identify whether a solution to their problem exists.	See if your product/service solves their problem.
Evaluation of Alternatives	Gather information to make an informed decision.	Learn more through watching a video demo. Request a brochure or download explaining more details. Contact a sales representative with a few questions via phone or live chat. Consult your location to see if you are within driving distance (for a service business). Submit an online lead form or quote request to get pricing information if it is not available on the website. Evaluate your product/service relative to competition by • Comparing features • Reading reviews or testimonials
Purchase Decision	Choose which solution.	Purchase online. Submit an online lead form or quote request. Email a sales representative. Call a sales representative using a number from the website.

Other Important Audiences

In addition to the potential customer, your website serves other noncustomer audiences, such as investors, job candidates, members of the press, and so forth. Ignoring these types of audiences can haunt you at the end of a web design project. A hidden stakeholder may appear and demand respect for one of these.

Including them is perfectly fine, as is prioritizing them low on the list. Just take them into account early in the project to avoid surprises later.

Table 5.2 roughly lists these categories. For each of these groups, you want to list out what you already know about your audience and organize it in a meaningful way. Think of what each group of website visitors is trying to do and how they might end up on your website to complete their task.

Table 5.2 Audiences, Goals, and Tasks

Audience	Goal	Tasks They Might Perform on Your Website
Potential customers	See Table 5.1.	See Table 5.1.
Such a diverse and important group that it deserves its own table.		
Current customers	Get the most from their product/service.	Submit a support ticket. Look up your hours of operation, phone number, fax number, physical address, or an email address of an employee. Be assured you are keeping up with the competition so they have no qualms at renewal time. Learn of complementary services you offer. Sign up for a user conference or webinar.
Investors	Keep an eye on the company financials.	Access financial performance information. Evaluate your product/service offering against that of a competitor.
Job candidates	Find a job with a great company.	Search through current job listings. Submit and track a job application. Learn more about the company and its future. Learn more about current staff. Share a current job listing with another job seeker, or perhaps their spouse or family.
Company staff	Do a great job, quickly.	Locate up-to-date marketing materials, such as a whitepaper, to email to a sales prospect. Send a friend a job posting. Research a new job within the company. Keep current on company news. Check whether website copy is up-to-date.

The next step is to prioritize your audiences, to define your target. The highest priority audience for most lead-generation or e-commerce websites is potential customers. The website is an online welcome mat to the store or warehouse, a way to start a new relationship.

Other audiences' needs may be served on the website, but the primary real estate of the home page is devoted to helping customers find products or services they need. Investors, job candidates, and employees might have a small portion of home page real estate, and they might merit website sections of their own, linked from the home page, but the website's main task is to attract and build the trust of potential customers.

Make your own list, and use this process to brainstorm information you need on your website, ranging from

- Specifics on the problem your organization (or its product or service) solves

- Specifics on your solution

- Calls to action to engage visitors

- Contact details

- Information about your offline storefronts or offices

- Information for investors, employees, and applicants

Having the information your visitors seek in mind, you'll be able to craft appropriate calls to action and create navigation elements with enough "information scent" to help visitors find what they seek. As you plan your content to address these diverse goals on your website, consider how these groups will find your website in the first place.

Listen to and Watch Your Audience

After you sketch out the possibilities, flesh out your understanding of your audiences by spending time with people who fit these categories. Spend time with individuals, either one on one or two on one (with two representatives from your team, one interviewer and one person taking notes).

For this type of work, we don't recommend a focus group or survey, because these methods aggregate information, and what you're looking for are individual stories and personal characteristics. Watch real people use your current website or a competitor's website. Then you use your observations to create multiple detailed user "personas" to represent the different kinds of people that visit your website. When you have a snapshot in mind of your future customer types with detailed demographics, it facilitates clear communication across the team and focuses your web redesign efforts.

As examples, we've shared some sample interview questions we have used, anonymized to be for the e-commerce puppy accessories store on the PupMed website. Take these questions and adapt them for your own situation. Go find a couple of folks who fit each of the highest-priority audience categories and offer them a $50 gift certificate for their time.

Ask them directly how they make decisions about online purchases, and then, because people are not always good at telling you how they really act, observe people researching your product or service on your website or a competitor's website. What follows are sample interview questions and observations for an e-commerce puppy accessories website, but most of these questions would apply to a lead-generation website.

Don't forget: You should work with your company's legal team to create or adapt an informed consent agreement for all your interview and observation participants. Many university websites post their research-based informed consent agreements. If you're not sure where to start, you might look to one of them as a model.

Puppy Accessories Interview Questions: An Example

Objectives: To learn about the participants' goals for purchasing puppy accessories (toys, leashes, and training tools) and the participants' purchasing process.

Interview Questions

- Why do you need to purchase puppy accessories?
- How do you know that you need to purchase puppy items?
- How far in advance do you actually buy puppy accessories, in relation to when you plan to use them?
- Do you purchase them for yourself or for others?
- Do you buy more than one type of puppy item at the same time?
- If so, why did you purchase more than one type?
- What puppy toys have you or would you purchase?
- Approximately how much do you spend on puppy accessories per year?
- Do you shop around and compare prices?
- Where have you gone to purchase puppy accessories?
- Why did you choose the PupMed website (if applicable)?
- What is the most important factor in determining where to purchase puppy accessories?

Purchasing Puppy Accessories Observation Scenario: An Example

Gathering context and information through observing people interacting with your websites or similar websites can be done in person in a usability lab, at the interviewee's location, or remotely using web conference software.

Budget at least an hour for this activity (or even better, 90 minutes) to give yourself and the participant time to become comfortable with the observation logistics. Otherwise, you might lose some of your precious observation time to learning how the web conferencing software does or does not work for this particular participant!

Look at PupMed Interface Together

Ensure that we touch on

- Role of item price
- Role of shipping price
- Role of delivery time
- How did the user want to complete the transaction? Phone? Online?

Let the Participant Control the Scenario

At this stage, we ask the participant whether he or she could search for a puppy accessory that he or she has bought in the past or would conceivably purchase. We then turn our attention to a computer with the participant "piloting."

"Can you think of a puppy accessory that you have purchased in the past or one that you may need to purchase sometime soon? We'd like to have you search for it online."

- Please go to the search engine that you prefer when you need to find information or are shopping for something.
- Please search for the item that you have in mind.

If the user's search brings up PupMed in the search results, ask the participant to click either the link in organic search results (preferred) or the paid search ad.

If the user's search does *not* bring up PupMed, note what the user searched for and ask him or her to tell us about the search if it does not correspond to a title or publisher.

Then, go on to ask the following:

- We'd like get feedback on the PupMed website. Could you go to www.example.com?
- Now that we're here, could you try searching for your item here?

Review Specific Pages

Last, we gather feedback from two specific pages from our website.

Item Category Page

- Tell us about this page. What do you see?
- Is the item that you want on this page?
- Tell us about the search box in the middle of the page
- Is there any additional information that you would have liked to have seen on this page?
- What would you do next?

Item Description Page

- Tell us about this page. What do you see?
- Would you buy an accessory at this point?
- Tell us about the items on the page.
- Is there any additional information that you would have liked to have seen on this page?

Develop Website Personas

Described by Alan Cooper in his book *The Inmates are Running the Asylum*, user personas are sketches of individual fictional people used during the design process. These personas are members of target audience categories. Personas serve two purposes: They are a tool for team communication and an input into the design process.

As a communication tool, they exist to make the target user more concrete during design discussions. They allow the design team to "get on the same page" as to what the target user is like, through empathy instead of designing based on personal preferences. They also tap into our ability as humans to empathize with others.

For this reason, personas have seemingly extraneous personal details and a portrait, which should be a photograph, not a cartoon. As humans, we respond strongly to faces; it's hard wired in our psyche. It's easier to dismiss the needs of an unknown faceless website visitor than it is to disregard the needs of a character that has been described in detail and has a familiar face.

Without the personas, the design team often unconsciously designs in terms of their own needs and goals. This phenomenon is known as the *mirror persona*. We all tend to design for users like ourselves, the one in the mirror, in the absence of an actual user. But, the folks who run businesses and make websites may not represent the audience for the website, and this might decrease the website's success. Personas remove this problem, providing a tangible (yet fictional) person to focus on, instead.

WEBSITE PERSONAS IN PRACTICE: AN EXAMPLE

"I wonder whether this page is getting too complicated. What do you think, Maria?"

"Well, let's go back to our user personas. We said that some users, like our Sam persona here, will be reading this page at work, perhaps on their lunch hour, so someone like that might be distracted. Other users, like the Nicole persona, are probably online at home after the kids are in bed... which could mean she'd be tired. Yes, I think you're right, it's getting a little busy on this page for a lot of our users, given their time or energy constraints."

Personas are more than facts—they are stories. They are not a deliverable to get out of the way before moving on, they are something that you live with throughout the project. Most important, personas don't solve any problems just because they exist. They only really work if they become an integral part of how you talk and even think about a website project.

After the user personas are complete, the design team should be able to tell the story of how the users would complete tasks using the website. These task-based stories are called scenarios, and ultimately, after being fleshed out, become diagrams showing the users' various task paths through the website.

Personas can support a "cognitive walkthrough" of the website's design, but also complement aggregate user data found in analytics packages such as Google Analytics. The combination of the specific user needs and the larger quantitative patterns provides deeper insight than either method provides on its own.

Persona and Scenario Development Process

Developing each persona is a five-step process:

1. Determine the target audiences. This prioritization is primarily the work of your business team. For a website focused on lead generation or e-commerce, the highest-priority audience and persona should be a potential customer or a buyer, with other people and actions on the website taking a distant second place.

2. Interview people who fit the target demographic and learn about their needs and the process they use to make decisions when completing a specific task supported by your website.

3. Describe the personas and define the specific goal that drives each persona's visit to the website. Which motivations must the persona fulfill to have a satisfying experience with your company? How do they think about this problem? How would they solve it? What do they think they need?

4. Describe the task. The task is the activity that brings the persona to your website, either directly or indirectly. What do they need to complete their task on the website? List specific conditions that the persona must meet to feel successful at completing the task.

5. Repeat steps 2–4 for other tasks and other audiences for your website.

Sample Personas

Let's look at a couple of sample personas we developed for Attendance on Demand, Inc., a vendor of time and attendance systems. Attendance on Demand, Inc.'s results from web design using these personas are covered in the case study at the end of this section.

Persona 1: Paul Stackhouse

Figure 5.1 shows Paul Stackhouse, the persona representing someone shopping for a replacement product.

Figure 5.1 *Paul Stackhouse, a fictional persona.*

Age: 54

Job Title: Production Manager for Plastica North America

Personal Background: Paul has been involved in plastics manufacturing since 1990. He went back to school to get a Bachelor degree in Industrial Management and was promoted to Production Manager of the Plastica North America film production plant. He is married, has three kids, and he has lived in Connecticut all his life.

Goals: Plastica emphasizes analytics in its operational goals, and as a result Paul is expected to help provide clear reporting as part of the integrated management team. He provides information for planning and scheduling production and maintenance efforts.

Paul is directly responsible for meeting production requirements, and his performance assessment is directly tied to technical and cost-saving improvement activities. Because Plastica's production line produces high numbers of short-run, diverse products that require the production shifts to quickly retool and reorganize production operations, this can be challenging to track and improve. Paul wants to identify the level of effort for retooling, and to identify which processes best help his teams during the retooling efforts.

Scenario: Currently, Paul is using a competitor software product to manage his workforce and generate reports, but he finds it confusing and often cannot configure it properly. Because he is charged with creating tools to better do his assigned duties, he searches for time and attendance software and finds the Attendance on Demand, Inc. website.

Paul is particularly interested in reporting and configurability for production environments. He is intrigued by the possibility that he could acquire a web-based software as a service tool without having to battle with the IT department for additional support or resources, and wants to get a demonstration of the product's value for his particular industry.

Requirements: Website must clearly describe the ease for reporting of workforce information for production managers:

- Tool must handle issues such as absenteeism, overtime, and idle workforce overhead time during retooling efforts.

- Website must include a clear cost/benefit description of hosted time and attendance solutions.

Persona 2: Carla Crowther

Figure 5.2 shows Carla Crowther, the persona representing someone in the initial product research stage of the sales cycle.

Figure 5.2 *Carla Crowther, another fictional website persona.*

Age: 37

Job Title: Payroll/HR Manager for Perla Corporation

Background: Carla is a CPA who discovered an aptitude for "softer" HR-related activities while working at an elementary school in her 20s. She took a job as a CPA and HR manager at Perla 4 years ago. She is single, and she lives in metro Detroit.

Goal: Carla provides overall leadership in the administration of Perla Division's multistate weekly and monthly payroll. She coordinates the efforts of department personnel, ensuring continuity, integrity, and confidentiality. She also coordinates with all of Perla Corporation's operation personnel to provide accurate and timely data in the most efficient manner.

Carla has seen the company try to integrate its workforce management and payroll systems twice previously, without success. Carla has a good reputation as a thoughtful member of her team, and her perspective will be highly regarded during the decision-making process.

Scenario: The chief financial officer (CFO) and chief operations officer (COO) decided to get input from their team this time around, so she has been tasked to find recommendations for an integrated workforce management solution that does not require them to stop using their current payroll system, but will allow them to enjoy better benefits reporting with an accrual feature for their production and sales staff. Carla comes to the website to identify the integration and reporting capabilities of the Attendance on Demand service.

She knows that the company is still 6 months away from making a decision, but she is intrigued by the hosted solution of Attendance on Demand, Inc. and wants to be able to share the information with her CFO, who also manages the IT resources of the company.

Requirements: Website must clearly describe the integration and reporting capabilities:

- Descriptions of front-loaded automated processes to reduce the month-end reporting and payroll resource crunch

- Descriptions of the reporting and integration capabilities of the Attendance on Demand system

Adapt Your Website to Your Personas' Needs

Now that you've characterized your website visitors and their needs, use this information when planning your website and negotiating with other stakeholders on website content, layout, and functionality.

Next Steps: Gather More Feedback

After you identify your target website visitors or personas (most websites have more than one), there are a variety of usability techniques and data sources to gather data and prepare recommendations for increasing your website's usability and conversion rates, explored in "Beyond Best Practices: User Research" in Chapter 7, "Making Websites That Work."

A website that answers visitors' questions and addresses their needs increases conversion rates and therefore your revenue. Gathering and organizing as much knowledge as you can about the different users of your website helps you address your customers in a way that satisfies their needs. By now you probably realize that knowing your audience is an integral part of your success!

Consider Their Path to Your Content

A good portion of your website traffic comes through search engines, though some of that search engine traffic is simply navigational. Over the past few years, direct visitors to websites (visitors who come through typing in the URL into the browser address bar or through a bookmark in their browser) have declined. People seem to have stopped maintaining lists of websites in their browser bookmarks to get back to websites they value. Instead, they just type brand names and even whole URLs into search engines to get to the website they're seeking quickly.

So, being found in search engines is important for both new customers and existing relationships. Folks may take other routes to your website, as well, such as through email or a link from another website. Table 5.3 lists how different audiences might arrive at your website. You might want to draw your own table for your audiences.

Table 5.3 Audiences and Potential Paths

Audience	How They Might Come to Your Website
Potential new customers, information search stage	Click through organic search listing or paid search ad on keywords describing their problem or needed service. *Examples for a nonprofit: Hungry in Poughkeepsie, pancreatic cancer, how to make my store more secure.*
Potential new customers, evaluate alternatives stage	Click through organic search listing or paid search ad on keywords describing their anticipated solution.
Potential new customers, purchase decision stage	Click through organic search listing or paid search ad on keywords describing their problem or needed service. *Examples: The name of a specific prescription medicine, 1.375 AR Level II Bullet Resistant Acrylic.*
Customers	Click through an organic or paid search listing on keywords, such as your brand name or URL.
Investors or donors	Click through an organic or paid search listing on keywords, such as your brand name or URL.
Job candidates	Click through an organic or paid search listing on keywords, such as your brand name, your URL, or general career/jobs keywords. *Examples:* *For a nonprofit: Volunteer in Ann Arbor, nonprofit jobs in Chicago.* *For a corporation: Jobs at Pharmotron, pharmaceutical jobs.*
Company staff	Click through an organic or paid search listing on keywords, such as your brand name or URL.

Links from other websites (for example, links from Twitter or Facebook) will influence your audiences, too, by showing up in organic search engine results and on their own merits.

Table 5.4 presents several scenarios of folks clicking through to your website from another website. These might be online press releases, social media sites like Facebook or Twitter, directory listings such as a list of members of a local Chamber of Commerce, or online reviews.

Table 5.4 Routes to Your Website from Social Media or Other Websites

Audience	How They Might Come to Your Website
Potential new customers, information search stage	Reading an online article on the problem that mentions your organization.
	A recommendation from a Twitter or Facebook friend with a similar business or personal issue.
Potential new customers, evaluate alternatives stage	Reading a review article.
	A link from a corporate Twitter account.
	A note from a happy customer on Twitter.
	A customer service mishap that got some publicity on a website like www.pissedcustomer.com.
	A Facebook promotion or post.
Potential new customers, purchase decision stage	Reading stories people have posted online about your company and examine your responses (or lack thereof).
	Reading tweets mentioning your company and evaluating sentiment (positive or negative).
	Reading Google Places reviews.
Customers	Newsletter or promo to existing customers.
	Click through an email from an employee.
	Via a Twitter or Facebook conversation with a customer service representative.
Investors or donors	Investment website, company press release.
Job candidates	Jobs listing website or online press release website.

Prepare your website to attract new customers and be found by folks who know you already through search engine optimization (SEO).

Case Study: Persona-Driven Redesign

Attendance on Demand, Inc. helps businesses manage time tracking, scheduling, and leave for their employees. Attendance on Demand, Inc. relies on its website for attracting prospects and communicating with existing customers. With a website full of valuable information and lots of online traffic, there were inexplicably few new leads. Conversion rates languished at less than half a percent. Why?

The project team measured visitor behavior using Google Analytics, benchmarked key website features against competitors, and gathered qualitative data through interviews. The team compiled the insights gained from interviews into two key personas and associated scenarios. Using the personas, the market description, and an assessment of Attendance on Demand Inc's competition, the team identified the four key aspects of the website that should be improved and how the architecture and layout could address this.

The new website design needed to focus on

- Communicating to new customers the value of the Attendance on Demand product and why they need it.

- Introducing users to the system and service and showing how their complex workforce management needs are met by Attendance on Demand.

- Addressing credibility issues up front. Potential customers needed to know more about Attendance on Demand, Inc. as a company. Credibility is an important issue for hosted web solutions, so the website needed to include enough information to allow users to know the organization better.

- Encouraging visitors to start the conversation about hosted time and attendance solutions, regardless of what stage of the sales cycle the visitor is in.

The team created a wireframe, a rough layout of the website, to focus calls to action and relay information to support these specific needs. When the new website design launched in early April, 2008, the results were immediate and dramatic, as shown in Figure 5.3. Conversion rates jumped from less than half a percent to 1.31%, quadrupling lead generation.

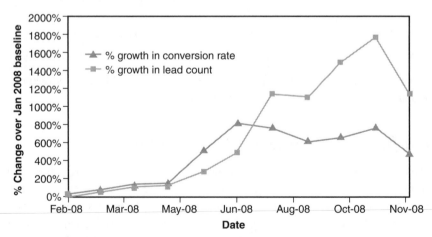

Growth in Leads and Lead Conversion Rate in 2008

Figure 5.3 *Growth in lead-conversion rate and lead count by month, from Google Analytics.*

For more information about Google Analytics and other analytical tools, see "Web Analytics: Information Rich Dashboard" in Chapter 4, "Breaking Down Silos to Get the Metrics You Need."

Speak Your Audience's Language: The Real SEO

The best way to establish rapport is to reflect that you've heard the other person. In conversation, this is known as *active listening* and often involves repeating back, in your own words or theirs, what the other person said to demonstrate your attention and understanding.

Well, SEO is the same thing. SEO involves making sure the web copy you write is successful because it uses the important terms and phrases on which your audience, your personas, are searching. And, because they recognize a little of themselves in your web copy, and because your website copy will be crafted specifically to support them in their decision process (reflecting their goals and tasks from Tables 5.1 and 5.2), website visitors may deem your website to be more persuasive and effective.

Bear in mind the words your target audience uses to describe your services. If your website uses words to describe your services that are different from those that people use when searching, those searchers won't find your website, and they may end up being directed to the website of a competitor.

Do Your Keyword Research

When identifying potential keywords and keyphrases, make sure you are reflecting your target audience's language. Do they use different keywords to describe your products than you use internally or in your industry? Quite likely. Writing for your audience means using their language, *not yours*. And, what's amazing is you can find out just what they're saying by asking the search engines. Search engines capture, store, and let you query information about what people are looking for, in their own words. What a treasure trove!

Start by generating a long list of options: brainstorm industry-related keywords, get a list of related websites in your industry and then harvest words from those websites, and then use a keyphrase research tool to expand this list to additional, related keywords.

Web Writing Term Evaluation: An Example

Let's assume you want to investigate web writing keywords. All you have to do is ask Google to show you what search keywords people are using, and you'll get guidance on how to speak to your audience and how to help them find you all at the same time.

Figure 5.4 shows that in 2009, the keyphrase "writing for the web" has been eclipsed by popularity of searches for "SEO writing." The data points shown here are the average search volume for each year extracted from worldwide searches available from Google Insights for Search.

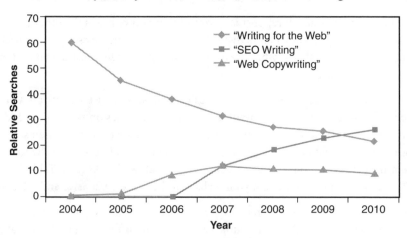

Popularity of Search Terms on Web Writing

Figure 5.4 *Relative popularity of searches on web writing.*

But, comparing sets of keywords in small groups on a visual tool like Google Insights for Search is limiting. You should go to a more data intensive keyphrase generation tool to characterize the larger landscape of words that describe your products and services, your word market.

Tip

You can access Google Insights for Search at www.google.com/insights/ search. This tool lets you review and compare search volume patterns across specific regions, categories, or time frames.

Evaluate Your Keyphrases in the Context of the Entire Word Market

A *word market* is the collection of keywords and keyphrases that people use when searching for products or services. An optimized website shows up for high-traffic words from its word market.

Optimizing a website for important keywords in the relevant word market creates two advantages. Traffic to the website increases due to higher search engine page rankings. More important, the traffic generated brings in better qualified visitors who are more likely to be interested in your products and services. Because of this, make sure you start your SEO work grounded firmly in research on what keywords your potential customers are using in conversation or when searching.

After identifying the word market itself, you need to determine the best keywords to use on a website, how much traffic those keywords can bring to a website, and how difficult it would be to become well ranked in them.

Word Market Analysis Process: List Generation and Evaluation

Begin by creating a list of keywords and keyphrases related to your products, services, and organization. You can scour your website for examples, and you may want to review competitor websites to see other language describing these things. You want to supplement your list by using tools such as Google's Keyword Tool to expand that list of keywords.

A cross section of keyword tools includes the following:

- Google AdWords Keyword Tool (free) (https://adwords.google.com/select/KeywordToolExternal)

- Paid programs such as

    - WordTracker (www.wordtracker.com/)

    - Trellian Keyword Discovery (www.keyworddiscovery.com/)

    - SEO Book's keyword tool (http://tools.seobook.com/keyword-tools/seobook/)

    - WordStream (www.wordstream.com/)

These tools enable you to start with a few phrases and provide longer lists of suggested keywords and supporting data from which to choose. A key criterion here is the average traffic on these keywords. However, more is not always better if the keyword fits other websites better than yours. (For instance, if you sell soup, the keyword "food" is relevant but not specific enough.)

Assess Your Keywords and Traffic

Next, assess both your competitors and the traffic for each keyword and website. With these insights, you can filter the list to only the most relevant keywords.

To categorize the keywords:

1. Group together those phrases that indicate a search for similar information.

2. Check the search results pages for all phrases and filter the categories, removing any category with search results entirely outside of your competitive market.

3. Assess the keyphrases within each remaining category to determine which are ideal targets.

Make Your Final Keyword Choices

To complete the keyword assessment, choose the words that have the best chance of success. You want to target the highest traffic keyphrases where you have a relatively strong chance of ranking. The challenge here is assessing the relative likelihood of getting good rankings. Your assessment of the "likelihood" is always relative to other websites and other phrases in your word market:

1. Determine the number of commercial type websites in the first page of search results. If the results are overwhelmingly reference websites, industry resources, and news publications, then there are fewer opportunities for a commercial website to rank.

2. Are the results mostly for websites that show up all over your word market? If so, those websites are likely highly competitive SEO wise, and this term is likely highly competitive.

3. Spot check some of the top results for basic SEO implementation as described in Chapter 7, in the "Define Your Market" section. If your competition on those terms is unsophisticated SEO-wise, ranking is easier here than against folks who have taken care of the basics and more.

Deciding What *Not* to Target

What you'll find, after reviewing competitor websites and keyphrases, is that some keyphrases have a better chance of success than others, both in terms of the total traffic and the chance of improving search engine rankings.

Obviously, to get the most return on your investment in website infrastructure (see the section "Crawler Control: Speak to Your Spiders" in Chapter 7) and website copywriting, you want to optimize your website for the keyphrases that have the most potential for success.

There may be other reasons to abandon a keyphrase as a potential SEO target, such as the following:

- **Single word:** Given the nature of SEO tactics, it's difficult to intentionally target single-word keyphrases. It's better to target two- or three-word phrases instead. Sometimes, a website increases ranking on the single-word keyphrase as a result of these efforts, but it is impossible to predict.

- **Informational resource prominence:** Search engines seem to treat informational resources differently than commercial websites. When informational resources dominate the search results, this indicates that the search engines have determined the query is typically noncommercial in nature.

In such cases, it is inordinately difficult for commercial websites to appear; and even if they do, they appear with a low ranking, below the fold.

- **High competition:** Attempting to target a large number of competitive keyphrases in your SEO strategy is highly resource intensive and expensive, and often provides only modest results (for example, below the fold, second page visibility, or worse... no results at all). Instead, try prioritizing the highly competitive keyphrases, and targeting a few top candidates. Based on the success of these, you can plan on targeting additional keyphrases (or not) in the future.

Case Study: Word Market Focuses Tutor Time on the Right Descriptors

In 2007, Tutor Time, a national provider of early childhood education and child-care, undertook a review of their appearance on keywords in their field. Until that time, their marketing copy had focused on keyphrases such as "childcare" and "learning center," and they were positioning their centers as schools. They had good visibility online for searches that included these keywords, and little visibility on phrases that included the keyword "day care" or "daycare;" see Table 5.5.

The brand was visible on a few daycare keyphrases (for instance, "toddler daycare," "learning center daycare"), but not general unmodified daycare keywords that were more common. The company had been intentionally omitting the phrase "daycare" from their marketing materials, in an effort to distinguish themselves from other daycare companies (that is, to let parents know that they offered more).

Table 5.5 Search Engine Rankings for Tutor Time in Summer 2007

Keyphrase	Rank
Childcare learning center	2
Preschool learning center	2
Childcare learning centers	3
Toddler childcare	3
Childcare centers	4
Preschool learning centers	4
Private kindergarten programs	4
Child learning centers	4
Learning center daycare	5
Toddler education	5
Child learning centers	5

Yet, the data showed that search engine visitors were using keyphrases such as "daycare" more often than "childcare" and much more often than "early childhood education." Competing brands had better visibility than Tutor Time did on the daycare keyphrases. And, when a searcher for "daycare" landed on the Tutor Time website, they had a higher conversion rate than "childcare" searchers.

"Daycare" keywords also had higher traffic and generated leads for Tutor Time schools at a higher rate than "childcare" keywords. So although Tutor Time offered more than just daycare, people used that familiar term when searching.

After 2007, when Tutor Time committed to including "daycare" keyphrases on their website, visits from these popular organic searches increased year over year, shown in Figure 5.5. The resulting jump in website visits for 2008 through 2010 was extracted from Tutor Time's Google Analytics. (The searches on "daycare" keywords declined somewhat in 2010 due to economic factors.)

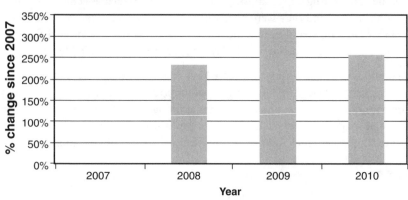

Percent Change in Visits to TutorTime.com via natural searches containing "day care" terms

Figure 5.5 *The percentage change in visits data comparing the number of visits to 2007.*

Summary

A simple, easy-to-use website is not easy to build. It involves making real tradeoffs, choosing a target audience and a message and focusing on that, instead of trying to satisfy everyone. Do the hard work of making design and language choices so your website visitors don't have to.

Making it easy for your visitors takes time. It involves learning from mistakes and a passion for listening, listening to the website analytics patterns and listening to the voices of the target audiences. This investment is worth the effort, saving waste and rework later, sparing your team and your website visitor from content that misses its target audience or is past its due date.

Ensure the success of your website by making it all about your target audience's needs:

- Analyze your audiences:

    - Develop personas and scenarios of use.

    - Keep these personas and scenarios in mind when writing web copy and to vet any proposed design and functionality changes.

    - Watch real users use your website to make refinements.

- Speak your audience's language so that they feel understood and can find you using search engines.

- Research the important terms in your word market.

6

Putting It All Together and Selling Online

You've got your user research and user personas for the people visiting your website. Now what? How do you turn that valuable information into a strategic advantage by building a better website? By applying a few techniques taken from the field of Information Architecture and defining "user paths" through your website's content.

In terms of Internet marketing, it's not all about the main website that everyone sees. The landing pages (behind the scenes, separate from the main website but critical for every marketing campaign) also need to be built. What makes a good landing page, and how do you decide when to make multiple landing pages? This chapter focuses not only on how to design a user-informed main website, but how to create compelling landing pages for your marketing campaigns.

Designing Your Website

Now that you've done your user research and developed personas (from Chapter 5, "The Audience Is Listening (What Will You Say?)"), you are ready to put that information to work and redesign your website. It's best to start from scratch, and not get tied down to your existing website's navigation or terminology.

To take the next steps, apply some of the best practices from the field of Information Architecture (IA). This ensures a thoughtful, user-centered approach based on the information or tasks website visitors are trying to accomplish on your website.

After developing a skeleton for the complete standalone website, you need to turn your attention to landing page design. Landing pages are often your potential clients' first experience of your website and brand (as they typically are accessed by clicking an ad or responding to a marketing campaign). Relevant, compelling landing pages with clear calls to action are critical to long-term campaign success.

You can set up your landing pages to act as a continuous survey of how your marketing message fares in the real world, getting almost real-time results to hone that message. We go into greater detail about what makes a good landing page later in this chapter, in the "Landing Page Basics" section.

Chapter 7, "Making Websites That Work," goes into more detail about the development process, rolling out a new version of a website, and related considerations. This chapter focuses on the initial website design process itself, instead.

Incorporating Information Architecture Techniques

Although building websites requires many specialized skills (team roles summarized in Figure 7.5 in Chapter 7), design by committee leads to the sure death both of a concept and team morale.

Someone has to be responsible for the design; some people's opinions, wants, and needs really do matter more than others'. The user advocate should overrule other team members' preferences, informed by user research and the agreed upon priority personas.

While the website's graphic design is informed by the branding and design standards of the company, the design of the infrastructure used to present the information fails if it doesn't help website visitors accomplish their goals.

So, the website's information architecture—the organization of its navigation and the flow of its content—must revolve around the user tasks, scenarios, and goals.

IA is a large field and includes the categorization of many things beyond websites. Within website design, the term *information architecture* can be used loosely in conversation and mean many things; a subset is listed in Table 6.1. Each item represents critical aspects of the website design process, and associated research activities involve direct contact with website users.

Table 6.1 Information Architecture Concepts and Outputs

Concept	Deliverable
Arrangement or organization of pages on a website	Sitemap
Mechanism for visitors to move around the website	Navigation specification (menus, breadcrumbs) On-site search specification
Labels for categories	List of words to be used in website navigation and headings
Critical elements needed on each page	Page-level information design—page layouts or wireframes (which are typically turned into Hypertext Markup Language [HTML] templates)

ADDITIONAL READING

For a great foundation on the tenets of website information architecture, refer to *Information Architecture for the World Wide Web: Designing Large-Scale Web Sites*, by Peter Morville and Louis Rosenfeld.

You'll get sound advice on how to meet the needs of website visitors when designing a navigation system, labeling system, and searching system for your website.

Experiment with an Unconventional User-Driven Architecture: McKinley.com

McKinley is a Michigan-based real estate company. Through user research and testing, it evolved a somewhat unconventional website organization that specifically addresses the needs of its visitors and its business goal of leasing apartments. The website has the "regular" website categories (About Us, Careers, News, Contact Us), but the design de-emphasizes that navigation by placing it at the top right of the page (see Figure 6.1).

Instead, the company devotes the main part of the home page to helping visitors hone in on specific apartment communities in their portfolio while featuring lovely photographs of the communities.

Figure 6.1 *The McKinley.com home page emphasizing the apartment finder over the "main" website navigation.*

One level down from the home page, McKinley's website navigation guides visitors through the apartment-finding process (see Figures 6.2 and 6.3). After visitors select a state on the left side of the home page, they are taken to a map and offered the choice of cities within that state.

The horizontal bar at the top of the page shows the visitor's position in the process of selecting an apartment: first select a state, then a city, then a community within the city, then a floor plan, and then a particular apartment with that floor plan.

Selecting a community is an interactive process where visitors choose the amenities they need (number of bedrooms, baths, other features such as school district, patio, bus accessible, and the like) and is shown McKinley communities that meet their criteria.

In the previous website organization, the website visitor had to choose a community without knowing its amenities, but many apartment-seekers did not have a particular community in mind and were more focused on certain features instead.

The Information Architecture Process

Information architecture can be created through careful and challenging work done by a trained expert. It can also be done by building elements from the ground up via user research activities such as card sorting.

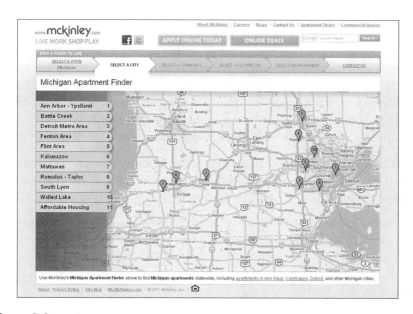

Figure 6.2 *Michigan apartment finder, leading visitors through the process of locating an apartment community.*

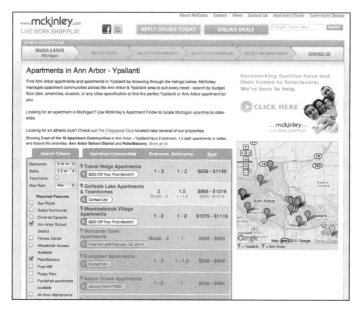

Figure 6.3 *Ann Arbor/Ypsilanti apartment finder, that interactively sorts the list of available communities based on specific selections of amenities.*

We generally approach it from both top-down (via expert analysis) and bottom-up (via interviews, content inventory of existing or competitive websites, card sorts) techniques, piecing together the website framework and content organization through many iterations.

Websites have some typical design patterns and categories. Many websites repeat familiar navigation structures. such as a single or multiple sections describing products or services or an About Us section with company information. About Us might also include some investor or job applicant information, or if the company is large, those sections might merit their own navigation sections.

There are usually fairly standard on-page conventions to follow, as well. On each page, there is typically a company logo, the navigation, the content itself, and a footer repeating or adding to the navigation.

For e-commerce websites, products in the database may have many descriptors, some of which are more important than others and deserve more visual emphasis. These are the "easy wins" in the process, though. The actual challenge comes in trying to organize nonobvious things. For example, do your visitors expect to locate your products by purpose, industry, or features?

So, the process of defining the information architecture (creating the sitemap, designing the navigation and on-site search, and designing the layout of individual page types within the website) is a combination of reusing existing and familiar elements with your own special customizations to suit the needs of your customers and the specifics of your product offering.

Take a collaborative and iterative approach to the information architecture development. Assemble the right team and proceed through the steps of envisioning and specifying your website through applying best practices and your user research. And don't forget to test along the way.

Investigate and Inform Your Information Architecture

At this point, we assume that you've already done your homework on who your website visitors and potential customers are. You've read the sections "Listen to and Watch Your Audience" and "Develop Website Personas" in Chapter 5.

You should have a few website personas that you've developed from audience interviews. The audience information you uncovered will help determine how your website's information architecture takes shape and exactly which words appear on your navigation system's labels.

Develop a Website Skeleton or Wireframe

Now that you have a good idea about who might be a potential website visitor, you need to think about how those visitors will move through your website content to become a customer (or take another specific action along a path).

These paths through your content are defined by the website's information architecture. Some of the paths support the goals of website visitors. ("I want to find information about a service" or "I want to buy a birthday gift for Aunt Nancy.") Other paths support the goals of your company (for example, to increase website conversions and generate more qualified leads or completed sales).

It's important to realize that these two distinct goal paths (website visitor and company) may or may not completely overlap. The trick is to find the sweet spot where both paths overlap enough so that both the business sales goals and the customers are supported.

After you've developed multiple visitor paths to support different personas and different goals, an overall picture of your website structure starts to take shape. Think of this as a bottom-up method of creating your navigation and website content hierarchy.

Most people instinctively start with a top-down methodology, defining the navigation labels on the home page, and then moving on to subsequent main pages. We find that the bottom-up method is more organic and yields better results because you're focusing on the website personas and their goals, not a predetermined idea about how a corporate website is organized.

Scenarios and Paths

Start with a website persona and a primary goal. What is a potential customer trying to do? Map out a scenario, or set of content chunks, of what a "good" interaction would look like. What would visitors want to do (and what information does your company want them to have at each step?)?

Does your company have additional business requirements that affect the scenario, such as website visitors must submit their email address before downloading a whitepaper? This impacts your interaction scenario.

Often, it's helpful to start by thinking out loud with a story about a website visitor. Then figure out what you'd need to make that goal path happen, and what information should be on the different pages throughout the scenario.

Arranging Multiple Scenarios

You might want to map out bits of content or interaction on sticky notes and start arranging them on a whiteboard. After you've got a couple of goal paths (or scenarios) defined, you'll probably start to see how some of them overlap or where some content can be reused. Fiddle around with the sticky notes to reuse content where it makes sense but doesn't negatively affect the scenarios.

Eventually, after working through each business goal and website persona (down to the potential new employee looking for job openings), you'll have a detailed idea of the myriad potential paths for the new information architecture.

Now is the time to draw on the content inventory you performed back at the beginning of the project (or do it now!). The content inventory is the list of the existing content and the new content that you want on your website.

Consider how users would look for your products or services. Does that change how you arrange the much larger set of content that you now have? And did you find that there are different ways in which users navigate or search your content based on your user research? You'll have to make choices to accommodate that. This might feed back into your scenarios that you've written up.

At this point, it really is a question of trial and error, putting pencil to paper (or using more sticky notes), and going through multiple iterations to make the magic happen. The end result is that you've created a large diagram mapping out all the primary and secondary scenarios for the website.

Define the Navigation Structure

Recall that we looked at the language your website visitors are using to talk about your products and services in "Speak Your Audience's Language: The Real Search Engine Optimization" in Chapter 5.

The same audience-oriented language research that informs your website copy to improve search engine rankings also informs your information architecture development. Why refer to a product page as "frozen milk fantasies" when everyone else simply says "ice cream flavors?"

Simply put, the more you learn about your website visitors and align the website language to their orientation, the more successful the website will be at gathering and converting potential prospects.

Define the structure of your navigation system to account for each of the content chunks (sticky notes) you identified earlier when you created scenarios and to accommodate the classification scheme that you applied to your content. Use the website visitor's language to create meaningful labels for the links that let visitors navigate through the website content. Leverage the keyword research you've done for search engine optimization (SEO) and paid search purposes for your information architecture's navigation labels and page titles.

MULTIPLE DATA SOURCES MAKE MAGIC

The ideal situation is when you can gather data from multiple sources to help with language choices for the website.

Can you access the "real language" work behind-the-scenes in your keyword programs (SEO and paid search)? What about gathering web analytics data to identify which pages are more popular than others? This can give you an idea of what labels and language resonates (or doesn't) with website visitors, and to identify which keywords drive more traffic.

We firmly believe you can never have too much data; it just takes a bit of effort to gather it and wade through it to make better decisions (and therefore a better information architecture).

Rough Out the Page Layout

Now that you've got an overall website structure, navigation labels, and individual page titles, you need to think about what the individual pages will look like at a more detailed level. Essentially, you'll create a content specification (you won't be writing the website copy—leave that to an SEO or marketing copywriter).

But the information architect on the project should specify which content chunks need to appear on specific pages. The information architecture not only includes the content specification for each page but also the general page layout for the individual elements. Will the navigation options appear on the left with mouseover text or flyouts for secondary navigation links? Where does the search box go? How do you lay out product descriptions?

The relative emphasis of various elements on each page also needs to be considered. Where should the visitor's eye go first? And second? What is the relative importance of the various information items on a given page?

For many of the industry's best practices, follow the web conventions identified in "The Basics: What to Fix Before Testing" in Chapter 7.

Many companies prefer to define the rough page layout and overall website "skeleton" in a flowcharting program such as Visio. You can use the flowchart, or simple paper prototypes, and conduct basic usability testing with these simple tools, before the first piece of HTML code has been written. See "Beyond Best Practices: User Research" in Chapter 7.

The Full Information Architecture

To complete the website information architecture, make sure you include all the various methods that someone can use to navigate through your website.

This includes defining a sitemap, which acts somewhat like the index of a book. If you think of your overall navigation structure as a table of contents, the sitemap is an index at-a-glance view of all the website content, just arranged thematically instead of alphabetically.

Do you have an on-site search function? Having on-site search is a goldmine, because you get to see the words your visitors type to find content and you can use their search terms to expand or revise existing web content. Yet, a poorly working on-site search can do more harm than good by frustrating your users. Sometimes the search engines built in to content management systems require a fair investment before they work well.

You might consider not using the out-of-the-box search, but using Google custom search, which at least lets you handle off-site SEO and on-site search with the same feature set and optimization strategy. If you cannot find something that you know exists on your website using your search function, take it out until you can get it to work properly.

Don't forget that a primary path for most website visitors' first visit to your website is via landing pages that are built as part of a marketing campaign, paid search program, or organic search program. Landing pages, by their very nature, are not part of the main website navigation or hierarchy, but act as standalone content "islands" for groups of keywords.

The development of landing pages is related more to the paid search advertising work, not the primary website information architecture. In some cases, however, you'll want to tie landing pages into the main website. Look at your website's traffic patterns (assuming you already have landing pages) to see how to best support this content path.

We cover landing page development in greater detail in the second half of this chapter.

Test the Information Architecture

Finally, when you've got a paper prototype or HTML wireframe of your new information architecture, run it by a small group of people who match your personas to confirm that the labels, placement, and hierarchy make sense to potential website visitors. The exact method depends on your timeline and budget. Several options are available and discussed in Chapter 7.

For more information, see "Qualitative User Analysis: Observations, Usability Tests" and "Beyond Best Practices: User Research" in Chapter 7.

Graphic Design Comes Later

To those of us untrained in graphic design, this part can feel like magic. In a good design, the designer and the design process recedes and the meaning in the words, pictures, and media are center stage. Yet, while part of it is an art, much of successful graphic design comes from the application of known principles of layout and emphasis.

Robin Williams, in *The Non-Designers Design Book*, boils graphic composition down to a few essential principles:

- Proximity

- Alignment

- Repetition

- Contrast

Good designs please the eye and convey meaning through grouping similar items together in *proximity* and leaving whitespace in between.

Good composition comes from placing items on the page intentionally and with visual connections (*alignment*) from one item to another: In a photograph of a plane for sale, the nose of the plane might point at the call to action link or phone pad.

Repetition of key elements and styles unify a design and a website. Basic repetition of font styles and shapes in the design can be accomplished and unified across a website through cascading style sheets. Yet it is more than mindless consistency.

And good design relies on repetition's seeming opposite: contrast. A designer can emphasize certain elements through implementing vivid *contrast* through elements such as a hierarchy of colors, typefaces, font sizes, or any visual element.

A Process Overview

A veteran graphic designer understands the relative importance of on-page elements and makes informed choices about what items to keep together, what to repeat, and where to apply contrast. Clear priorities from the user research and business goals of the website inform the design. At this stage, the work of the information architect is to collaborate with and guide the designer.

Designers may want to subtly stylize the links or use a clean simple approach, which was shown in Figure 6.1. In this website, the site's navigation is intentionally de-emphasized with low contrast and tucked up against the upper-right corner.

Instead, the emphasis is placed on the "find an apartment" element, which is in the place where some websites have their main website navigation. Unconventional arrangements like this one come from a strong working relationship between the information architect and the graphic designer.

This approach of handing off the rough layout to a designer will sound like a "waterfall" project management approach, where individual project stages must be completed before the next phase starts. Of course, the best approach comes where the graphic designer is involved throughout the project at a low level, asking questions that will help the information architect and the stakeholders prioritize website elements.

Having more people involved in the process for a longer period of time helps access the wisdom of a larger group and leaves time for the participants' subconscious mind to process and solve conflicts. However, our sense is that the results are better when there is clear ownership of certain stages.

The graphic designer benefits from agreement on the elements to include in the design before the design work starts. Page elements are much easier to revise within a simple Visio website mock-up than in beautiful, layered Photoshop designs.

Information Architecture Case Study

We recently collaborated with a nonprofit debt-counseling organization to develop a new information architecture for their website, and to guide them on which phrases would be useful to emphasize for SEO. To handle the SEO work, we applied our word market analysis technique, outlined in "Evaluate Your Keyphrases in the Context of the Entire Word Market" in Chapter 5.

User Personas and Keyword Analysis

First, competitive research, stakeholder interviews, and user research helped to define user personas for their target website users. Next, we did a content inventory of their existing website. The user personas helped the team to identify meaningful paths based on user goals through the website content.

We performed the keyword analysis process simultaneously to help define the navigation system's labels in the new information architecture. There was much discussion between the information architects and the SEO analysts as the group identified the best keywords to use for both organic search and the information architecture.

High-Level Information Architecture

Next, the team identified a new page structure and hierarchy, based on the content inventory and the user paths through that content. Figure 6.4 shows the website's top-level structure.

Figure 6.4 *The website organization, including a proposed Community section.*

After identifying the two versions of the home page content, one for the blog and one for the main website with community pages, the team worked on the information architecture for the next level down (see Figures 6.5 and 6.6).

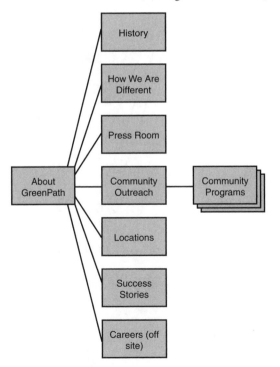

Figure 6.5 *The structure of the About set of pages.*

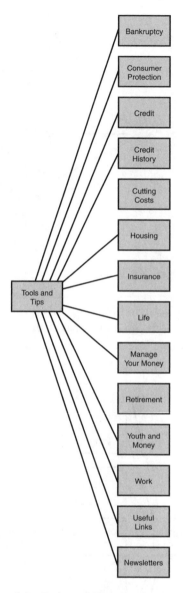

Figure 6.6 *The structure of the Tools and Tips set of pages.*

Figure 6.7 shows what the overall website content structure looks like.

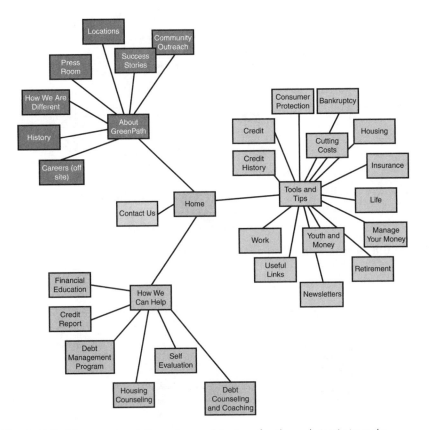

Figure 6.7 *The complete information architecture for the website (minus the Community/Blog section).*

Page Templates with Content Specified

We collaborated to develop a couple of different page templates, illustrating how a new layout and organization could provide more room for content while removing irrelevant (off-goal) aspects of their existing pages (see Figures 6.8, 6.9, and 6.10).

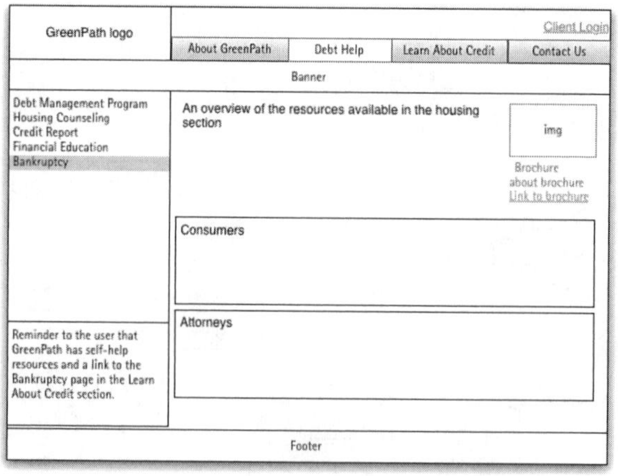

Figure 6.8 *A content specification from a deeper-level page.*

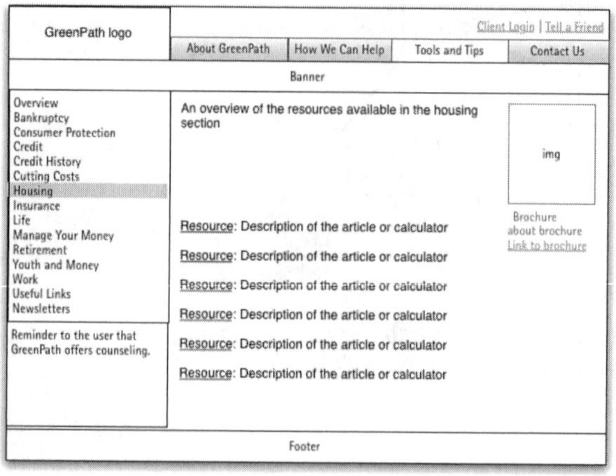

Figure 6.9 *Another website page template well below the home page.*

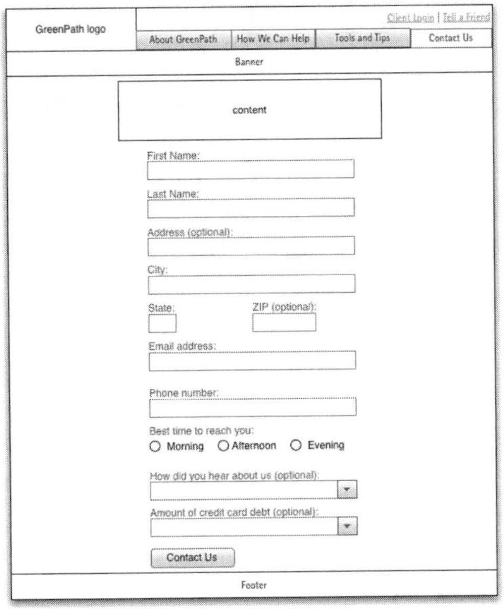

Figure 6.10 *The specification for the contact form.*

How the Website Mission Can Affect Information Architecture

GreenPath Debt Solutions, a nationwide, nonprofit organization, is committed to providing high-quality financial education to consumers struggling with debt. One of the purposes of GreenPath's website, www.greenpath.com, is to provide helpful money-management resources.

When a visitor lands on educational content within the website, GreenPath considers this a successful outcome. Because of this particular measure of success, the information architecture and navigation system labels took on an even greater significance. This also impacted the measurement criteria for success. Instead of counting the number of website visitors who completed an online form (for example, a sale), the team closely monitors traffic for the educational pages.

Designing Your Landing Pages

Landing pages, in their most basic form, are the website pages that you show when a potential customer clicks an advertisement. The ad could be a text ad or banner on a search engine or on another type of informational website. You may consider using landing pages for email marketing, billboards, broadcast, or direct mail drops.

Some people use the term *landing page* to mean the top-level page in each navigation section of a website. (That's definitely not what we mean throughout this book.)

Ideally, each ad or promotion would have its own custom landing page. In practice, people use a mixture of custom landing pages and existing website pages in marketing campaigns. Custom landing pages that are separate from your website typically have a look and feel similar to your website, are hosted on the same domain, but are unreachable except via clicking a link in your campaign or by knowing the exact URL.

They are often almost self-contained mini-websites, with context about your brand, your services, and, usually, a targeted offer or contact form, all on one page. The landing page typically displays sales copy that is a logical extension of the offer in the ad.

Let's walk through a few landing page design basics, including what makes a good (or a bad) landing page, and how you decide when you need a separate landing page in your marketing plan.

Landing Page Basics

Landing pages are a critical component to online advertising that many savvy marketers miss. You need to deliver the exact information that someone is looking for, in a compelling way. For this reason, landing pages are not a "one size fits all" undertaking. You generally want to have multiple landing pages for multiple marketing needs.

These are pages that are skimmed quickly, so large and legible fonts, simple language, and clear next steps are critical.

To continue the conversation with the website visitor you started in the ad, the landing page should

- Reinforce the ad clicked by the visitor
- Be long enough to provide proper context, but be easy to skim
- Have a visual focus
- Have clear calls to action (phone call or contact form, or both), avoiding distracting elements
- Most important, offer something of value to the website visitor

Reinforce the Offer in Headline and Copy

The landing page is the point of entry for someone new to your website. To get there, visitors have clicked a paid search ad, a banner ad, or email that interests them. To avoid disorienting your new visitors, it's important to repeat and support the offer that initially drew them there.

So, the landing page should be consistent with the advertising used to attract the visitor. Reinforce the offer in your page's headline, images, and copy. Use persuasive copy that supports the claims made in your ad that triggered the clickthrough in the first place.

The headline should refer directly to the place the visitor came from or to the ad copy and relevant keywords that drove the clickthrough to the landing page.

Write Just Enough, Clearly

A key misconception about landing page copy is "the shorter, the better." Good landing page copy is well organized and easily scannable, but that doesn't translate into short. Good landing page copy can be actually very long.

All subheadings and links should be written with clear language. Opt for "Request More Information" rather than "Got 2 Minutes?" and use "Testimonials" instead of "Don't Take Our Word for It."

Make liberal use of the following:

- **Subheads and bulleted lists:** Make it easy to scan.

- **Descriptions:** Support their information needs.

- **Testimonials:** Leverage the human need for reinforcement in decision making.

- **Guarantees:** Put your buyer at ease.

Avoid any graphical or navigational elements that might imply that visitors are at the bottom of the page before they actually have scrolled down through all the page content. A long landing page is fine, as long as the visitor knows to scroll.

Help with Hero Shots

Ensure that your landing pages appeal to both visual and textual learners. Often, the primary visual focus of a landing page is a "hero shot"—a picture or drawing of the item you're marketing. Limit the hero shot to the main product or a single element.

If you're selling something that doesn't lend itself well to pictures, try a diagram of how it works or the value it provides. Avoid inserting obvious stock images of smiling businesspeople or indecipherable abstract images.

Show something that has meaning, if at all possible. Figure 6.11 has a hero shot of a beautiful room featuring the product (interior wood paneling). The page emphasizes product benefits and invites visitors to call. A link to a brochure request/contact form is available, but de-emphasized.

Figure 6.11 *A landing page with a hero shot at left.*

Figure 6.12 has a hero shot of a before and after dental work, directly featuring the results: a beautiful smile.

We Practice Dentistry as a Fine Art

Dr. Kirk Donaldson and Dr. Kristin Guenther provide excellence in comprehensive cosmetic, restorative and implant dentistry. At Donaldson & Guenther, we incorporate a wide variety of dental disciplines to orchestrate optimal care and results. Our dentists have advanced training and talent in cosmetic implant treatments. Our focus is always on fulfilling our patients' individual needs, preferences and priorities.

Whether you require small or large implant work Donaldson & Guenther have experience with all types of implant needs.

Let Donaldson & Guenther make you smile again, contact us below or call us at (734) 971-3450.

Donaldson & Guenther Excels in Dental Implants

Your Name:
Your Email:
Your Phone Number:
Comments:

Before
After

Office Hours:
Monday thru Wednesday 7am-4pm, Thursday and Friday 7am-1pm. Closed Saturday and Sunday.

Submit

Donaldson & Guenther

© 2007 Donaldson & Guenther. All rights reserved.
3100 Eisenhower Parkway
Suite 300
Ann Arbor, MI 48104
(734) 971-3450

Figure 6.12 *A landing page with hero shot and a web form.*

Requirement: Clear Call to Action

Both above and below the fold, each landing page should repeat the call to action that you want the website visitor to take. There's nothing worse than seeing a call to action in the header scrolling out of the way so that the website visitor can get to the "meat" of the page, only to have nowhere to go after reading your copy.

If you've opted for a contact form on the landing page, make sure that it captures the absolute minimum amount of information required at that step in your sales process for the next step with the prospect. Always assume that you can get more data from a lead, after it's been qualified. There's no need to pry.

Interactive details on forms, such as slow load times of optional fields, do affect the conversion rate. Make sure the form is clearly identified and is visually distinct from the rest of the page content.

Place the call to action on the click text or Submit button itself. Make it easy for visitors to complete the action. And don't just label the button Submit. Instead, label the button with what action the user is taking, such as Sign Up or Request Information.

Reduce Distractions

Clarity comes from what you eliminate. Many landing pages eliminate the website's navigation, perhaps offering a few links to supporting content but looking to capture the visitor's attention and motivate the next step entirely on the one page.

Other distractions include the following:

- **Illegible text:** Strive for 12 point text. It's a good standard size for most body text fonts.

- **Unrelated copy and graphics:** Make sure the landing pages match the creative campaign look and message.

- **Long wait time to load media and animations:** If you plan to use rich media on the landing page, make sure the page is designed to be usable before it loads completely.

Offer Something of Value

Always remember: *People convert because you offer them something they need.* Reciprocity is key.

You are asking someone for contact or credit card information. Make sure you offer something equally valuable in return. That's the idea behind a whitepaper: In return for getting to read some helpful information, you're sharing your own information.

The Design Cycle

Your sales process is the primary driver behind your landing page scheme, and your marketing plan helps you identify how granular to make your landing pages.

You should develop a landing page strategy by asking a couple of key questions:

- At what point in the sales process are people reaching this landing page?
- Who are these people? Have we developed user personas?

To design a landing page strategy, you

1. Develop the strategy based on your sales process and marketing campaign needs.

2. Define the conversion or conversions.

3. Build a landing page template, collect graphic elements, and create a design concept.

4. Write targeted copy for each landing page.

5. Track, test, and modify the landing page concept, copy, graphics, and so on over time.

Your user personas, developed as described in Chapter 5, guide your Internet marketing strategy and your landing page design, as well.

Getting More Granular: When Do You Need a New Landing Page?

Many people are confused about how many landing pages to create for their website. Let your sales process and marketing efforts define the level of granularity. Are you reaching out to prospects in a specific print ad or a paid search campaign based on a group of keywords?

Think about how, why, and when leads are converted into sales. This is where you'll find the answer to the question of landing page granularity.

Needs During the Sales Process

You can create a unique landing page for each need during the sales process. Recall the sales funnel (Figure 3.1) from Chapter 3, "Building a Metrics-Driven Practice."

In the beginning of a search for a solution, searchers may only be aware of their pain, without an ultimate solution in mind. They might need help taming their fun (but a little too exuberant) puppy, or they might need to research software to help automate certain business processes. Whatever the situation, people typically start researching their need rather than their solution.

Then, they move through an information-gathering phase into identifying what categories solutions will help them. It might go like this. My old car keeps breaking down. Should I get a different car or should I consider a combination of public transportation and car sharing through a service like Zipcar?

I might look at informational websites in the beginning of the process and then settle on a general solution set (for example, an electric scooter) that is the intersection of all of the known solutions to the issue and my individual preferences.

After a category of the possible solution has been selected, people look to individual vendors within that type. They compare features, benefits, and costs to make a decision between a known set of products or services.

Draw on your user research to define the phases relevant to the searching and decision process for your products and services. Then, prepare materials to support people at different phases.

You might start by spending time interacting with the content on your website, downloading several files, and "reading up" on your company. Look to learn not just about your company, but about how the industry or solution space works overall.

Completing this homework helps you identify what information you're currently offering to the information needed. It might identify gaps in the process that need to be filled by new website content or new landing pages.

Here's the key take-home message: Include multiple conversion points for different stages of the buying process. Each conversion point is a potential landing page opportunity.

Long-Term Maintenance Is Critical

Maintaining your landing pages is critical to their success. Not only does optimizing them continuously drive improvements in paid search conversions, but a failure to maintain landing pages long term can have the opposite effect.

Unfortunately, because landing pages are "disconnected" from the main website, landing pages can be "out of sight, out of mind." Returning visitors, including the team that maintains the website, do not typically view these pages.

Yet, because landing pages are the most common point of entry for new visitors, and specifically for visitors where you are paying a third party to get them to visit your website (search engine, email campaign management software, banner ad network), it is critical that these pages be included in your periodic website reviews.

Otherwise, landing page content can become stale or out-of-date, promote the previous year's trade show, flaunt a copyright date a few years old, or even showcase old versions of whitepapers, products, or services you no longer offer.

In rare cases, changes to website infrastructure or content with expiration dates might send visitors you're paying for to a Page Not Found page. Ugh! (See "Plan for Graceful Failure" in Chapter 7 for help on avoiding Page Not Found glitches.)

If you build landing pages, you must commit to maintain them. Visit and review these pages during regularly scheduled website maintenance. It's best to prevent the error, but if you have bad landing page content out there, an alert paid search manager can tell from the numbers in the paid search account which landing pages are beyond their expiration dates.

How? These pages typically perform more poorly than up-to-date pages, converting fewer visitors to leads or sales. Following the metrics trail can show your team which pages need life support or at the least, a refresh. A savvy paid search manager can alert the website design team to issues on the website that have not yet been discovered, such as pages whose content has expired or web forms that have gone awry.

Maintenance "gotchas" you can periodically check for include the following:

- Broken links from these pages to your main website
- Broken contact forms
- Broken calculator or other interactive elements
- Outdated copyright information
- Outdated descriptions of products or services
- Promoting last year's trade show dates
- Promoting whitepapers that have been replaced by newer, better content
- Layout errors where template elements (such as a promo banner linking to content within your website) do not play nice with on-page content

We have seen these issues occur on websites, and when you've paid to have a visitor find these glitches, it's a bad experience all around.

Optimizing Your Landing Pages

So, after lists of best practices, we have to offer the following caveat: It depends. Your website, your product offering, and your users might be different from the users and websites that inspired our best practice guidelines.

For instance, a commonly recommended landing page design principle is to remove the website navigation elements at the top or side of the page. To conform to the expectations of your visitors and the terms of service of any paid search you may be running, you still need to retain the types of links commonly relegated to the footer (Contact Us, Privacy Policy, or Terms of Use for the website) on your landing pages.

When we remove the primary website navigation and compare the performance of two similar pages, we often see that for certain kinds of services, pages with links to relevant information perform better than isolated pages. If your readers need more information to make a decision, then by all means offer them more.

All of these best practices are good things to test on your situation. The best thing you can do is to get landing pages up and test alternative versions to improve your landing pages incrementally. This section walks you through the basic testing design and analysis to optimize landing pages.

When to Optimize

Over the course of your campaign, after you've identified which keyphrases are your best performers, the landing page conversion rate becomes the critical point to improve.

We delve a little more deeply into paid search metrics in Chapter 3, in the "Paid Search KPIs" section, and into paid search management in Chapter 7, in the section "Extending Your Reach with Paid Search Advertising."

The cycle of paid search optimization and management starts with keywords and ad copy, but over time the emphasis in a mature paid search account turns specifically to conversion rate optimization through landing page testing and improvements.

In addition, the quality of your landing pages affects the costs for your paid search advertising quite directly. Google AdWords evaluates landing pages to determine minimum bids. Low-quality landing pages are assumed to represent a low-quality website. Landing pages do not affect ad rank, however.

Table 6.2 shows the performance from a sample, fictional paid search account for the lead-generation company Happy Puppy. In the first months, the paid search management focused on increasing performance through keyphrase and ad copy optimization, focusing on the keywords that were most relevant to searchers for doggie daycare and training.

The numbers in bold in the first two rows of Table 6.2 show areas of improved performance leading to improvements in the key metric in bold (see bottom row), cost per lead.

Table 6.2 Example Paid Search Performance over Time

	Month 1	Month 2	Month 3	Month 4	Month 5	Month 6	Month 7
Average cost per click	**$4.40**	**$3.72**	**$3.61**	$3.61	$3.61	$3.61	$3.61
Lead-conversion rate	0.8%	0.8%	0.8%	**1.0%**	**1.2%**	**1.44%**	**1.7%**
Number of clicks for a lead	125	125	125	100	83	69	58
Cost per lead	**$550**	**$465**	**$451**	**$361**	**$301**	**$251**	**$212**

The benefits of keyphrase and ad copy optimization show a lower cost-per-click amount, month over month. Starting in the fourth month, the Happy Puppy team focused on improving performance through targeted landing page changes. Although these landing page changes did not increase the number of visits to the website or clicks on the ads, the landing page adjustments improved the conversion of visits to leads, lowering their overall cost per lead.

Never forget that landing page management is your most important long-term paid search activity.

Use Your User Research

A critical aspect of landing page optimization is to consider for whom you're actually optimizing the landing pages. To optimize a landing page, consider the design of a landing page based on both

- How Google AdWords (or any paid search vendor) interprets the page, which in turn affects your bid and campaign costs

- How visitors interpret the page (for example, whether it is a compelling page that generates qualified new leads)

Landing page categories often vary in their conversion rates. Some of the variation in conversion rates is due to the specificity of the search terms used. For example, product pages might be linked with the most specific search queries.

Often, the key to optimizing conversion rates on landing pages that pass the "good landing page" design tests is to revisit the needs of website visitors. That means going back to your user personas developed in Chapter 5 and conducting user testing as described in Chapter 7.

The goal is to align landing pages as closely as possible to the needs of website visitors. In addition to user personas and usability testing, you can use user interviews to learn more about your website visitors.

These interviews can include such questions or prompts as

- What information did you expect to see on the landing page?
- How easily can you identify product details, price, or shipping costs?
- What information would help you make a decision to buy from this company (or contact this company for more details)?
- What criteria will you use in your purchase decision?
- Tell me about the last time you purchased a product like this.

You also can examine similar pages on competitor websites to gain insight about the methods of your competition. Just locate and click your competitor's ads to see their landing pages.

In addition, try to gather quantitative behaviorial data from your analytics accounts to learn about visitor behavior on individual landing pages. This data helps you locate potential problems for follow-up in the scripted interviews and help define the direction of landing page usability testing.

Then, get the next version in front of users and test again. If it's quick to build a new page in your content management system (CMS), build a new page. If it's tedious and labor intensive to build a new page, try a noncoded visual mock-up showing potential changes to selected landing pages. You can use the visual mock-ups during usability testing and prioritize changes to landing pages based on supporting visitors in accomplishing their goals (and yours).

How to Measure

First, you need to set up alternative landing pages, direct traffic to them, and measure which one results in more of what you want: web leads, phone calls, sales, or perhaps all of these. This stage is where your "close the loop" details come into play, because you don't want to optimize your pages to get you more leads if the page brings in more but *poorly qualified* leads that result in *fewer* sales.

The key to clear interpretation of test results is to define how to measure success ahead of seeing the results and with enough time to get a true sample to interpret.

Essentially, landing page testing is hypothesis testing, just like you might have learned in school. You put two (or more, but two is simpler for a start) alternate pages into play, with the null hypothesis being there is no difference between them. Then, you collect data on how they perform, measuring against predetermined key performance indicators (KPIs).

Here's where we'll get a little statistical. You are looking to determine whether there is a difference between the performance of your two alternates. So, a critical question is what size difference over what sample size is "different enough" to make a decision to eliminate one of the two options.

The good news is that you don't have to work this out from scratch. You can take advantage of existing calculators to determine the appropriate difference you need to see in conversion counts or rates over what sample size to call one alternative the "winner" over another.

You can find free online tools that have the statistical test baked right in such as Google Website Optimizer. You can also use online calculators such as splittester.com to do the calculations for you.

Google Website Optimizer randomizes testing of landing pages from Google AdWords campaigns. It can also be used outside of AdWords paid search advertising to manage website or web page versions for testing. Google Website Optimizer interprets the test data for you, letting you know when you've reached a threshold of "enough difference and enough samples" to make a change.

Figure 6.13 shows an example of something that looks like a large difference in conversion rate, but is not yet "high confidence" for an actual decision.

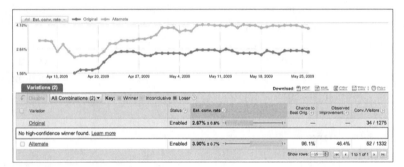

Figure 6.13 *Google Website Optimizer test results for a landing page test.*

In this case, the original version and the alternate had different conversion rates (2.67% versus 3.90%). The sample size was 1,275 visitors for the original version of the page and 1,332 visitors for the alternate. Yet, according to the graph, we have not yet achieved high confidence in this test. The tool advises us to run the test longer to increase the confidence that the alternate landing page is the winner.

Granular Testing Within the Page

Several tools provide data at a more granular level than web analytics or Google Website Optimizer. If you want to see what users are doing on the page before they leave or fill out a shopping cart or web form, you can use tools such as Crazy Egg or ClickTale to capture mouse movement and clicks.

You can also use ClickTale to gather analytics on form fields, such as which ones are filled out before the page is abandoned, which ones are avoided, and so on, to streamline your web form.

You can find more information about on-page and form analytics in the "Quantitative User Research: Form Analytics and A/B Testing" section in Chapter 7.

You Have Data. Now What?

The two goals when using the data from these tools are as follows:

- Take all that you've learned from the data and begin a conversation with your team about what you like and don't like on the suggested landing pages.

- Determine what changes you could make immediately to your landing pages and what approach could improve them long term.

Summary

To ensure that you're following a solid information architecture process, make sure that you

- Use user research to inform your website's sitemap and page layouts.

- Are willing to do unconventional things to support your website's primary personae and their most common scenarios.

- Test your website's arrangement and layout (using paper prototyping or with coded pages, whichever is faster and simpler).

- Use the information architecture developed to collaborate with a professional graphic designer to make your pages pop.

Follow best practices in landing page design, but test everything so you know what fits your market and your prospects.

Good landing pages are

- Strongly aligned with the marketing and keyphrases that visitors used to reach it.

- Useful. The landing page provides clear value in exchange for the visitor's time or personal information.

- Have one or more clear calls to action.

- Simple and focused. You lose visitors if they have to work hard to find the information they need by reading through irrelevant copy or clicking to other pages

- Asking for the bare minimum. Avoid asking for too much; capture only as much information as you absolutely need at this point in your sales process.

- Usable. You don't want to frustrate or confuse the landing page visitor.

- Up-to-date and working. Commit to your landing pages for as long as your campaigns are running. Check them periodically for glitches or out-of-date content.

7

Making Websites That Work

Building and maintaining a website is challenging work: The web team needs to balance technology, design, branding, functionality, and the needs of multiple types of website visitors, while maintaining the security and freshness of the website. When making decisions about website enhancements or revisions, you need to balance the needs of website visitors, search engines, and the technical and marketing staff who maintain the website.

All too often, a critical voice is missing from these discussions: the voice of the website visitor. Ensuring that the website supports visitors completing tasks can make a dramatic difference in the effectiveness of a website and give you a critical competitive edge. This chapter covers the basics for optimizing the user experience of a website to improve conversion rates (for example, leads and sales). We also touch on the management tasks underpinning successful websites.

Improving User Experience and Conversion Rates

Driving website visitors is not enough. The route to turn a website visitor into a lead or customer hinges directly on the website's quality and the difficulty of the process leading to a "conversion."

A website *conversion* occurs the moment a prospect (a visitor to your website) becomes a lead or a customer by submitting an online contact form or purchasing online, respectively.

Because web traffic may vary season to season or day to day, we focus on the conversion rate above raw conversion counts. The *conversion rate* is the number of visitors who complete a transaction divided by the total number of visitors, expressed as a percentage in Equations 7.1 and 7.2. The more conversions, the better. The higher the conversion rate, the better.

Equation 7.1: Lead-Generation Conversion Rate

Lead generation = [(Visitors who complete forms) / (All visitors)] x 100

Equation 7.2: E-Commerce Conversion Rate

E-commerce conversion rate = [(Visitors who buy) / (All visitors)] x 100

We are often asked for a ballpark conversion rate, an objective standard by which to judge the performance of a website. Whether your conversion rate is good or bad depends on your market, and is influenced by things completely beyond your control (such as the purchasing power of the people who want to buy your stuff).

So instead, we evaluate whether the rate is increasing or decreasing compared to the same time last year (to eliminate seasonal and even day-of-week effects) and what changes to the website or web content influence the rates positively or negatively.

The ways to improve conversion rate include affecting the numerator or the denominator of the percentage (refer to Equations 7.1 and 7.2).

Businesses can increase conversion rates by improving the pool of people in the denominator: the total number of visitors. Businesses improve the denominator through bringing qualified visitors to their website through targeting search engine optimization (SEO), paid search, or banner ad campaigns (covered in the sections, "Evaluate Your Keyphrases in the Context of the Entire Word Market" in Chapter 5, "The Audience Is Listening (What Will You Say?)" and "Define Your Market" in Chapter 8, "It's All About Visibility").

This chapter focuses on improving the numerator: increasing leads or sales by providing quality information and an easy transaction on the website.

There are several levels of user experience (UX) sophistication in website design and development. The most basic level is simply to avoid annoying your users. Instead, follow web conventions, visually highlight user goals, shorten difficult activities (simplify forms or reduce screens in the shopping cart), and handle errors carefully.

Beyond the basics, tease out the nuances for your market and your website by applying user research and testing on your website with real potential customers or clients.

The Basics: What to Fix Before Testing

One of the sadder days in our recent professional life was a meeting with a branding and web design firm to discus a design composition ("comp") for a joint client. The comp was an evocative image with minimal text, beautiful in its simplicity. Unfortunately, the company logo was at the bottom right rather than the standard top left. The comp looked like an inviting print ad, but not like a usable website.

The dominating image and minimal text would have made the home page invisible to search engine spiders, and the placement of the company logo in the bottom right of the design meant that any users who did find the website would have to relearn years of training that client logos, and the click back to the website's home page, reside in the top left.

Worse, when we challenged the team on this, they replied something like, "This company's audience is smart and tech-savvy, so they will figure it out. We don't have to follow web conventions." Sigh. Although perhaps that's true on one level (motivated people will figure it out), the merely curious or unmotivated will just leave.

Follow Web Conventions

Instead of asking your web visitors to learn the one-of-a-kind interface you've designed for your website, let visitors use the few moments you have of their attention to engage with the content (media, prose) of your website to determine whether to stay and learn more.

Here are a basic set of web conventions for web design and development:

- In Western languages, we read from top left to bottom right, and we have come to expect (generally) the company logo at top left, clickable to link back to the website's home page.

  Some websites that have alternate language versions with different expectations (for example, one English version that is read left to right and a Hebrew version that is read from right to left) will actually swap the position of the logo in different languages to adjust for the change in reading direction.

- Place a search bar or quick links (to a shopping cart, for example) in the upper-right corner for Western languages.

- Make desired actions stand out visually. Buy buttons should look like buttons and stand out from the text. Conversely, items that are not clickable should not receive visual button-like treatment.

- Support navigation on your website for folks who like to browse and for folks who like to search.

  Caveat: If you implement website search, make sure it works well.

- Links to other content should follow typical web styling, using underline and different colors for both unvisited and visited.

  Some usability experts suggest that links should always be web-standard blue when unvisited and purple when visited, following the original web conventions. That's a judgment call, but certainly don't make links look like regular nonclickable text.

- Consider accessibility. Make sure your website can be understood and function without JavaScript and images.

- Check the visual design against standards for the colorblind. This can be done via third-party websites, such as http://colororacle.cartography.ch or www.vischeck.com).

On Key Pages: Form Optimization Basics

For a lead-generation website, make the form as simple as possible to get your first contact sales team the minimum information needed to contact the prospect. Essentially, you need to balance the amount of information you request against the prospect's interest in your services and your company.

You don't ask people their salary or the cost of their home or car when you first meet them at a networking party, so why is asking for the visitor's company's annual budget for [your service] in your first encounter acceptable?

What's our ideal lead-generation contact form length? Try the absolute minimum needed for someone on your team to contact that person back to have a conversation: name, email, phone number, and preferred contact method.

For an e-commerce website, simplifying and signposting the path from product selection to purchase should decrease shopping cart abandonment and increase sales.

The process might be something like this:

1. Choose items.
2. Provide shipping information and choose shipping method.
3. Provide billing information.
4. Confirm purchase.

Let shoppers know where they are in the process and let them move between steps to make corrections. Best case is to use persistent information (shipping choices) in later sections if visitors need to go back to previous screens (perhaps to change a quantity, for example).

In addition, because a credit card purchase is involved, it is important to signal that the website has taken the appropriate security measures to be safe (and, of course, to actually to do so). These include Hypertext Transfer Protocol Secure (HTTPS) transactions, but can go as far as displaying badges from transaction security firms, such as VeriSign.

Template-Level: Automated Attention Analysis

An easy way to take advantage of known UX design best practices is to submit website or page layout designs to automated analyses before coding them. Online tools such as AttentionWizard.com review a design and predict where the viewer's attention would focus on the design.

It applies rules drawn from studies of human visual processing to create "virtual heat maps" predicting where the viewer will look on the page design. The website's software analyzes contrast, the presence of objects, and visual emphasis (whitespace, size). It can help identify whether all the visual emphasis, say, is on the Privacy Policy link rather than on the Buy Now button.

In Figure 7.1, you see that the image and logo at the top of the page is predicted to absorb most of the visitor's attention, with the top of the form attracting some attention. The form itself and the Submit button at its end have little visual impact.

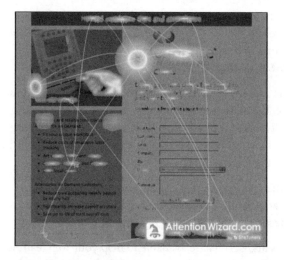

Figure 7.1 *Automated analysis of a landing page by AttentionWizard.*

Caveat: These types of tools predict where people's eyes focus in the first milliseconds that the visitor reaches a page.

They can't take into account

- Any of the context that people bring to the website

- The actual content (such as labels) of the website

These tools only help you predict what people immediately notice on a page and can never replace studying how people actually use your website.

On Every Page

On each and every page of your website, you should do some key checks: Is your page-load time as short as possible? Is your copy at the right reading level? Are your calls to action obvious and easy to use?

Minimize Visitor Wait Time

Now that we're used to 24/7 Internet connectivity, we hate to wait even for a handful of seconds for anything. Ever.

Usability expert Jakob Nielsen's research has been consistent over the years that website response times less than 1 second feel "seamless" to website visitors, whereas responses between 1 and 10 seconds seem increasingly long to people, and over 10 seconds people will just leave the website (www.useit.com/alertbox/response-times.html).

The Site Performance tool within Google Webmaster Tools places the line between fast and slow websites at 1.5 seconds, which is the 20th percentile value. So if your website pages load in less than 1.5 seconds, your website is faster than 80% of the other websites. Something to strive for!

The converse is something to fear: Your website needs to avoid making visitors wait; otherwise, they'll go somewhere else. You can see an example of a slow website in the results from Google Webmaster Tools shown in Figure 7.2. You can find more information about how to access Google Webmaster Tools in "Submit These Files to Google Webmaster Tools" in Chapter 8.

Looking for other reasons to minimize wait times on your website? How about this: Google uses load time for your website as part of its input into its ranking algorithm, so it affects your organic search position.

Several websites and scripts are available to help your web team identify, prioritize, and optimize slow-loading resources. Google has even included reports on load time and optimization tips right into its Google Webmaster Tools dashboard.

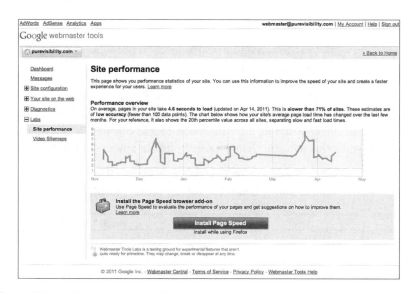

Figure 7.2 *Website load time information in Google Webmaster Tools.*

Calls to Action

Items to review on every page include the presence of calls to action. Thanks to search engines and external links, people can land on any public page of your website as their entry point.

They could start deep into the customer service FAQ or deep in your product catalog. Is it clear to them where they've landed? You might consider going through Keith Instone's navigation stress test, detailed on his website http://instone. org/navstress.

Key checks: If a user wants to make a purchase or contact a sales representative, is it clear from each page template in your website how to do so? Review each to make sure. Double-check that your calls to action are in view in the content area on each page within the common screen resolutions of your visitors (available from your web analytics).

If your website has a decorative header that users immediately scroll to get out of the way, and your calls to action are in your header, they won't see them when they need them.

As Figure 7.3 shows, companies can reap large increases in prospects' willingness to share their contact information once they can find where to submit it.

There is some noise in this data, but the conversion rate was generally much higher after two website improvements:

- Separating buttons on a web form to reduce data entry errors

- Placing a call to action to find a nearby location (by submitting a ZIP code via search) on every page

You can see that lead form conversion rates increased over than the same time the previous year, resulting in over 100 more lead forms completed in 2009 compared to same period in 2008. Assuming a constant lead-to-sale conversion rate after the web form submission, this increase should have resulted in more sales for the company.

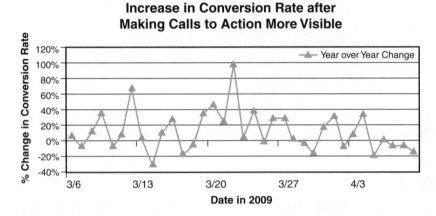

Figure 7.3 *Increases in lead conversion rates after increasing emphasis on and prevalence of the call to action.*

Check Your Reading Level

Another item to check on every page is the reading level of on-page copy. Make sure your copy is not overly technical or difficult to skim, because website visitors tend to skim before reading closely.

Jakob Nielsen's studies suggest that people read about 20% of the words on a page (www.useit.com/alertbox/percent-text-read.html). You can check the reading difficulty of your pages through online reading-level tools, but you can also check reading level within most common word processing programs.

Rules of thumb for website reading level targets range from grade 5 to grade 8. It can be more useful, however, to assess the reading level of your website copy against your competitors' website copy and against trade publications or news outlets important to your audience.

The average reading level of a technical website used to support a high-ticket software subscription purchase can inch a little higher than one aimed at busy folks on the go who might be using smartphones to surf the website.

Imagine Your Website Through Your Persona's Eyes

The previous list covers many best practices, and because you used the process described in "Develop Website Personas" in Chapter 5, you can get much more specific. With your personas and scenarios in hand, you can "test" your website by performing a cognitive walkthrough.

In a cognitive walkthrough, a group of usability professionals not responsible for the design take the website's target personas and (in his or her imagination) walks through a scenario or task flow to identify stumbling blocks. This should be done iteratively with different personas, and it can identify any show-stopper issues to remove before testing with end users.

Beyond Best Practices: User Research

Looking at aggregate data about what people do on your website is fascinating. It generates endless questions and hypotheses about why people behave the way they do.

Quantitative user analysis helps gain more insight into behaviors on forms and individual pages of your website. Surveys may give you some broad motivations and summary statistics on interests.

However, the only way to answer the "why" questions is to get in touch with individuals in the pool of website visitors, ask them to perform some typical tasks, and observe their interactions with your website or prototype.

Where Do Surveys Fit In?

Surveys are quick, easy, and automated. It's possible to whip up a quick survey of 10 questions on an online tool, such as surveymonkey.com or zoomerang.com, to blast out your questions to an email list.

These tools tally responses in a spreadsheet to give you quantitative insight into what people say they do or want to do. The types of round statistics useful in framing discussions (X% of U.S. households with incomes over $Y use search engines on a daily basis) are obtained through surveys.

Surveys are often used in website brand assessment, to see whether the brand name is recognized, what associations people have with the brand, and what competitors others may be using. They are less useful in UX research in part because sometimes you have to ask "why" three, four, or five times to get to the real underlying motivation for a preference or an action, and the quickness of a web form interferes with that deeper level of inquiry that can unfold in a one-on-one interview.

In addition, survey design is a discipline all of its own. Without effective question design, your data may be useless. Beyond that, people do not always do what they say they do, so actually observing them is critical to real understanding.

Like web analytics, survey data can be used to point out areas to research more closely, but doesn't replace user inquiry.

Quantitative User Research: Form Analytics, and A/B Testing

When you set up your website to gather data on visits, goals, and exits, you can mine your web analytics data to determine the UX pain points you should research more completely.

Review metrics such as page abandonment to determine problem areas:

- Where in the search results or shopping cart process do people give up and leave the website?

- Which are the highest traffic parts of your website where a small change in conversion rate of visitors to leads or customers could make the biggest impact?

Use your web analytics to discover and prioritize website problem areas for deeper investigation. The highest priority areas are typically landing pages for paid activities (because you're paying to get people there) and product selection and shopping cart processes.

After you've identified priority areas for close study, your next step depends on the type of pages you want to optimize.

Form Analytics

If it's a form page within your lead-generation system or shopping cart, you can review abandonment rates on a page-by-page basis through setting up a conversion funnel in Google Analytics. To do so, you let Google Analytics know the expected sequence of pages or steps in the shopping cart, by pasting each step's URL into the Goal Settings dialog (see Figure 7.4).

A review of your funnel analytics (Figure 7.5) tells you on a page-by-page basis where your lead contact process or shopping cart is failing.

For a simple lead form, this might be only one page: the form itself (see Figure 7.5). In this case, it's hard to drill into what about the form is deterring visitors.

You can get deeper form analytics on a field-by-field basis through a third-party tool such as ClickTale.com. Among other items, ClickTale can tell you how long people spend on the form, how they move their cursor or mouse around when interacting with your form, and which fields people fill out before abandoning the form (see Figure 7.6).

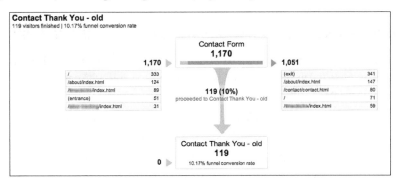

Figure 7.4 *Goal Settings dialog within Google Analytics.*

Contact Thank You - old
119 visitors finished | 10.17% funnel conversion rate

Contact Form
1,170

1,170 ▷ ▨▨▨▨▨▨▨ ▷ 1,051

/	333
/about/index.html	124
/index.html	89
(entrance)	51
/index.html	31

119 (10%)
proceeded to Contact Thank You - old

(exit)	341
/about/index.html	147
/contact/contact.html	80
/	71
/index.html	59

Contact Thank You - old
119
0 ▷   10.17% funnel conversion rate

Figure 7.5 *Conversion funnel for a one-page form in Google Analytics.*

▦ Drop Report

11.9% of visitors dropped in the middle and stopped filling this form.
Field number 1 had the most drops (5.5%).
A field with a high drop rate may mean that it or the following field might be scaring away your visitors.

Percent of Visitors Dropping at Each Field

1	5.5%
2	0.7%
3	1%
4	0.7%
5	0%
6	0.3%
7	1.4%
8	0%
9	0%

0%   2%   4%   6%   8%   10

This report displays how frequently your visitors drop in the middle of filling your form.

This report was generated from 293 visitors that interacted with this form.

Figure 7.6 *Form analytics report from ClickTale.*

A/B Testing

If a problem could be solved in a couple of different ways, you can compare options by building out both versions and observing goal conversion rates on each. Google Website Optimizer tool can randomly show alternate versions of the page to the visitor to allow seamless testing.

"How to Measure" in Chapter 6, "Putting It All Together and Selling Online" touches on page-level landing page optimization tests using Google Website Optimizer. Depending on the ease of creating and deploying alternatives, however, you might test "paper prototypes" of the redesigned pages to get feedback from your users before you invest in building new pages.

Qualitative User Analysis: Observations, Usability Tests

Usability testingis an important part of creating a website that works. It is often ignored because it can be expensive, time-consuming, and ultimately a messy way of collecting data.

Your sample sizes are usually small, forcing you to try to look past the idiosyncrasies of individuals to try to find commonalities and underlying problems. Your data may conflict, forcing you to choose what issues to address and what to ignore for now.

You're not going to find every issue. Yet, it is immensely cheaper than wasting your web investment and frittering away the attention of potential customers in wrong-headed websites and forms. It's also quicker, in the long run, to design the website so that it's easy to use from the beginning, instead of uncovering problems after you've launched and need to redesign and relaunch.

So yes, you won't find every issue, but you'll likely find the big ones, and will save time and money in the long run. We encourage you to embrace usability testing as an essential step in your design process.

Initial user research can start with as few as 5 to 10 observations or scripted usability tests, as long as the participants represent real clients and customers. Although to students of statistics that is an indefensibly teeny sample size, that small number usually suffices to identify the underlying problem for the rest of the user population.

The larger and more expensive the fix or the more critically important the website (say, heart transplants versus emailed Valentine's Day cards), the more users you'll want to include in your preliminary testing before rolling out the new feature or tweaked process.

Table 7.1 summarizes many research activities involving direct contact with website users. The goal is to combine multiple sources of information to produce a rich recommendation to help you maximize your return on your website investment.

People may not always do as they think or say they do, so our top choices here are observations and usability tests which focus on what people do (instead of what they think or say).

Table 7.1   User Research Techniques

Type	Description	Application
Card sorting	An activity where users organize and sort labeled index cards to create categories.	Categorize keyphrases for SEO (see "Word Market Analysis Process" in Chapter 5). Redesign your website's information architecture or navigation. Prioritize information.
Interviews	Scripted questions to understand motivations, context, and goals.	Understand people's motivation and workflow.
Observations	Watch your participant use your website or a competitor's.	An excellent starting point. Understand what people actually do on the website. Identify concerns outside the investigator's pre-conceived notions or priorities. For this reason, observations may not result in consistent data from different user observations.
Usability testing on prototype	Testers create prototype versions of website designs (such as a sketch on paper, a design comp, or an interactive online prototype) with a scripted scenario.	Understand what people would do with a system that has not yet been built. Test early design concepts; useful on a shoestring budget as it involves little or no coding, depending on what kind of prototype you use. Good if your IT department is overwhelmed or your content management system (CMS) is cumbersome and you can't make test pages.
Usability testing on working website	Instruct participants to attempt scripted actions on the website. Observe their efforts via web conference software, usability testing software, or through a one-way mirror.	Understand what people actually do on a specific task. Test an existing website to prioritize updates. Test late stage design alternatives. Our "go-to" technique for identifying barriers to better performance.

Logistics: Test Scenario, Recruiting, and Rewards

You have bought the argument. You're ready to test your website with some real, live users. What next? Well, you need to create your test plan. Will you go to the user? Or will they come to you?

Outline the goals for the test and the scenario you'll ask the participant to attempt to follow. You should test your test scenario on a colleague before running it on real folks, just to make sure it is clear, accurate, and simple.

Then, go and get some test participants. You can try

- Online classified websites, such as Craigslist

- Recruiting from associations who meet your target user's characteristics (for example, have a particular job title or professional affiliation)

- Recruiting from your own network (which is kind of circular, because you should prefer people you don't already know)

- Drawing names from contact or customer databases

- Recruiting visitors who visit your website using a pop-up recruitment form, such as what is provided by Ethnio.com

We tried all these methods for different projects, and it's easy to get bogged down in recruiting for very narrow characteristics for specialized websites. Recruiting users on the website for remote usability testing via web conference software is our favorite method for most situations.

We're catching people when they're on the website of interest, much easier than trying to attract them when they're doing something completely unrelated (such as reading their email from a professional listserv or shopping for a new coffee table on Craigslist). Simply provide the minimum instruction to get them started.

In the recruiting email, ad, or online pop-up, we usually offer a small gift for participation, something like a $50 gift certificate to a popular store.

Don't forget to explain the purpose and activities of the user research, and ask for the website visitor's consent to participate in the study. You can see one version of this type of consent request at http://www.lapetite.com/consent-form/. You should view this as a legal document and keep good records for all participants.

Moderating a Test

While moderating usability tests, it's temping to intervene. Your own empathy draws you to help the person you can see is struggling to "get it right." Don't.

Watch, take notes, and intervene only if the person comes to a complete stop, if it looks like the study is about to be derailed, or both. Watching real users interact with your website is your goal, and because your website typically does not come with a human guide, it's best not to jump in and provide one during your usability tests.

It **is** your job, however, to probe the participant for more information. You should ask questions like "what are you thinking right now?" or "tell me about what this means?" or "I don't know; what do you think will happen when you click that?"

Of course, it's important that your questions don't lead the participant or color his or her impressions of the website.

🔍 Tip

Want to learn more about practical, hands-on usability methods?

A good starting point is Steve Krug's *Rocket Surgery Made Easy: The Do-It-Yourself Guide to Finding and Fixing Usability Problems.*

I've Got Data, Now What?

After you've tested with enough folks that you're seeing some repeating patterns in the results ("wow, almost everyone misses the call to action in the header because they scroll below it"), it's time to review, reflect, and prioritize.

Noting the prevalence of some problems with the website and their relative severity (did they prevent the person from buying or filling out a form?) should help when prioritizing issues. Check what you saw in the usability testing against your web analytics. Are the patterns in agreement?

After you decide what to do, you might need to convince your colleagues. For that, you can rely on their human powers of empathy.

Video clips of tests are particularly useful in persuading people to make changes on the website. The pain you and your team felt while people struggled with the website?

Use the clip from the test showing the person flailing between pages on the website that don't have the information she needs, saying out loud, "Gee, I thought I would find it here, but yeah, I've been here already and it isn't on this page." It'll speak volumes and can help motivate change.

UX Checklist

Use this UX checklist to make sure that you've covered all the bases:

1. Do the minimum:

    a. Meet web conventions and standards.

    b. *Minimize waiting times* for page, media, and form results to load.

    c. Make your *forms simple* to fill out. Don't pry beyond the context of the initial inquiry. Let your sales team get that context when the time is right.

    d. Ensure you have *clear, appropriate calls to action* in every page template.

    e. Make sure your reading level is appropriate to your audience.

2. Optimize by watching people trying to use your website:

    a. Schedule observations or user tests.

    b. Use your web analytics to identify and prioritize user stumbling blocks for deeper inquiry.

    c. Optimize your forms using data from specialized form analytics tools.

3. Head off disaster by testing designs and pages prior to launch:

    a. Check your design with automated attention tools to ensure the right elements of your design pop out at users when they first see your website.

    b. Confirm new designs before coding by using "paper" or digital prototyping with real users.

Website Planning and Maintenance

A website is not a short-term project where a team drops in, sets up a beautiful, easy-to-use, content-rich website and then disbands to other commitments, leaving a never-changing online brochure. Internet marketing requires a long-term plan to maintain and enhance your content and engage with your target audience.

Launching a website redesign or refresh is a particularly risky period for online marketing campaigns, so we pay special attention to website relaunch planning and checklists.

Plan for Graceful Failure

Of course, when you're planning your website, most of your time is focused on the niceties of the new design, perhaps the color scheme or the exact placement of the logo and tagline. A common hobgoblin in web design is not planning for... well... when links go awry and pages move.

Eventually, visitors try to get to a page on the website that doesn't exist, either because a link was broken, because of a problem with the server, or because they just typed in the wrong address. The ability of a website to help people return to pages that exist is a good measure of its resilience, and is a fundamental part of any complex, well-maintained website.

The default action of a web server when someone requests a page that does not exist is to show a 404 error page, so named because 404 is the status code returned when a requested item is "not found." The default 404 page is typically uninformative and outside of the look and feel of the rest of the website.

Figure 7.7 shows the default page offered up by the Apache web server. Similar default pages are shown by other web servers. Figure 7.8 is the default Page Not Found error page from a Microsoft Internet Information Services (IIS) web server. You might be shocked by what you see when you go to big name websites, or even your own, and type in a nonsense filename. Try it!

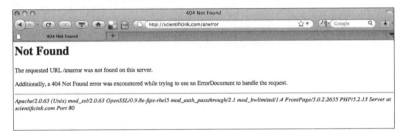

Figure 7.7 *A standard (but disorienting) file not found error for an Apache web server.*

The page cannot be found

The page you are looking for might have been removed, had its name changed, or is temporarily unavailable.

Please try the following:

- Make sure that the Web site address displayed in the address bar of your browser is spelled and formatted correctly.
- If you reached this page by clicking a link, contact the Web site administrator to alert them that the link is incorrectly formatted.
- Click the Back button to try another link.

HTTP Error 404 - File or directory not found.
Internet Information Services (IIS)

Technical Information (for support personnel)

- Go to Microsoft Product Support Services and perform a title search for the words **HTTP** and **404**.
- Open **IIS Help**, which is accessible in IIS Manager (inetmgr), and search for topics titled **Web Site Setup**, **Common Administrative Tasks**, and **About Custom Error Messages**.

Figure 7.8 *The standard File Not Found error page on a Microsoft IIS web server.*

Default 404 error pages don't provide links to navigate to the intended website after someone has come in via a broken link, so anyone hitting one of these pages has landed on a dead end. Anyone who mistypes a page or hits a broken link will be stranded on a page without the website's global navigation.

This page runs the risk of losing qualified, engaged visitors, and can be improved with a resilient 404 page with navigational links back to the website.

All websites should have a custom 404 error page that provides website navigation and help for visitors but does not redirect them automatically. Figure 7.9 shows the real custom 404 page for a personal blog. Figure 7.10, however, is an example from a lead-generation website, the Accuri Cytometers website.

In both cases, the error page is contained within the look and feel and navigation of the website. The Accuri Cytometers page (see Figure 7.10) also contains calls to action in the footer and the search box is prepopulated with the name of the file that was not found.

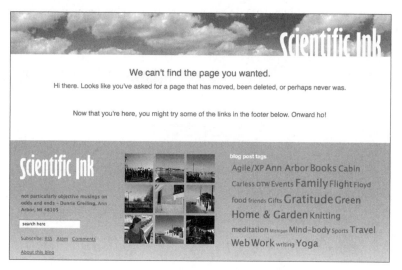

Figure 7.9 *A custom File Not Found page for a blog.*

Automatically Track Your Page Not Found Errors

You should work with your web development team to capture information about 404 errors, even when you have a nice user-friendly page like Figure 7.10, because your visitor should connect with your content immediately. Your team can use a server-side script to catch the filename not found and the referring web page (on your server or another).

Then, use this information to retouch broken links on your own website, or identify incoming broken links from other websites that you can ask be retouched.

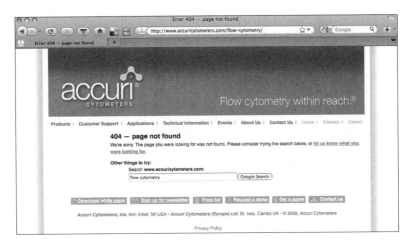

Figure 7.10 *A custom 404 error page triggered by an attempt to visit a page on the website that doesn't exist.*

Another nice option is to add custom web analytics tracking to your 404 page so that you can view and count files not found within your web analytics package, instead of asking your web team to investigate server log files or the like.

This option should be available within standard analytics packages. For Google Analytics, search "404 tracking within google analytics" or go to www.google.com/support/analytics/bin/answer.py?hl=en&answer=86927.

Website Maintenance Tasks

To help you plan your efforts, here's a rough guide to tasks (and their frequency) for website maintenance and enhancements.

Weekly/Daily Tasks: Monitoring and Implementation

These jobs need to be done on a daily or weekly basis:

- Keep an eye on your paid search program numbers.
- Review, approve, and publish blog posts.
- Review mentions of your brand on social websites through an RSS reader subscribed to an open search, a web "clipping service" such as Google Alerts, a free dashboard such as NetVibes, or fully featured dashboards such as Alterian SM2 or radian6, available by subscription.
- Consider or delegate addressing issues that merit a public or private reply.
- Participate in conversations on Twitter, Facebook, LinkedIn (or social website du jour) as applies to your target audience.

Monthly Tasks: Implementation

Handle these tasks every month:

- Review progress and assign the next step for tasks within ongoing Internet marketing initiatives.

- Check the parts of your website that you intend to be dynamic, such as news or events.

- Take care of open job descriptions; archive or note which positions are no longer open.

- Check the events calendar and news or press release section. Make sure it's up-to-date with your planned editorial calendar.

- Review your website analytics, and see whether anything appears to have gone awry with the numbers. Large changes in the numbers may indicate real seasonal or market changes, or it could be as simple as a tracking script that was inadvertently deleted from the website and needs repair.

- Does any of your new content have a full set of <title> and <meta> description tags? See "Page-Level SEO Best Practices" in Chapter 8 for guidelines.

- Does any new content have full web analytics tracking in place? Sometimes landing pages created for special email or banner ad (or even paid search campaigns) may lack tracking scripts. Make sure all website templates carry web analytics scripts as a default.

Quarterly Tasks: Trends and Planning

On a quarterly basis, you should

- Review your organic rankings on key terms and plan to address any losses and build upon gains.

- Ask your technical team to double-check your infrastructure:

  - Do you have the most up-to-date version of your CMS? If not, do you need it?

  - Does your development team need to deploy a security patch for your CMS or blog?

  - Do you have the most up-to-date version of your comment spam filtering plug-in for your blog?

- Plan for new content, based on your editorial calendar.

- Make assignments and deadlines for this quarter's anticipated press releases and events.

- Leave placeholders in your schedule for a few blog posts or unanticipated website content updates.

- Review all pages of the website and landing pages for outdated information.

Annual Tasks: Planning

Tackle these planning tasks on a yearly basis:

- Plan the editorial calendar for the year based on your seasonal cycle and any new market initiatives (new product or service launches, software upgrades, and so on).

- Plan your budget and schedule for infrastructure updates.

- Review your information architecture against current web analytics and the requests of your UX or customer service team. Plan any updates.

- Update and extend the copyright years covered in your copyright notice at the bottom of every page. This can be done with a script to always include the current year.

SEO: EXCITING OR BORING?

We can't tell you the number of meetings we've attended where we've heard about shiny new custom-coded CMSs that a company is putting into place for a website redesign. But because the crackerjack developers have been so busy fiddling with the fun under-the-hood mechanics, they haven't had time to implement a few basic items such as unique and descriptive Hypertext Markup Language (HTML) title for each page or redirects from the old website navigation to the new one.

We have struggled with why this is, and ultimately, we have to come back to the idea that SEO infrastructure is not sexy. It isn't as cool as coding something from scratch and it isn't as pretty as an evocative Flash animation of a sunset or lighthouses that create an emotional connection with your brand.

It feels boring, rote, and like something you'll make time for when you have time to do things like floss between your bicuspids, which is never.

It is consistently deprioritized by web teams during website redesigns, and this neglect is more than a lost opportunity because it often entails a loss of search engine ranking for some period after a redesign launches.

Planning a Website Refresh or Relaunch

A website redesign is a project. Like any project, website redesigns sometimes get delayed, off-track, or even canceled. The common threats to web redesign projects come in the forms of scope, schedule, quality and cost.

Typically, website projects require scope vigilance because

- IT infrastructure concerns may derail or take over a marketing project.

- A new technology or plug-in may ease some concerns at the cost of changes in resourcing or cost.

- Competitive landscape changes may require scope or schedule to be renegotiated partway through the project.

Overcommitted IT or marketing resources might not be able to complete critical path tasks on schedule. While overburdened internal resources may be able to out-source some activities to maintain the schedule, outsourcing comes at the cost of subcontracting work that was budgeted to be performed in-house.

In addition, lateness from missed deadlines early in the project should never be made up by skipping quality control or user acceptance testing at the end. These tasks are consistently undervalued in website launch planning.

In our experience, SEO and UX considerations are frequently considered too late in the web development decision-making process to have significant impact. SEO and UX tasks get placed on the change request log instead of driving the design.

When critical UX and SEO visibility requirements end up on the change request log or prelaunch punch list, they get prioritized against items that are "actually broken" in bug triage discussions.

This is a terrible outcome for everyone, because it requires the technical team to do costly rework at the project's end. If these items are not done, these omissions negatively affect the website user, search engine users, and thereby the company's bottom line.

Redesign Project Roles

Essential roles in a website redesign process are as follows:

- **UX designer**, the person or team who specifies the website user interface to achieve project goals (such as to increase browse-to-buy ratio on an e-commerce website). This person may also be the information architect designing the website navigation.

- **User researcher**, the person or team who learns about your target customer to create useful and meaningful personas, and who plans and

conduct usability tests. This person may also be the information architect who designs the website navigation. (Different organizations divide
up these activities differently.)

- **Graphic designer**, the person who prepares the visual layout, look, and
  feel of the website. This includes color schemes, graphics, and cascading style sheet (CSS) specifications.

- **Technical team**, the people in charge of the website infrastructure
  planning and implementation. These folks implement the UX and
  graphic design in the existing website infrastructure.

- **Content team**, the people in charge of writing or creating all the copy
  needed for the new website and all media (images, sound files, videos)
  required to populate the website's information architecture and content
  plan.

- **Testers**, the team in charge of verifying that all pages, links, forms, and
  transactions on the website work as planned. This includes verifying
  web analytics and conversion tracking scripts.

- **Marketing metrics owner**, someone in charge of making sure that the
  website is as trackable (or more) after launch as before and that the
  launch doesn't disrupt ongoing marketing campaigns, including organic
  SEO, paid search marketing, and any email campaigns.

- **Project manager**, the person who maintains the project plan, coordinates project details, and communicates divergence from agreed-upon
  schedules to project stakeholders (project team, executive sponsors).

These might not be individuals, but teams of people. These roles have different
concerns in the project and ask different questions. The dilemma illustrated in
Figure 7.11 is that the website's technical team may receive requests and requirements from most of the other roles.

The technical team implements the graphic and UX design in the website. It also
receives infrastructure requirements from the marketing metrics folks about tracking scripts and landing pages for ongoing marketing campaigns, etc.

If the project is not managed well, the technical team may be asked to broker conflicting requests from different teams.

Hard decisions on conflicting requests and requirements should be the negotiated
by key stakeholders, and shouldn't be the burden of the technical team. Business
requirements and cost/benefit analyses should drive these discussions.

Planning tradeoff and requirements prioritization conversations with all stakeholders involved is the key to building a successful website.

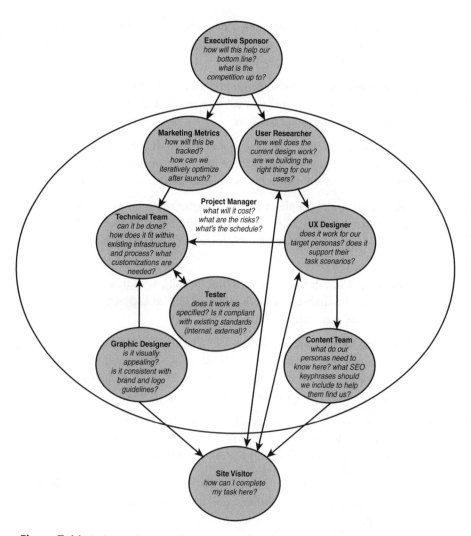

Figure 7.11 *Roles and areas of concern in a website redesign project.*

Alternatively, in small companies or on small projects, some of these roles may be played by the same person. For instance, you may have a UX designer who is also the graphic designer and content team. The drawback of having one person play multiple roles is that one role may be favored and the obligations of other roles may slide.

Common pitfalls include neglecting the testing phase entirely, skipping user research, or omitting Internet marketing requirements during project planning. The only way to avoid a web redesign morass is to start with clearly defined, shared goals and return to those project goals at junctures where tradeoffs need to be made.

Have the project team identify risks to the agreed-upon project scope and schedule. Meet regularly with all team members, including outside vendors, to ensure all parties are in agreement on next steps.

For the greatest ease and control, see whether you can break up a large project into smaller components to plan for many smaller victories for the project team. Vary either the infrastructure (CMS) *or* the design and templates (look and flow), instead of changing everything at once.

Simultaneously changing out the underlying infrastructure and the page content, information architecture, and the graphic design creates additional complexity and risk. It's tempting to do all of it at once, but much more risky and time-intensive.

If everything is new, it's impossible to ascertain which change had which effect. If there's a beautiful new skin and architecture, but the technical infrastructure is rough, it puts the entire effort at risk.

From the perspective of maintaining and building on existing SEO and paid search gains, transition things subtly, in as controlled a fashion as possible.

Website Prelaunch Punchlist

Quality control is critical ahead of a website launch. Yes, your team can update the website post-launch if there are any glitches, but best to have things as close to perfect as you can prior to launch and then plan post-launch work for optimization and enhancements rather than bug fixes!

Here's a checklist you can use before you launch a new website version:

1. Check links! http://validator.w3.org/checklink.

2. Spell check! http://www.spellwonder.com

3. Complete test cases identified in project planning activities.

4. Proofread the website.

5. If there was a previous website, please ensure the names of the pages stay the same. If the pages names cannot or should not stay the same, then redirects *must* be done.

   - Do 301 redirects from the old website structure to the new website structure, see the section "301 Redirects: Critical and Little Used," later in this chapter.

   - Update inlinks from other websites, including Google Places and other local directories if relevant.

6. People will still go awry. Create a human-friendly File Not Found (404 error) page.

7. Avoid removing within-site links to SEO critical content. If you remove a link to a deeper page from the home page, it could affect the ranking of that page. If you change the linking text of a page, that can also affect rankings.

8. Implement SEO best practices on all new content. See the section, "Page-Level SEO Best Practices" in Chapter 8.

   Spot check `<title>` and other `<meta>` tags for completeness.

9. Triple-check that analytics tracking code is available from *all* pages.

10. Check landing pages for consistency and check all links from landing pages for URL changes.

11. In case there is a host transfer, double-check the Contact Us form to see whether it's still working. Check the script:

    • Test the contact us form by filling out *all* fields and having it sent to yourself. Make sure it collects pertinent information for returning the contact, including some background on what their specific interest is.

    • Test all other forms in the website in the same way.

12. If the website is an e-commerce website, run trial orders.

13. Test any search functionality. (For example, if a search is supposed to work by name and stock-keeping unit or SKU number, test both names and numbers.)

14. Call all phone numbers on the website to make sure they're correct. (If there are too many, at least check the sales line.)

15. Test websites in multiple browser and operating system configurations. Prioritize the browsers and operating systems that make up sizable percentages in your website analytics. You might consider third-party services such as CrossBrowserTesting.com that prevent you from having to retain old hardware/software combinations for web testing.

16. Archive a copy of the old website, in case data is lost or incompletely migrated or to retrieve old copy or images for before and after comparisons.

301 Redirects: Critical and Not Often Used

Whenever a page moves through a name change or a directory name change, or perhaps because it was eliminated, folks and search engine spiders will see an error page. In this situation, your team should put in place two items: a helpful error page, and a permanent redirect to get visitors to the correct location.

This content mapping step preserves your "search engine equity" from the old page and tells the search engines where to find that content on your new website.

Define a signpost where the same or similar information can now be found on your website through a "301 redirect." Depending on your server configuration, the redirects are specified differently, but in general, they map from the old URL set to the new one.

The 301 redirect is an HTML status code, indicating that the page has permanently moved to a new location. It's different from the often-misused 302 redirect that indicates to spiders that the file's move is only temporary and that the old URL should stay valid.

A visitor simply receives a seamless redirection to the new page on the website regardless of the redirect status code, as long as the page is redirected. But search engine spiders pay attention to this status code, so please use the right one for your situation.

Reserve Budget for Post-Launch Enhancements

Website optimization is an ongoing commitment, and the best-designed websites can always be improved incrementally.

For this reason, it's wise to reserve a budget of 10% to 20% of the website cost to prepare and launch revisions and enhancements to the website driven solely by user behavior and user feedback on the post-launch website.

Case Study: Poor SEO Execution Hurts

Missing steps in a website launch can decrease your website's visibility immediately. Do this at your own peril!

Figure 7.12 (from an unnamed company) shows the impact on the organic visits to a website after a poorly curated website launch. In this case, the new website launch had improved content, an improved information architecture, and upgraded website infrastructure, but the team did not carry out basic SEO tasks.

When the URL structure changed from the old website to the new website architecture, the previous URLs on the website were not redirected (using 301) to their new locations. Folks arriving on both inlinks from referring websites and search engine spiders were stranded. In addition, the website launched with over a hundred duplicate page titles, denying spiders the critical information needed to categorize each page.

Although the year started strong, because of the impact of the website launch the website finished the year down by 10% over previous year's organic visits. Just after the website launch in week 15, the organic visits was about half of its previous benchmark, though it recovered to two-thirds quickly, it took many weeks to get back to the previous year's level.

Because of this website's high-quality content and its efforts in creating links to its new architecture, this website's organic position and organic traffic recovered within 3 months after the website launch.

In the interim, the website had to pick up the missing organic traffic with increased paid search spend. Closer attention to SEO during the website migration would have minimized or eliminated the loss of visits.

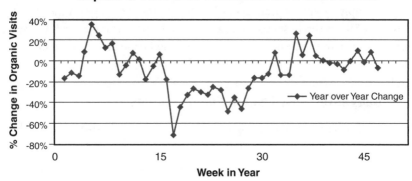

Figure 7.12 *Year-over-year comparison of organic traffic to a website with a poorly curated website launch after week 15 of the year.*

In contrast, a website launch project that attends to SEO details can avoid losses and even achieve quick increases in organic visits compared to previous year benchmarks. Figure 7.13 shows the organic impact of the launch of Childtime's new website November 19, 2010.

Comparisons are to the same day (not date) in the previous year to account for day-of-the-week differences in traffic for this website. The spike comes from changes in visits during a traditionally low traffic time, Thanksgiving.

Gain in Organic Visits after a Website Launch

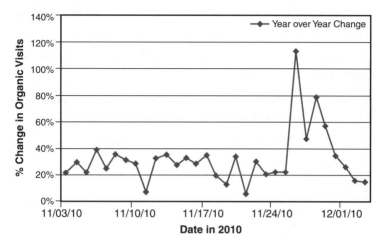

Figure 7.13 *Year-over-year comparison of organic visit increases through an SEO-attentive website launch.*

Summary

To make websites that work for your visitors, make sure you use Internet best practices to fix what you know you should, before you start to test your design. Put your best foot forward by

- Following web conventions. Only violate them intentionally and with good reason.

- Optimizing your contact forms, particularly on key pages.

- Analyzing your website template using an automated attention analysis tool, such as AttentionWizard.com.

- On every page, making sure you minimize visitor wait time, improve calls to action, and check the reading level.

- Imagining your website through your persona's eyes.

Now you're ready to go beyond the best practices and conduct some user research. Including usability testing and user data is a critical piece in any website enhancement process.

To research user behavior on your website

- Consider using a quick and automated user survey to get immediate quantitative insight.

- Look at abandonment rates for form pages by setting up a conversion funnel in Google Analytics.

- Compare two different solution options by observing the goal conversion rates on each, with A/B testing.

- Refer to the qualitative user testing techniques listed in Table 7.1, and conduct one or more of the following:

  - Card sorting

  - User interviews

  - User observation

  - Usability testing on a prototype website

  - Usability testing on your working or existing website

Finally, you should consider your website as an ongoing business-critical effort rather than a one-time project. Make sure you

- Undertake revisions and relaunches to the website carefully, including marketing metrics as a vocal part of the website project team.

- Attend to SEO concerns at launch or suffer traffic (and conversion) losses. This includes using 301 redirects for any URL changes.

- Don't strand your visitors. Plan for graceful failure (404 error pages).

- Reserve budget for post-launch optimization.

8

It's All About Visibility

This chapter looks at the critical tasks for getting your message found on the web. Now that we've discussed how to prepare a clear targeted message using the right words (Chapter 5, "The Audience Is Listening (What Will You Say?)"), we describe how online visibility depends on search engine optimization (SEO) "eat your broccoli" basics, such as lightweight and crawlable website code, targeted content with useful labels, and inlinks.

In addition, you can raise the visibility of your website, products, and services online through online advertising such as paid search advertising, outreach through social websites, and display advertising.

Who Sees What and How

Two different tribes visit your website: people, and entities known as web spiders (or crawlers or robots). People will experience your website differently based on their own characteristics (their visual acuity or impairment), their browser (Internet Explorer, Chrome, Firefox, and so on), and the machine they're using to view your website (a TV, a giant computer monitor, a laptop screen, or a mobile phone). Figure 8.1 shows a page on a website as it appears to website visitors through a browser.

Figure 8.1 *Screenshot of a story page on Model D, a web magazine about Detroit, Michigan, www.modeldmedia.com.*

What Search Engine Spiders See

The web spiders are computer programs critical to your business because they help people who don't know about your website through your marketing efforts find it through the search engines. The web spiders "crawl" through your website to learn about what it contains and carry information back to the gigantic servers behind the search engines, so that the search engine can provide relevant results to people searching for your product or service. The web spider reads the source code of the web page and linked files.

Generally speaking, web spiders do not see anything beyond basic HTML, so any content on the page that's generated through JavaScript, Flash, or digital images on your website will not be indexed by them.

You can approximate what a spider sees by viewing your website through a screen-reader, like Lynx. Or you can "fetch as Googlebot" from within Google Webmaster Tools. They see the source code shown in Figure 8.2.

```
<h1>Features</h1>
<div id="main-content" class="content-block" >

    <h1 class="featureTitle">Art of walking: Going the distance in Detroit's inner space</h1>
    <div class="byline">
        <span class="author">Steve Panton</span> |
        <span class="date">Tuesday, January 25, 2011</span>
    </div>
<div class="featureMasthead">
    <img src="/Images/Features/Issue 269/alh.jpg" alt="Field with Goldenrod" />

    <div class="photoCredit">Field with Goldenrod</div>
```

Figure 8.2 *What a web spider sees on this page, its underlying source code. On line 228 of that source code is the headline "Art of walking."*

Web spiders index your content so that they can provide relevant results to search engine users. In this way, web spiders are gatekeepers for finding new visitors for your website. People may click through the search engine result (organic search or paid search) and become a website visitor. Enticing them to do so is your goal!

What Search Engine Visitors See

Because search engine visitors are a potentially huge source of traffic and business for your website, it is important to consider how your website appears in search engine results pages (SERPs). A sample SERP is shown in Figure 8.3.

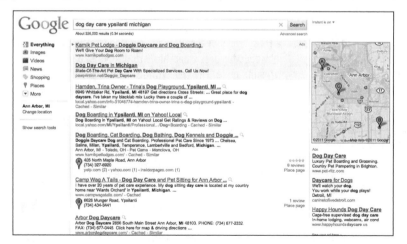

Figure 8.3 *SERP for search for "dog day care ypsilanti michigan," showing the organic results in the main part of the page and paid search ads above the organic results in the shaded box and on the right sidebar.*

The search engine results display and blend different content types. They show organic and paid search results, as detailed in Table 8.1. The organic search results contain several types of information; "classic" text results, local search listings, images, videos, news, and even recipes may also appear on organic SERPs, depending on the search keywords.

Table 8.1 Types of Content on SERPs

What	How
Text organic search results (that is, natural search results)	Results are shown from all pages indexed by the search engine crawlers based on the search engine's determination of which pages are relevant to the search query. The SERP displays the `<title>` tag and the `<meta>` description from your website's code. The `<title>` tag is linked to your web page.
Google Places listings	Places listings may or may not appear. Their presence depends on whether the search keywords have a local component. These are similar to text search results, but are extended with a physical address and phone number. These listings can be identified easily with the lettered map "pins" adjacent to the address information within the entry on the left column. These pins refer to locations in the map at the upper right.
News, images, videos, real-time results, recipes, books	These may or may not appear, depending on whether these information types match the search keywords. These categories of results are not shown in Figure 8.3. These types of results have a category title (for example, "videos for best smoothie") that links to a longer search results page. The "everything" search results page shows the top results taken from the longer page. See Figure 8.8 for an example with images in the search results page.
Paid search results (that is, pay per click [PPC] or sponsored search)	Results are shown from the set of advertisers on the user's query based on the advertiser's bid for that phrase and the search engine's determination of relevancy or quality. The paid search ad displays a headline, one or two lines of content depending on where it is placed on the page, and then a website URL. The headline links to the advertiser's website.

SEO is the process of making a website more visible on the SERP for relevant keyphrases. According to the Pew Research Center, half of all Americans use search engines on a daily basis,[1] so optimizing for organic search can have a huge impact on your overall traffic.

Search engines crawl websites across the Internet to identify which websites to display in response to a search query. Different web crawlers seek out and index different types of information. For instance, Google has specific web crawlers for news, images, video, and even mobile websites.

They then assess the content and display the websites that have content matching the words used in the search. At a tactical level, SEO involves making sure that your website is properly configured to allow these crawlers to find your content and easily identify its theme.

The core of SEO is the website content. Search engine crawlers consider what words you use, where they are positioned, and whether they match the terms that people actually use when searching. Google, Yahoo!, and Bing then determine the rank of a website based on their assessment of how relevant it is to the particular goals of the person executing the search.

Writing Web Content for Users and Spiders: On-Site Optimization

So, we know that we need to create information that is visible to both people and search engine spiders so that the web spiders can help the people who do not yet know you find your website. Good news, though. These two audiences need pretty much the same thing: content relevant to keyphrases used for search.

Search engine ranking algorithms on the gigantic servers owned by the search engines match user queries with website results. The algorithms use information that is seen by the website visitor in their indexing and ranking of the website.

However, search engine spiders have a more limited understanding than people and pay attention to information that regular website visitors will not even see: the metadata about the content of the web page. In this section, we discuss on-page optimization for the pages on your website, as either part of your main website or part of a blog associated with your website.

Page-Level SEO Best Practices

A best practice for people and spider satisfaction is to focus each page of your website on a single concept, keyword, keyphrase, or set of related terms. Make the website a great destination to learn more about your topic. If that's the case, you won't be keyword stuffing your page; you just need to use the phrase a few times to explain yourself.

For spiders especially, provide clear and consistent labeling of each page in associated metadata, such as the page's URL, its Hypertext Markup Language (HTML) title, and in structurally important elements of the page, such as header text.

"On-page" SEO is what you need to do on your own website. We also discuss off-page optimization in the "Increase Your Findability via Local Search and Link Building" section, later in this chapter. On-page optimization starts by targeting a single keyword or keyphrase (or occasionally two or more closely related keyphrases) on individual pages of your website.

Each page in the website should target unique phrases that are not already targeted by other pages. In general, the keywords or keyphrases that you choose to target should be ones that a search engine user would type into a search engine.

The core on-page factors are as follows:

- **HTML page title:** Include the exact keyword phrase in the HTML page title. Try to include the most important phrases at the beginning of the HTML page title and, at least, make sure they are within about the first 64 characters.

  For punctuation, use a colon, pipe character, or hyphen (: | or -) to separate words or phrases in your HTML page title. Include a space between words so that they do not run up next to each other.

  Take advantage of this space to say something unique and useful about each page on the website.

- **Page narrative/content:** Include the exact keyword phrase (and possibly variations) in the body text of the page a few times, while keeping the content meaningful and "human friendly." Incorporate the target keyphrase into heading tags (particularly the <h1> tag) wherever possible.

  Note: When you target a particular page with a unique keyphrase, you can still use that phrase in the copy on other pages.

- **Inbound links:** Link to the page from other pages or from your website's navigation using the keyword phrase (or variations) as the link anchor text.

- **Image alt attributes**: Use descriptive phrases in alt attributes of images and image links, incorporating the target keyphrase where reasonable. <img> (image) alt tags are becoming less critical for search engines, but remain important for accessibility for the vision impaired.

- **Page URL:** Incorporate the target keyphrase in the page URL. Use dashes rather than underscores to separate words within the phrase.

Generally, the most important elements for optimization are the HTML title and the anchor text of the links pointing to the page. <Meta> descriptions are also included in on-page optimization, although they are not factored into Google rankings.

<Meta> descriptions are used for a website listing's description on a SERP, however, so it is important to have an accurate and enticing <meta> description to engage those reviewing search engine results to click through to your website. If the <meta> description is not filled out, interesting and nonsensical things can happen, as in Figure 8.4.

Figure 8.4 is a search for one of the four high schools in Ann Arbor, Michigan: Ann Arbor Pioneer. Figure 8.5 is a search for Ann Arbor's Huron High School. Although these two public high schools are in the same school district, they have different content in their search results because Ann Arbor Huron has taken more care of the tagging on its home page.

From the SERP, it appears that Ann Arbor Pioneer lacks a <meta> description, and so Google has substituted some text from the page for the description. Ann Arbor Huron has a <meta> description and therefore has a better description displaying on the SERP.

Figure 8.4 *A screenshot from a search for Ann Arbor's Pioneer High School.*

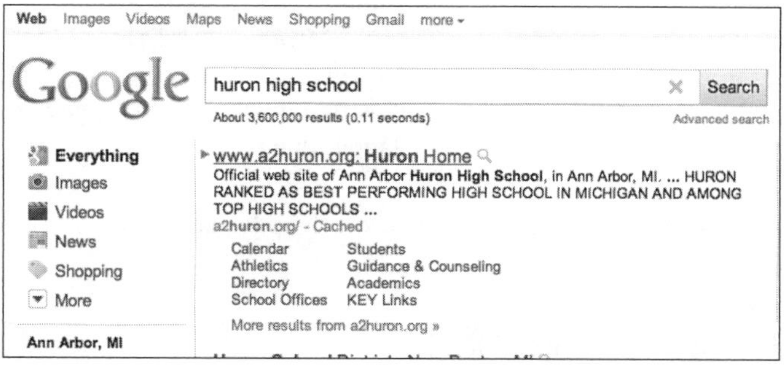

Figure 8.5 *A search for Ann Arbor's Huron High School.*

Page-Level SEO Guide: An Example

When retouching on-page content to increase its visibility for key terms, we typically go page by page through a website, emphasizing a key target phrase or concept on each page. In Tables 8.2 and 8.3, we detail the current state and recommended updates for a hypothetical puppy training company website, Happy Puppy.

Table 8.2 Proposed HTTP Meta Tag Changes

Tag	Current	Recommended Update
URL	http://www.example.com	
Targets	puppy training	
Title	`<title>Home - Happy Puppy </title>`	`<title>Train your puppy now - First Classes Free - Train your dog with Happy Puppy</title>`
Meta	`<meta name= "description" content="PupCMS - the premiere and secure Content Management System for Puppy Training Companies."/>`	`<meta name="description" content="Puppy training from Happy Puppy allows you to enjoy a well-behaved, happy dog."/>`
Alt	Missing	`http://www.example.com/images/home/ start-puppy-training-happy-puppy.gif alt="Start your Puppy Training at Happy Puppy"` `http://www.example.com/images/ learn-more-puppy-training.gif alt="Sign up to Learn More about Puppy Training at Happy Puppy"` `http://www.example.com/images/ trained-puppy-happy.jpg alt="A trained puppy is a happy puppy at Happy Puppy"`

Table 8.3 shows the current narrative text on the page and the proposed SEO improvements to the content.

Table 8.3 Proposed Narrative Changes

Current Narrative	New Narrative
Bulleted points saying "First classes free"	**"Puppy Training Classes Free"**
You will train FAST & EASY with Happy Puppy!	You and your **puppy** will enjoy **training** at Happy Puppy! **Puppy training** is FAST, EASY, & ENJOYABLE at Happy Puppy.
Start your training.	Start your **puppy training**.

Case Study: Call It What It Is to Increase Findability

In 2008, we consulted with a company that had named its website categories by internal categories rather than by what its target customers were calling its product. They thought of themselves as a real estate company, and they had called their apartments "properties" in the navigation and in the directory structure of their website. Well, their potential customers were not looking for "properties," they were looking for "apartments."

Our client made one change to their website navigation, holding the rest of the website relatively static as they were in the midst of a website redesign. They changed the link to this section and the directory holding this section to "apartments" from "properties," and realized a 10% increase year over year in organic page views within this section as a result. We also built a few links for them during the year in between, but renaming that directory was a least a contributor to that jump in visibility.

Special Considerations: Blogging for SEO Benefit

Blogs definitely increase the search engine-relevant content on your website. They provide a less-formal venue to discuss timely topics and keep your website up to date. For some clients, they can generate as much as two-thirds of the organic visits to the website (see Figure 8.6). The book *Blogging to Drive Business: Create and Maintain Valuable Customer Connections* by Eric Butow and Rebecca Bollwitt (Que Biz-Tech, 2010) provides a thorough overview of the whys and hows of corporate blogging.

After you've committed to an editorial schedule, recruited your authors, and set up your blog platform, it's time to make sure it is optimized for search. Blog posts should have the same level of on-page optimization as a regular website page has, which means making sure whatever blog platform you are using allows the `<title>` tag, `<meta>` tag, and `<alt>` tags to be edited. Many blog platforms, such as WordPress, have SEO-oriented plug-ins to accomplish this.

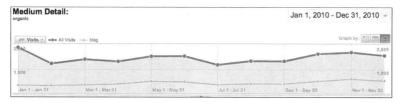

Figure 8.6 *A screenshot from Google Analytics showing blog visits (orange) and all visits (blue) to a website. In this case, the blog is generating about one-third of the organic traffic to the website.*

Any entry on your blog may be your "front door," the first experience of someone who has not previously visited your website or knows your company. For this reason, your blog template should include context on your company and prominent calls to action for folks to take the logical next step: learn more, purchase something, or sign up for a newsletter.

Blogging Best Practices

To maximize the SEO effect from your blog posts, make sure you

- **Blog frequently and regularly:** In a survey of Fortune 100 companies in early 2010, the Burson-Marsteller Evidence-Based Communications Group found that 33% of these companies had blogs, and of those that had blogs, they posted an average of seven posts per month.

- **Keep posts succinct** and focused on a single topic.

- **Turn on "human-readable" or "clean" URLs** so that your optimized blog titles get fed into your blog post URLs.

- **Make it clear how the visitor can learn more** or become a contact through prominent calls to action.

- **Use a descriptive title** that emphasizes key terms you are targeting. A blog is a nice place to target variations of your website's keyword phrases. Use your priority keywords or keyphrases in the beginning of the title to gain the most SEO benefit.

- **Use SEO plug-ins** to allow authors to customize the metadata (<title> tag, <meta> description tag, <img> image alt tags) for pages and page content. Then fill these in! You might want to appoint a separate SEO editor from the writer if this is too detail oriented for the people you have tapped to write blog content.

- **Consider a third-party SEO plug in**, such as Scribe for WordPress (http://wordpress.org/extend/plugins/scribe/), to provide feedback to authors on their posts prepublication.

WHERE TO HOUSE MY BLOG?

A common question is where to host the blog. Should it be at the subdomain blog.example.com? Or should it go in a subdirectory such as example.com/blog?

The answer is, it depends on your goal:

- For SEO purposes, it is better that your blog be a subdirectory on your main domain, because Google thinks of blog.example.com as a different entity than example.com/anything. As a subdirectory, all the inlinks to your blog entries and the rich content will be associated with your domain.

- But, for reputation management, if you want to really own the first SERP, you get another entry or two if you use the subdirectory, as shown in Figure 8.7.

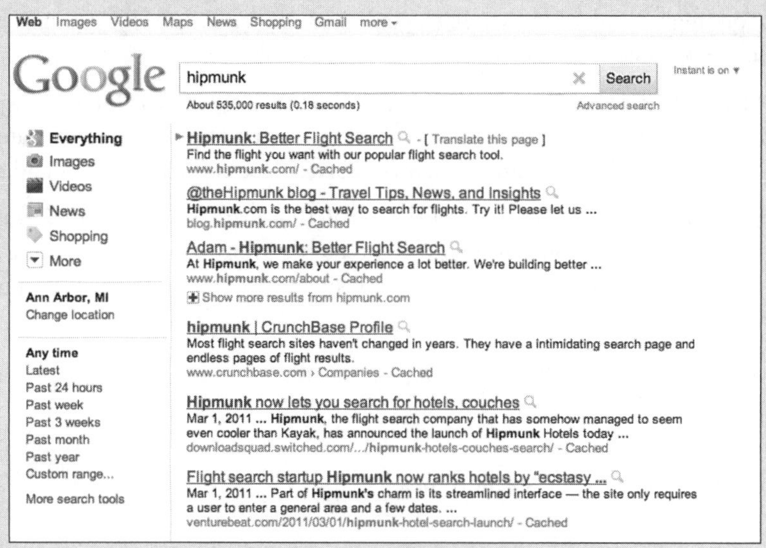

Figure 8.7 *The blog subdomain earns travel website Hipmunk an "extra" entry at the top of this SERP, useful for reputation management.*

Get Out of Your Own Way: Make Sure Your Content Is Findable

Now that you have the creative messaging planned out, the technical side of SEO is a matter of making sure you don't get in your own way by impeding the search engine spiders from finding your message. It's the "eat your broccoli" basics of web design and development: making sure that you have checked off a bunch of little details on a list.

We start by going back to basics. We outline the mechanics of web pages just enough to understand the requirements for online visibility through the technical side of SEO. Our goal is to provide a working knowledge of the components so that you can have a conversation with your development team about the business requirements for findability online.

A Digression into the Guts of Web Code

You won't need any coding experience for this book, nor for this chapter. But a few of the concepts require a basic understanding of web code to digest the screenshots of actual web code supporting some of the technical discussion.

A web page consists of text and images that can be displayed in a web browser. The browser knows what to display by reading the source code of the page in HTML, which defines the content (words, pictures, videos), its layout, its structure, and format. You might think of HTML like detailed set of instructions for a painting we're asking the browser to draw.

An HTML file is a text file that can be read by a browser (such as Internet Explorer, Firefox, Chrome or Safari, to name a few) or by a text editor on your computer, such as Notepad on a PC or TextEdit on a Mac. The text file contains content and tags.

The tags, which start and end with brackets, define structural elements/formatting. Each HTML file has some basic tags wrapping the information: the opening and closing HTML tags and the opening and closing tags defining the <head> and <body> sections of the file.

In the abstract, here is a basic HTML page:

```
<html>
<head>
   Here are my page descriptors
</head>
<body>
   Here is my page content
</body>
</html>
```

The <head> tags contain basic data about the file, called metadata, which is simply data about the data in the file. This includes items such as the character set of the information about the page and some descriptors of the information such as its <title> and summary (<meta> description). It can contain links to useful things like style sheets in use to format the display of the information, and links to script files in use on the page such as Google Analytics.

The <body> tags contain what is shown on the page in the browser, the body copy, links to image files, links to video files, the on-page navigation and so forth. Within the <body> tags, we can specify a hierarchy of information, from first, second, and third level headlines <h1><h2><h3> on down to bulleted lists and general paragraph text <p>. The body also contains links to other media that will be displayed on the page, such as an image or a YouTube video:

```
<body>
  <h1>Here is my Headline including key target phrases for SEO</h1>
  <p>This is my text. I might use this paragraph to describe a con-
cept that needs an illustration using the target phrases that sounds
natural. </p>
  <img src="http://example.com/images/target_phrase.jpg" alt="text
describing my illustration, with target phrases if appropriate." />
  <h2>Second level headline</h2>
  <p>More text. And here's a <a href="http://example.com/different-
page.html">link to a different page of my website</a>.</p>
</body>
```

WEB CODE IN THE WILD

When viewing a web page in a browser you can always request to view the underlying source code by choosing View Page Source from a right-click menu or the View menu (specifics of where to find this menu item depend on your browser). Websites vary in their complexity. Google's very simple home page, a white page with a search box, has complicated-looking source code, as shown in Figure 8.8.

Figure 8.8 *Just for fun, a screenshot of some of the source for Google.com. This is all formatting code, to control the display of the few elements on the page (in essence, the Google logo and the Search box).*

Watch Your Web Technologies

Some ways of creating web pages are better than others for SEO. For instance, some website navigation menus are created with JavaScript. Others with cascading style sheets (CSS). Some are beautiful images of words, whereas others are actual text. Text menus are better for search engine spiders than menus that have pictures of words in them.

Use JavaScript appropriately. Search engine spiders don't execute JavaScript. CSS is better for navigation, but if JavaScript is used, be sure to include <noscript> tags for search engine spiders to follow, elaborating on your website's content.

For example, some websites accidentally hide interesting information behind search forms on their website. We had a client who sold used expensive vehicles, and their sales listings listed the vehicle make, model and year, and then had a (Learn More) button that was wrapped in JavaScript with an onClick action.

When clicked, it took the visitor to a longer detailed filled page, with specifications and photos, of that vehicle. As far as the search engine spiders knew, that detailed page did not exist. We had them replace the image with a text link so that the crawlers could find and index the page.

Content management systems (CMSs) provide unique challenges and opportunities for SEO. Many available CMSs have useful SEO plug-ins available to enable search engine best practices.

You should enable these key functions:

- Human-readable URLs. Some CMS systems allow you to automatically create customized URLs based on title, taxonomy, content type, and username. Think carefully, though, about how you want URLs to look to comply with guidelines for including key terms in the page URL.

- Customizable <meta> description tags and <title> tags.

- Ability to create and update <alt> descriptions for images.

- Automatically creating/maintaining a sitemap.xml in the root directory, if possible.

- Customizing your robots.txt file to point to your sitemap.xml if it is not in the root directory.

Take Advantage of Universal Search: Tag Your Media Files with Target Keywords

Media such as images and videos are increasingly included in SERPs. A query for "day care" turns up images on the first page. These include a few still images from the movie *Daddy Day Care*, a logo for a particular daycare provider (which has the term *day care* in its filename), and an image of blocks with the word *daycare* in its filename (see Figure 8.9).

A query for "learn to knit" turns up video tutorials on Google's first page. Optimizing your multimedia files for key terms gives your company a chance to appear on page one of Google, even for competitive terms. This is in part because people have not yet turned their full attention to optimizing their media files, which gives those who have done so an edge over their sleeping competition.

Because the spiders understand the content of video and image files less well than the text tagging applied to these files, take advantage of all of the tagging you can. Label your image and video files using a keyword-laden filename, provide relevant and informative <img alt> text describing what is contained in the file, and place the image or video on a page relevant to those terms.

Figure 8.9 *Google SERP showing day care images in the middle of the first page of results.*

Avoid Using Multimedia for Critical and Unique SEO Content

Web spiders, for the most part, understand what is written out in the web page's source code. So, the very best place to emphasize key target terms is within the on-page text elements within the <body> tag of your HTML file.

The corollary to this rule is do not limit key terms to elements that are invisible or less visible to spiders, such as videos, images, Flash animations, or the cool new multimedia type of the moment. Search engine spiders do not read and index information within image and media files as well as they capture text information; they read text best.

Sometimes, an animation or a video is crucial to communicate a complex topic or to provide a particular experience desired or required by branding or other concerns. If Flash is critical for some reason, consider externalizing the text elements from the Flash SWF in an XML file as described here, or providing alternative text versions for all content contained in Flash files. This substitution, though, will not replace the value of on-page *text* content for SEO, because greater emphasis is placed by the search engines on content on the page.

Similarly, if a video conveys something you would like people to find, make sure you provide appropriate metadata on the video content to help someone find the video. And, if your video will be hosted off site, such as on YouTube, include a call to action within the video itself and within your YouTube profile to entice people to take a next step by calling you, purchasing something from your online store, or whatever action may be relevant.

By all means, use video and Flash animations on your website, just do not make them the sole source for your content. Be sure to incorporate the information within your video or Flash animation into the adjacent text on your website.

Have Fun with Widgets, but Avoid Putting Interesting and Relevant Content Inside Frames

Frames were initially used in web design and development to provide consistent navigation elements across a set of pages. You might remember them, the "page" in your browser was chopped up into many sections, typically the top navigation, and maybe a sidebar on the left, and then a larger content area in the middle/right. Each of those subsections might have had its own scrollbar. The frameset typically had a single URL with changing content based on clicks in the top or left-side frame.

Frames prevented the easy retrieval of content deep within a website, because without a few tricks, it was difficult to link to information in the content section of the frame directly. Better technologies have replaced frames for consistent website navigation, so the era of frames should be over.

Yet, frames seem to be sneaking back into websites in the form of iframes from third-party widgets. Be aware that many widgets offered by third-party websites (including Google Maps, Google Calendar, and some social feed widgets) are iframes and therefore obscure the content they contain from search engine spiders.

For this, we use ourselves as an example. We wanted an easy-to-maintain calendar for our upcoming speaking events on our website, so we used Google Calendar (Figure 8.10). Yet, the titles and dates of these events are not content available to web spiders from our website (Figure 8.11). Note: Since the time these screenshots were captured, we've replaced the calendar widget on our website.

Figure 8.10 *This Speaking Engagements list includes details for a couple of our "Donuts and Search Marketing" talks.*

Figure 8.11 *Yet, the code for the calendar widget is an iframe, and so information a visitor sees is actually not "on the page" for the search engine spider to find.*

Widgets can be a nice shortcut to get information from other sources, such as external calendars, Facebook, Flickr, Twitter, LinkedIn, or more, onto your website. Just make sure you're not shortchanging your SEO by using them. Check out your own website's widgets. You can tell by inspecting the code. Is the content of the widget written into the source code of the page? Or is it a reference to an external script?

Don't Spread Yourself Too Thin: Consolidate Your Content Power on Your Main Domain

Sometimes corporate marketing departments use microsites to promote temporary events, such as a user conference or as a destination page for an offline marketing campaign. Sometimes these microsites are used to get around restrictive or over-whelmed internal IT departments who cannot create suitable pages within the main website's domain.

Ideally, all your content should be available from your domain, interlinked and providing the web spiders with the complete picture of your offering and communications. If you must build a microsite, consider placing it in a subdirectory on your main domain; so instead of exampleuserconferencemay2011.com, make it example.com/microsites/userconferencemay2011.com.

Crawler Control: Speak to Your Spiders

Although web spiders try to index as much of a website as possible for a search engine, it is possible to manage and influence these web spider programs. Crawlers look to a specific file on your web server, robots.txt, to guide their behavior. Help them get information that they normally would be unable to get, such as any data that is dynamically generated through a query to a database.

Use Robots.txt to Guide Crawler Behavior on Your Website

If you want all of your website to be crawled, you need not bother with a robots.txt file. If you want to limit crawler behavior, however, you can share your preferences about which crawlers go where, by providing rules in your robots.txt file.

You might want to limit crawler behavior on your website to inhibit crawlers from soaking up too much of your web server's bandwidth (when working on your website they can request lots of files very quickly), but more likely you would do this to influence which of your pages would appear in search results.

The robots.txt file is a simple text file with a specific syntax. It starts by identifying which user-agent should be restricted by the rule to follow. You might choose all user-agents with the asterisk character or name a particular user-agent, such as Googlebot. Then, you specify any rules for the crawlers by listing all files or directories where the agent is not allowed.

If you have many PDFs on your website that are printer-friendly versions of content already available on the website as HTML, you might let the robots know not to bother with the PDF files. The motivation for this restriction is that you'd prefer that the HTML pages show up in search results, instead of the PDFs, because opening another program (and the extra delay in loading the PDF) provides a worse user experience.

To disallow all PDF files, you might place them all in a /pdf/ directory and restrict crawler access to that directory on your web server, like this:

```
User agent: *
Disallow: /pdf/
```

You can find more information about syntax and use cases for the robots.txt file at www.robotstxt.org. You can use Google Webmaster Tools to create and test your robots.txt files.

Keep in mind that simply not allowing access using robots.txt is not sufficient to protect private information. Password protection and a secure https:// connection are minimum requirements for online security.

Using Sitemaps to Expose Content Behind Firewalls and Within Databases

Websites that contain either content behind a firewall or large amounts of database-related content that can be retrieved only by filling out a web form often face serious SEO challenges. It is very likely in a Google-driven world that visitors will search on terms that can be surfaced on a website only through a database search, or that is not directly available without a login. But those very searches can be tremendously valuable to drive traffic to a website.

The solution to both problems is the use of the Extensible Markup Language (XML) sitemap, which explicitly surfaces pages of content that can be used to guide web spiders unable to manage the complexities of firewalls or database forms. You can find information about the sitemap.xml protocol at the official website: http://sitemaps.org/protocol.php. This excellent website provides you with both the protocol details and its history.

We recommend this as your starting point. The next step is to prepare your own sitemap, by hand coding it if you are ambitious, using a plug-in for your CMS, or using a third-party spider to locate the pages and then editing the results. You can generate a basic sitemap for your website using this free tool: www.xml-sitemaps.com. Google Webmaster Central also provides thorough documentation on the use of XML sitemaps.

Managing Database-Driven Content Through Sitemap.xml

The essential function of sitemap.xml in database-driven environments is to explicitly surface page results that normally would be delivered through a database search. The only technical requirement in this model is that the database-driven search be returned to the browser using explicit uniform resource identifier (URI) parameters that also can be placed into the sitemap.xml file to regenerate the results of this search for the search engine spiders.

Here's an anonymized example from a client's sitemap.xml file, where the URI for a map search in East Green Bush, New York, includes the following parameters:

```
start_city=East+Greenbush&amp;start_state=NY&amp;start_zip=12061
```

This URI needs to be included in the <loc> parameter for the XML entry so that the page can be resolved by web spiders examining the sitemap.

The following is an example from the website's sitemap.xml file to instruct the spiders to find this URI-parameter pages that would normally be delivered after a form-based database search. It shows the specific URI for the Greenbush location within the tags of the sitemap.xml format:

```
<url>
<loc>http://www.example.com/locate/start_city=East+Greenbush&amp;start
_state=NY&amp;start_zip=12061</loc>
<priority>0.3</priority>
</url>
```

Managing Searches for Content Hidden by a Firewall

Content behind a firewall is a different challenge. Even if a website's content is behind a firewall, the content may still be a candidate for search. The goal of a sitemap in this situation is to create "landing pages" that effectively tell the visitor a website is capable of delivering this content but that it requires a login to do so.

The implementation of this from the sitemap's perspective is similar to database-driven page results. The website developer must then generate these pages, either dynamically or otherwise, that act as a call to action to the visitor to enroll for the service that is hidden behind the firewall.

Implementing Your Sitemap.xml

Bring any content on your website behind filters or search queries to the surface by populating your sitemap.xml with a parameter-based URI that leads directly to the content.

1. Create an XML sitemap (sitemap.xml) that includes a full list of eligible uniform resource locators (URLs) that return content behind filters or web forms.

2. Place the sitemap.xml into the root directory of your website. If you can't place the sitemap.xml file into the root directory, point to its location in the robots.txt file.

3. Double-check your page count within Google Webmaster Tools to ensure Google's spiders count the same number of pages you expect.

4. Update the sitemap.xml as new information is added by appending additional lines to the sitemap.xml document for new available results.

You can use the robots.txt file to tell the web spiders where to find your sitemap.xml file. Simply add this line to your robots.txt file:

```
Sitemap: http://www.example.com/sitemap.xml
```

Your development team may be able to automate the process of building and updating your sitemap.xml behind the scenes, as part of your deployment process.

Submit These Files to Google Webmaster Tools

Let Google know about your robots.txt and sitemap.xml files by submitting their location within your Google Webmaster Tools account. Submit your sitemap.xml file under Sitemaps and your robots.txt file under Crawler access, shown in Figure 8.12.

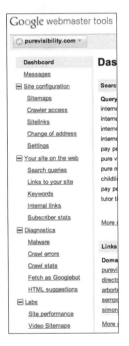

Figure 8.12 *Google Webmaster Tools sidebar, available at https://www.google.com/ webmasters/tools/home?hl=en.*

Technical Requirements: Canonical URLs

You'll have noticed that there are several ways to type a URL:

• http://www.example.com

- http://www.example.com/

- www.example.com

- www.example.com/

- example.com

- example.com/

These should be entirely synonymous, but are sometimes treated differently by web servers. We've encountered many websites where the URL that is not preceded by "www." returns a 505 Page Not Found error. Yikes!

Ideally, all these variants of your URL would redirect to each other. You can set your preference for with or without the "www." subdomain for Google in your Google Webmaster Tools dashboard, as shown in Figure 8.13. However, you also want to review your web server settings to handle URLs with and without a trailing slash.

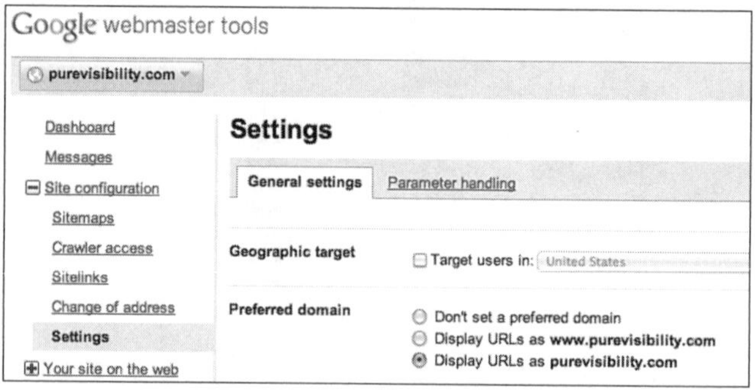

Figure 8.13 *You can set your preference for "www." or not in Google results, using the Google Webmaster Tools settings.*

Advanced Canonical URLs   Database-driven websites have some other potential issues for web crawlers. If you can get to the same item in very different ways through searches or categories on a larger database driven website, and if the searches or categories are reflected in the URL, your website may have a factorial set of URL possibilities.

For instance, if you can get to a particular leash (the Frisky Freddie leash) on the Happy Puppy website a couple of different ways, perhaps by browsing within the leashes category (arriving at example.com/leash.php?item=frisky-freddie) and by browsing within the small dog accessories (arriving at example.com/small-dog-accessories.php?item=frisky-freddie&category=leashes).

This duplication of content across multiple retrieval methods causes issues for a couple of important reasons:

- **Slowed web server response times:** The web server would be crawling your website and attempting to access all of the unique filenames. Having it access the same information through different URL paths could put unnecessary demands on your web server and potentially slow response times for actual shoppers on your website.

  After it reads the content, Google would then realize it's a duplication and ignore the "extra" copies, picking one of the copies from its list. So, you wouldn't benefit from "extra entries" in the index for your extra pages.

- **Valuable inlinks may be squandered:** People would link to your content across the set of possible URLs. Yet, Google, having discarded the extra copies of your information in its index, would only use inlinks to the indexed URL. Therefore, inlinks to nonindexed URLs are wasted.

You could construct your website so that each item of content cannot be accessed by multiple URLs. You might use robots.txt to suppress certain categories or directories in your website if they contain duplicates. But the best way to preserve the value of your inlinks is to tell Google which is the correct (canonical) URL for the information served in multiple places.

To do so, you would add a `rel="canonical"` tag in the header of the page's HTML indicating which URL is to be used. For the Happy Puppy example, it might look like this:

```
<link rel="canonical"
href="http://www.example.com/leash.php?item=frisky-freddie" />
```

For more information about specifying canonical URLs for database driven websites, see http://googlewebmastercentral.blogspot.com/2009/02/specify-your-canonical.html.

AN EXERCISE TO SEE WHAT GOOGLE SEES

Google Webmaster Tools is a useful resource where Google shows you how it sees your website. Take a peek at what Google knows about your website by first verifying you deserve access to this information. Next, look into the Fetch as Googlebot tool in the Labs menu. You might be surprised by a gap between what you experience on your page and what Googlebot actually sees.

You can find more information at www.google.com/support/webmasters/?hl=en. See Figure 8.14 for what "Fetch as Googlebot" returns in the Webmaster Tools dashboard.

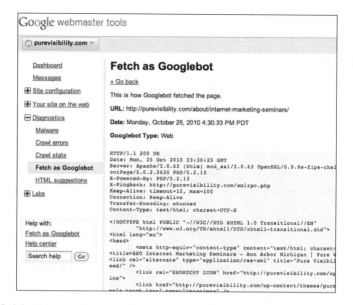

Figure 8.14 *"Fetch as Googlebot" results in Google Webmaster Tools.*

Increase Your Findability via Link Building

Search engine rankings take into account how your content is regarded by others. Google's algorithm includes the number and quality of links to your website. So, write content that is linkworthy (sometimes that means writing something attention grabbing or sharing data that others may need to make a point) and cultivate inlinks directly.

Link building is a real art in the modern SEO world, largely because links guide the way that web spiders think about and organize their taxonomy of your website. Link building is specialized, steady work. It involves developing relationships with other websites, cultivating linking opportunities, and developing tools to promote the website's marketing message.

External linking is probably the most important factor for getting ranked for competitive terms. Credibility is based on how many websites link to your website, especially if those websites are authoritative sources that are related to the content of your website.

Get links to your website from other websites including directories, related websites, and industry resources. Try to get links from those other websites with anchor text containing keywords relevant to your website.

Popular places from which to build inlinks include the following:

- List in major general pay directories: the Yahoo! Directory, Business.com, BOTW.org.

- Find highly related pay directories for your niche. Although Google is making an effort not to count paid links toward rankings, this can bring direct traffic, and probably still counts a bit toward rankings if it isn't obvious the link was paid for.

- List in free directories.

- Do searches for websites with information about related companies and request links from them.

- Seek relevant blogs where you can contribute a guest blog, offer the same opportunity back. When you blog elsewhere, if it fits, provide valuable and relevant information in keyword-rich inlinks to your website. Just don't be heavy-handed.

- Use memberships in organizations to get links.

- Syndicate articles that link back to the website with keywords.

- Look up links to competing websites by using tools like Yahoo! Site Explorer (search linkdomain:competitorsdomainhere.com in Yahoo!). Request links from websites that linked to your competition.

- Use existing business relationships to solicit links.

- Viral strategies, such as videos, interesting widgets, and so on.

- Use press releases and links to speaking engagements.

How to Approach Website Owners for Links

After you've found a website that has relevant content and some authority, prepare a message to the website's owner outlining how your information may be valuable to the website's audience. Request an inlink, ideally with some relevant phrases in the anchor text.

If your website is about puppy training, ask for the link to read "puppy training" not www.example.com. The easiest way to get keyword links like this is from business partners who already trust you and may be willing to help you define how they portray you on their website.

Increase Your Findability: Claim and Maintain Your Local Business Listings

Search is becoming more personal and more local. Traffic from local searches (for example, from Google Places and local.yahoo.com in web analytics) has increased dramatically for our clients over the past years. Search behavior is changing; searchers are typing in search queries with ZIP codes or city, state modifiers to get targeted results (for example, "handyman services, ann arbor, mi" or "maid service 48103").

In addition, search engines like Google are using information about the IP address of the visitor to serve up local results even for general queries. For instance, this search from Ann Arbor serves up local pet care facilities for the general query "pet care" as shown in Figure 8.15.

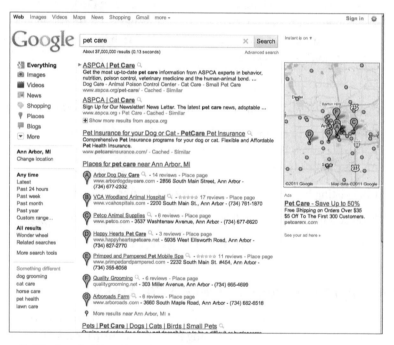

Figure 8.15 *Google SERP showing local listings.*

When Google launched Universal Search and began including Google Places results within the search results content, local directory listings became more visible and more important than ever. Managing this information for a single location can be tough and companies with extended networks of store or office locations have that same challenge hundreds of times over.

Here are a few tips to get you started:

- Ensure the completeness of your listings in Google Places, local.yahoo.com, the Bing local listing center, and directories such as InsiderPages that come up when you search your business name.

  Follow the instructions on each website to claim and populate your results with a full description, relevant categories, and all applicable fields. Augment your listings with videos, images, hours of operation, and payment types accepted, as apply.

- Keep your listings current; update with new additions, address changes, or closed locations.

- Submit consistent and complete information to the directories that feed into Google and Yahoo! listings such as Internet yellow pages directories, infoUSA, and other local directories. This can be done via bulk upload through third-party vendors such as Localeze or Universal Business Listings.

Monitoring, Responding to, and Encouraging Reviews Online

After you review your listing in Google Places, you're going to see (or note missing) online reviews of your business. At the same time you may be asking how you can increase your ranking visibility. These two questions are related. Local search rankings are influenced by several factors, including the same relevancy algorithm used to rank natural search listings.

An additional factor seems to be the number of online reviews. Google Places listings display reviews provided to Google directly, but they also pull in reviews from other review websites such as Yelp.com, ApartmentRatings.com, and InsiderPages.com, to name a few. Definitely encourage happy customers to post a review of your product or service online; it will become part of your online presence and benefit you by sharing a good story about your business with searchers and may just increase your visibility by increasing your rank in local searches.

You might also need to address negative comments with delicacy and resolve their root cause if possible. The Air Force has developed a great decision tree to guide responding to online negativity (see Figure 8.16). It takes into account the context and provides clear instructions for how to address the review: Be honest about who you are, cite your sources, respond in a way that reflects well on your business and yourself.

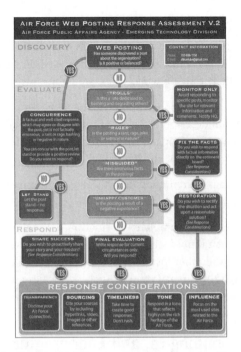

Figure 8.16 *The Air Force's Web Posting Response Decision Tree, available from www.globalnerdy.com/2008/12/30/the-air-forces-rules-of-engagement-for-blogging/.*

Advanced Visibility Strategies: Going Social

Everyone is talking about Facebook, Twitter, and social strategies. Potential customers consider mentions on social websites as impartial reviews by people like them (people they can trust), so these websites provide "social-proof" needed in purchase decisions. For this reason, you should definitely pay attention to social mentions of your business brand name and your trademarks.

Since the launch of Google+, Google no longer indexes Tweets in a real-time way. Yet items posted to Twitter and Facebook can be quite public (depending on your settings) and public posts are searchable. The spiders are certainly crawling these websites often, with real-time results for many queries.

However, the benefits of links from social websites like Twitter or Facebook to your corporate website are only indirect for SEO. The social websites like Twitter and Facebook explicitly put nofollow tags onto user supplied links, so these confer no direct SEO benefit at all (see Figure 8.17).

```
490         <span class="entry-content">Our book on Metrics
       Driven Internet Marketing. This time with a link. <a
       href="http://amzn.to/gOTTqE" class="tweet-url web" rel="nofollow"
       target="_blank">http://amzn.to/gOTTqE</a></span>
491         </span>
492      <span class="meta entry-meta" data='{}'>
493      <a class="entry-date" rel="bookmark"
       href="http://twitter.com/dunrie/status/56006321367040000">
494      <span class="published timestamp" data="{time:'Thu Apr 07
       14:52:02 +0000 2011'}">7:52 AM Apr 7th</span></a>
495      <span>via <a href="http://www.linkedin.com/"
       rel="nofollow">LinkedIn</a></span>
```

Figure 8.17 *Source code of a personal Twitter page, showing the nofollow tag automatically attached to tweets.*

Some have argued that the spiders might notice your link being mentioned by others on these websites and may index your website more quickly or pay more attention to your website because of its popularity in social websites. Possibly. What getting social will do is get your message in front of visitors to these social websites, which is a benefit in itself, as people are spending more time on these websites than search results pages, according to a study by comScore and ValueClick Media.

However, because search results pages are shown to people when they're looking for products and services rather than looking to chat with their friends or build a shed on Farmville, we recommend social strategies be pursued alongside, but not at the expense of, SEO and paid search advertising.

Extending Your Reach with Paid Search Advertising

It's funny. Whenever I share that I work in Internet marketing, people tell me that they never, ever click those sponsored search listings. I always laugh. Someone definitely is clicking the ads. From a spot check of clients in our portfolio, we see paid search advertising to bring them from 25% to 85% of their website traffic.

Paid search typically brings a higher proportion of new visitors to the website who are searching on more general terms related to their products or services, and paid search visitors buy things and raise their hands to become sales leads. It's worth testing.

Because the advertiser only pays for people who take a particular action, typically paying for a click on the ad to the advertiser's website, paid search advertising is the most targeted and trackable advertising around. It can be used to complement and extend SEO.

Setting up and optimizing your own paid search advertising is a book unto itself. In this section, we hit the highlights and include a few definitions to give you a working vocabulary to have the next conversations with your internal or external paid search management team.

Paid search ads are typically text ads, which makes them easy to build and update. They are paid for on a cost-per-action basis, typically cost per click, where the advertiser pays for clicks on the ad.

There are two types of paid search ads: ads that are shown on SERPs, and contextual ads that are shown alongside web content on a publisher's website. Figure 8.1 shows contextual ads, known in AdWords as the display network. Display network ads can either be text ads or media ads, such as images or display ads.

Search Engines as Paid Search Vendors

There are many paid search ad vendors. Google AdWords delivers the greatest clickthrough (and therefore has the greatest reach). The combination of Yahoo! Search Marketing (YSM) and Microsoft adCenter is second, at less than 30% of the searches. Ask Network and AOL trail in this market.

Table 8.4 shows comScore's March 2011 U.S. search engine rankings for paid search services.

Table 8.4 Search Engine Paid Search Rankings

Paid Search Vendor	Market Share
Google	65%
MSN AdCenter (Yahoo! and Bing)	28%
Ask Network	3%
AOL	2%

Facebook also offers ads, and they most closely mimic Google content or display network advertising. We've experimented with Facebook ads, matching to target audiences by demographic characteristics, including geographic location, but haven't found them to be as successful in terms of driving traffic, or close to the cost-per-lead efficiency of AdWords. Perhaps this will improve over time.

The drawback to choosing a smaller (less-expensive) vendor rather than Google is that they don't drive as much traffic, some don't have adequate safeguards against click fraud, and you may spend more time managing the campaign because of the less robust toolset.

Google AdWords (and its associated tools) is the market leader in this space.

Effective Paid Search Management

There are several paid search management tools or automated services available for a spectrum of use cases, from ReachLocal for basic management and reporting, through Clickable.com for more sophisticated bid management, to more powerful and comprehensive solutions like Omniture.

We've experimented with homegrown and commercially available bid management system and have always reverted back to human management of paid search. We simply have never found a better way than optimization by a talented analyst.

And, regardless of what you turn to eventually, human and automated paid search management follow the same general outline. So, following this framework should be useful if you do it by hand or in bulk via a third-party dashboard.

In the first phase of implementing paid search, you spend a lot of effort up front on keywords, ad groups, bid management, and ad copy management. As time goes on, you identify which ads and keywords work best for you, and therefore landing page management and conversion rates become more important.

Managing paid search campaigns involves five basic steps:

1. Choose appropriate profit-driven goals. See "Which Metrics Matter Most" in Chapter 3, "Building a Metrics-Driven Practice."

2. Define your market:

   - Target the right audience (or persona). See Chapter 5 for more details.

   - Set campaign region, time period, and so on.

   - Generate keywords and define ad groups with closely related, tightly themed keywords.

3. Qualify your market. Write targeted ads featuring your keywords to interest potential website visitors.

4. Convert your visitors into customers by create goal-driven landing pages with clear calls to action. Target your keywords directly and focus on user goals.

5. Repeat and refine. Revisit the campaign to determine which ads, which keyphrases are the best performers.

Tip

Improving the performance of a paid search effort requires accurate tracking of campaigns and comparison of clickthrough rates, costs per click, conversion rates, and the costs per conversion.

Define Your Market

Start with your profile of your ideal customer. If you serve your customers or clients through local storefronts, you don't want to advertise where you have no brick and mortar stores. If your product is only licensed in certain states or certain countries, limit your advertising to where it is legal to sell it.

If your product has prohibitively high shipping costs to certain regions of the country, you might want to focus your advertising on areas that result in sales. This kind of targeting is available within Google AdWords; you can set the language, geography, and schedule for advertising.

You also need to know the language your potential customers are using to find your service, covered in Chapter 5. After you've built a large set of keywords, group them into themes so that you can write paid search ads and set bids at the group level rather than for individual keywords.

Keyword Research   Here's the approach we take to tackle a new keyword research project:

1. Look through your website and identify major themes.

2. Research the competition for your root terms.

3. Use a keyword research tool to generate variations from your list of core terms.

4. Choose the right set of keywords.

Choosing the right keywords is extremely important. Although it might initially seem advantageous to show up on ultra-broad terms for wider exposure, extremely generic terms are often costly, and less relevant than more specific "long tail" keywords.

For example, if you sell sweaters, you will probably get a better return on your investment if you advertise on keywords specific to the *types* of sweaters you sell (red wool sweaters, cashmere sweaters, and so on) than broad terms (clothing, sweaters).

Why? Because the user has already told the search engine that they are looking for exactly what you are selling. These long tail terms also tend to have a lower cost-per-click minimum bid than higher-volume terms, and also have higher quality scores.

The key to finding the right keywords is to test and refine them over time. Although specific, long tail keywords often perform best, it's certainly worth testing a variety of different keywords and then making decisions to keep or delete the terms based on data. Paid search ads are very easy to track, so you'll be able to pause or delete any terms that aren't successful.

Define Ad Groups   After you've identified your keywords to target, organize them into ad groups, or sets of related keywords and keyphrases. You'll find that campaign management becomes easier when working at the group level rather than individual ads.

Why not write just one or two ads for all your keywords? The broader, simpler approach doesn't enable you to write very specific ads for well-focused ad groups. Each ad group is likely to resonate with a different type of user (or persona) for the website, because different people use different keywords when searching online.

🔍 *Tip*

Group your terms according to theme, bids, and common words. While some groupings are readily apparent, others may be more difficult to identify.

Ask yourself what types of ads you can write that best describe the keyword in question. You'll start to see more groups when you look at it from the other direction.

In general, *smaller ad groups are better.*

Qualify Your Market with Specific Ad Copy

You've seen search results pages; the ads are sometimes shown above the natural search results in the main column, and then down the right-side column. A Google AdWords ad has a few components: a title (up to 25 characters), two description lines (35 characters each), and a display URL, as shown in Figure 8.18.

On the back end, we also prepare a destination URL which is on the same website as the display URL but is typically a page more relevant to the user's query. In this example. the page might show only AT&T phones.

Figure 8.18 *Sample AdWords paid search ad from MobileKarma, a vendor of refurbished used cell phones.*

Ads make sure the right people in your market are getting to your website and that they are properly prepared when they get there.

Good ad copy

- States a benefit

- Has a call to action

- Gives a reason to act

- Uses a relevant landing page both in the display URL and for the destination URL

- Tempts or engages search engine users

Your team should be evaluating ad copy variants and then testing to find out for which ads have the highest clickthrough rates.

Mechanics of Paid Search Optimization: Quality Scores   The AdWords Quality Score encapsulates a few parts of paid search optimization activity:

- The fit of the keyword or keyphrases

- The fit of the ad

- The fit of the landing page to the user's query

The first two items are within the "qualify your visitors" stage of paid search optimization. The last falls into "convert your visitors into customers" and is about their experience on your website.

An AdWords Quality Score is a numeric index given to keywords or ad groups that characterizes the quality of an ad. The goal behind the scoring system is a good one; search engines look to provide a good user experience, so that their ads are helpful and relevant, rather than distracting and annoying.

If you search for "flights to florida" and a search engine returns advertisements for wool socks, those ads and their landing pages are irrelevant to your search. However, if the search engine serves ads for different airlines, those are likely highly relevant ads.

Many factors go into a quality score calculation, but most of the weight is on the clickthrough rate (CTR) in the search network, and the relationship between keywords on both the ad copy and landing page. Quality scores range from 1 to 10, with 10 being an extremely high quality score. We see good campaigns with quality scores in the 7s and 8s.

Quality score can influence ad position and the cost-per-click price. The following formula is used to determine ad position:

Bid x Quality score

Therefore, the higher your quality score, the less money you have to pay to rank in a higher position.

The best way to achieve a high quality score is to optimize your account to ensure that each of your ad groups has highly descriptive ads that match closely to the ad groups' keyword list. You should also have a landing page that is relevant to the keywords, rather than simply leading users to your home page.

Convert Your Visitors into Customers

Finally, make sure your money is well spent by giving your paid search visitors relevant, useful, and compelling information when they land on your website. After all, you've paid to get them there, why disappoint them? This is covered in more depth in the "Designing Your Landing Pages" and "Optimizing Your Landing Pages" sections in Chapter 6, "Putting It All Together and Selling Online."

Revisit, Refine, and Refresh Your Campaigns

Managing a paid search advertising program takes vigilance and attention to detail. It can be improved by eliminating words that do not produce good leads, testing and refining ad copy and landing pages, and keeping in sync with your website's and your customer's seasonal concerns.

COMMON ADWORDS PITFALLS

We've all clicked ads that lead nowhere or that make you feel like you've been subject to a bait-and-switch scheme. Avoid wasting your money and frustrating the visitors you're paying to get by avoiding these gotchas:

- Insufficient tracking. Don't forget to track visits and conversions with your web analytics and conversion tracking through the paid search program.

- Poor global targeting. Showing ads globally using eastern standard time, so the ads only show in Australia during the night. See more on global paid search in the section "Basic Mechanics for Global Paid Search Configuration" in Chapter 10, "Special Considerations for International Organizations."

- Focusing too heavily on your brand/trademark terms rather than general terms. Folks who are searching on your brand name already know how to find you. Make sure you're visible for folks who don't yet know your name.

- Bringing folks to your home page, where they'll have to hunt for content relevant to their query, or might just leave. Instead, place them deep into your website on a page relevant to their query.

- Taking folks to a page that doesn't reference the reason they clicked the ad. For instance, if they click an ad offering a whitepaper to help them reduce their puppy-training woes, but land on a page without a whitepaper, you will have frustrated your visitor.

- Being diffuse and wasting ad clicks in the display network. Start first in the AdWords search network and learn what is successful for you there before branching out into other paid search vendors (such as adCenter, which powers sponsored search on Yahoo! and Bing) and before experimenting with Google's display network.

- Managing the search network and the display network as if they were one and the same. The search network shows ads on searches, while the display network shows ads next to content. In the search network, CTR can affect your quality score and therefore your costs. CTR is not relevant to quality score in the display network, so the two campaigns can be managed very differently.

- Assuming all visitors are equal. Eventually, you might decide that certain terms deserve higher bids than others because of the quality and type of leads they produce.

Advanced Visibility Strategies: Display Advertising

We are all familiar with display ads (also known as banner ads). They can be intrusive, covering the content of an interesting article on an online news website, and visually noisy, blinking or animated and otherwise distracting you from your goal on the website. The dislike of banners by some web surfers is such that there are browser plug-ins (such as Safari AdBlock, Firefox Adblock Plus, AdBlock for Chrome, Adblock IE) to suppress banners and show only the "real" content of a web page.

However, these ads are ubiquitous on websites that publish content, such as the websites of newspapers such as the *New York Times* and *Washington Post*, as well as portal websites such as Yahoo.com and WebMD.com, and niche websites that offer free services such as flight tracker websites (for example, www.flightaware.com).

Display ads are critical to funding many useful websites that provide free or low-cost content and need a way to pay for writers, coders, designers, and server space. As an advertiser, these ads extend your reach beyond search engines, and typically reach users at an earlier stage of the buying process than paid search ads.

If you are a content provider online, you may accept advertising directly from individual advertisers or through an ad network that brokers transactions in bulk. Ad networks include Google AdSense (the network where Google AdWords advertisers appear when they sign up for the display network and Yahoo's Right Media Network). Ad networks also include publishers themselves, such as Fox Audience Network.

There are two main distinctions between paid search and display ads. Paid search ads are typically (but not always) text ads, whereas display ads are typically media files such as animated GIFs, Flash SWFs, or video formats. Paid search ads are almost always paid per click (therefore the acronym PPC, for pay per click) to the advertiser's website.

A display ad can be paid for in many ways, including cost per click. Another common way to pay is cost per impression or CPM, cost per 1,000 impressions, with the M denoting the Roman numeral for 1,000. A third way available on some networks is cost per acquisition, where users pay for a designer action on their website, such as a purchase or completing a contact form. This distinction is key. With banner ads, the advertiser may be paying for clicks or actions such as leads or purchases, but is often just paying for visibility. With paid search, the advertiser is almost always paying for the action of a click.

Therefore, banner ads are typically used in consideration campaigns, where an advertiser is looking to familiarize or reinforce the website visitor with its brand. Most businesses in the early stages of search engine marketing do not need to bother with consideration or branding campaigns. This is an advanced strategy, which should be tested only after all the other tactics in this chapter are producing good results and your team has extra bandwidth and advertising funds for experimenting.

A recent study by comScore shows that the proportion of people who click display ads online has decreased from 32% in 2007 to 16% in 2009,[2] and according to Doubleclick the percentage of display ad impressions that were clicked in 2009 ranged from 0.06% for financial services ads to 0.15% for automobile advertising.[3] These ads do not often result in website visits. So, showing your ads to a targeted subset is critical.

---

2 See Figure 2 in www.comscore.com/Press_Events/Presentations_Whitepapers/2010/
   When_Money_Moves_to_Digital_Where_Should_It_Go.

3 See Figure 10 in http://static.googleusercontent.com/external_content/untrusted_dlcp/
   www.google.com/en/us/doubleclick/pdfs/DoubleClick-07-2010-DoubleClick-Benchmarks-
   Report-2009-Year-in-Review-US.pdf.

The Best Ways to Target Display Ads

Advertisers can place display ads via several options, including the following:

- **Contextual ads:** The ad is shown next to content that matches certain keywords defined by the advertiser.

- **Audience targeting:** The ad is shown to consumers matching a particular criterion, such as demographic characteristics.

- **Retargeted ads:** The ad is shown only to people who have previously visited your website.

A 2010 comScore study using data from 2 million consumers, 1 million of whom were in the United States, found that retargeted display advertising resulted in the best outcomes, measured by visits to the advertiser's website and follow on searches of the advertiser's trademark terms. Audience and contextual ads showed about half of the lift of retargeted ads, according to the comScore and ValueClick Media study.[4]

Google AdWords offers retargeted and contextual ads through its display network. Given that we recommend starting out with an AdWords paid search campaign before moving to display, testing display ads through Google's display network is a great starting point.

You can work with your graphic designer to build the ad creative, work within their available marketplace of designers, or use standard templates in the AdWords interface. And then, after the ads are up and running, AdWords reports the display campaign within the reporting structure you are already using from AdWords, using the same units and your already established goals. (See Chapter 3 for more information about choosing goals and setting them up for measurement.) If display ad campaigns garner leads or sales at the same rate or better than your text ads, you might want to consider expanding this campaign and looking at vendors other than Google.

---

4 See Figure 8 in www.comscore.com/Press_Events/Presentations_Whitepapers/2010/
When_Money_Moves_to_Digital_Where_Should_It_Go.

Summary

After you've invested in building a website, make sure it will be found through creating content, not hiding that content from web crawlers, and ensuring that you reach out to relevant directories and websites to build inlinks into your website.

You can also increase your visibility through social media outreach, targeted paid search, and display advertising.

- **Create targeted on-page content** for your website visitors and web spiders.

    - Use keyphrases in your URLs, on-page copy, and page tags such as the <title> tag, <img> image alt tags.

    - Tag media files with relevant target terms.

    - If you use a content management system, allow your content creators to modify page tags and media tags to make the content findable on your target search terms.

- **Maintain your local business listings** to ensure your business shows for local searches.

    - Encourage people to leave positive reviews on review websites such as Google and Yelp.

    - Constructively engage with negative reviews.

- **Build quality inlinks to your website** to increase your authority to web spiders and visitors alike.

- **Build out a targeted paid search campaign** in the AdWords search network, landing visitors on appropriate pages with clear next steps for them to take. After you have success in the search network on Google, consider extending your paid search to contextual advertising in the AdWords display network and other paid search vendors such as Microsoft adCenter.

- **Consider social outreach and display ads** as extensions of your existing visibility strategy, not as substitutes for good on-page optimization and content creation.

After you're done making your content findable, new visitors might arrive on *any* page of your website. So, don't neglect to place clear calls to action on every page of your website, including blog pages.

9

Running the Feedback Loop

Many teams suffer from the dysfunctional misperception that their job is just to get raw materials to the next team. Marketing should just dump a bunch of leads at the door of the sales team, the more the better, regardless of quality. If the sales team cannot convert them into business, that's the sales team's responsibility. This kind of "Balkanized" thinking is a recipe for conflict and under-performance. Instead, build collaborative teams that agree on goals and tactics, and collaborate to win!

In this chapter, you review the sources of data for analyzing Your Online Sales Engine, learn about common analysis pitfalls, and connect the dots to return on investment (ROI).

Revisiting the Project Goals

Remember the Heisenberg uncertainty principle from high school physics? Among several other things, it posited that the process of measuring the position of a particle changed its trajectory. Put quantum mechanics to work in your marketing and sales team. Regular measurement and reporting will put your goals in front of a larger team regularly, keeping them top of mind, reinforcing alignment.

Set a reporting rhythm, stick to it, and accommodate new information as needed. Your rhythm might be weekly reviews of key numbers with your core team and then, monthly and quarterly reflection with other stakeholders. Which metrics to review when was included in the "Web Maintenance Tasks" schedule description in Chapter 7, "Making Websites That Work."

Your Goals Will Change as Your Process Matures

After following a process to identify your goals (see "What to Measure" in Chapter 3, "Building a Metrics-Driven Practice") and track against them (see "A Checklist for Getting the Metrics You Need" in Chapter 4, "Breaking Down Silos to Get the Metrics You Need"), it is time to feed new understandings back into the process.

Often, after some initial data has been gathered, some goals or metrics recede in importance and spark ideas for new replacements. Even better, by sharing information between systems and groups within your company, you will foster questions about data quality and marketing and processes. Your process will evolve as you go, gaining momentum and becoming tighter and more efficient, over time.

Maturing Goals: Happy Puppy

A lead-generation-focused company, such as Happy Puppy, might track online marketing activities in a dashboard or table such as Table 9.1. In this example, Happy Puppy followed the influence of different marketing activities in generating leads or sales by marketing channels.

But, after some initial data collection, they decided to consider an intermediate step, the number of qualified leads, as in Table 9.2, and drop retention, which was constant for all channels. Assessing the number of qualified leads gave the team a way to assess lead quality during the sales cycle, instead of waiting for the sale to close (or not) to assess quality.

Table 9.1 Initial Matrix of Metrics and Their Data Sources for a Lead-Generation Company, Happy Puppy

Channel	Site Visits	Phone Inquiries	Web Inquiries	Sales	Retention
Organic search	10,000	400	200	$30,000	40%
Paid search	20,000	900	400	$100,000	40%
Direct visitors	4,000	200	120	$22,500	40%
Email	6,000	50	350	$25,00	40%
Data acquired from	Web analytics	Call center or phone tracking system and CRM	Web analytics and CRM	CRM	CRM

Table 9.2 Second Draft of Metrics and Their Data Sources for Happy Puppy

Channel	Site Visits	Phone Inquiries	Web Inquiries	Qualified Leads	Sales
Organic search	10,000	400	200	60	$30,000
Paid search	20,000	900	400	200	$100,000
Direct visitors	4,000	200	120	45	$22,500
Referral	12,000	480	240	90	$45,000
Email	6,000	50	350	30	$25,00
Data acquired from	Web analytics	Call center or phone tracking system and CRM	Web analytics and CRM	CRM	CRM

Maturing Goals: TropiCo

As an e-commerce company, TropiCo is less concerned with leads and can jump to counting sales and revenue from phone calls and web transactions. E-commerce web analytics delivers information about marketing channels (for example, organic visitors and conversions within Google Analytics), and if you set up custom phone numbers for different channels, you can track call outcomes by channel.

In this example, TropiCo (our global tropical fruit reseller) has set up initial tracking by channel and used raw sales as a metric (see Table 9.3). Their customer service team has a more aggressive style tactic, so their average sale is higher than web transactions (which tend to hover around the "free shipping" mark of $50).

Also, returns are also a little higher from phone transactions. But, questions from the operations group prompted them to change course early on, and instead of reporting raw sales, they switched to sales adjusted for returns, termed *net* in Table 9.4.

Table 9.3 Initial Matrix for an E-Commerce Company, TropiCo

Channel	Site Visits	Phone Sales (#)	Phone Sales	Web Sales (#)	Web Sales
Organic search	20,000	400	$30,000	400	$20,000
Paid search	35,000	560	$42,000	525	$26,250
Referral	12,000	220	$16,500	180	$9,000
Direct mail	10,000	80	$6,000	80	$4,000
Email	9,500	76	$5,700	76	$3,800
Data acquired from	Web analytics	Call center or phone tracking system and CRM or order fulfillment	CRM or order fulfillment	Web analytics and CRM	Web analytics and CRM or order fulfillment

Table 9.4 Second Iteration Tracking Matrix, Redefining Income and Sales Counts to Remove Returned Merchandise

Channel	Site Visits	Phone Sales (#)	Net Phone Sales	Web Sales (#)	Net Web Sales
Organic search	20,000	400	$25,000	400	$19,050
Paid search	35,000	560	$35,000	525	$25,000
Referral	12,000	220	$13,750	180	$8,750
Direct mail	10,000	80	$5,000	80	$3,810
Email	9,500	76	$4,750	76	$3,620
Data acquired from	Web analytics	Call center or phone tracking system and CRM or order fulfillment	CRM or order fulfillment	Web analytics and CRM	Web analytics and CRM or order fulfillment

Analyzing Across the Online Sales Engine

Until you tie together information from separate parts of your company, you cannot optimize the online sales engine. After you have the data, celebrate, and then get down to analysis. Just getting the data is the critical first hurdle. But the numbers take careful review and some slow thinking to interpret them.

Pulling Data from Various Silos

As Tables 9.1 through 9.4 illustrate, the data you need to evaluate marketing initiatives from initial contact to a sale are typically contained in multiple systems, from web analytics, customer relationship management (CRM) or sales force automation (SFA) systems, and order-fulfillment systems.

After you start to integrate ROI calculations, as discussed in "Proving ROI," later in this chapter, you start to include other systems and groups within your organization, such as the finance and operations teams and the software or systems that they use.

Businesses that have grown through acquisition may be even more challenged in the data assembly, having to report from several legacy point of sale CRM systems. (We know of one client that has nine customer contact systems in operation, some carrying duplicate data, some with unique information.) Enforcing process compliance and data integrity across a patchwork of systems is tricky at best.

The data you need is held in separate systems:

- Traditionally managed by the marketing team:
  - Web analytics
  - Search engine marketing tools
  - Platforms managing paid search
- Traditionally associated with the sales or customer service teams:
  - CRM software
  - SFA tools

"Marketing" Metrics from Web Analytics

Your web analytics holds critical online sales engine data such as visits to the website by marketing channel and web form lead submissions. You can find more detail about what is contained within your web analytics system and how to configure it in the section "Web Analytics: Information Rich Dashboard" in Chapter 4.

You also need information about costs and lead counts (which should match your web analytics information, plus or minus 10%) from your paid search dashboard, as well as information from any display campaigns you are running.

Additional information might be found in marketing automation systems coordinating things such as email campaigns or coordinating across paid search and other types of campaigns.

You can extract these numbers into Your Online Sales Engine dashboard either by hand or "automagically" by a script that pulls from your web analytics' application programming interface (API).

"Sales" Metrics from Your Analytics and CRM

If you have an e-commerce website, you can get more from your analytics, such as counts of the number of sales and revenue (both overall and by marketing channel) from your web analytics dashboard.

Your CRM or SFA system holds other key data, such as

- Phone call counts and outcomes

- Web form submissions (used as a cross-check against your web analytics)

- Qualified lead counts

- Conversion of leads to sales

- Size of opportunities

You can use it to calculate other derived values, such as conversion rates along the process from lead to qualified lead to sale and average value of a lead or a sale.

Ideally, if you import marketing data into your CRM with the lead data, you can break these metrics out by marketing channel. If not, you might start by just assuming that all marketing channel leads are of equal quality (a poor assumption, but better than not connecting the dots to sales at all) and use standard rates for progression along the path from lead to sale.

If your data integration among different tracking systems (web analytics, phone calls, CRM) is incomplete, you may not have specifics on lead-to-sale ratios or retention rates by channel. You might start by assuming that all channels produce sales from leads at equivalent rates and have equal retention characteristics. Or, you could simplify the sample tables in this chapter into fewer channels for which you *do* have some data, such as grouping all web leads into one channel.

Similar to your web analytics data, you can have your metrics hand-pulled or you can automate and script the reporting through a software API.

You can find more information about obtaining this data in the section "Web to Lead to CRM Analysis: Close That Loop!" in Chapter 3, and in the "Lead Management: SFA/CRM Integration" section in Chapter 4.

Mastering the Mechanics of Data: Dashboard Assembly

We start with the obvious, because your data spans several systems, and because you cannot analyze it that way, you must assemble a unified dashboard. Create a single reference that spans the online sales engine.

Perhaps there is a well-priced, easy-to-use enterprise system that covers this spectrum end to end, but many sophisticated companies are using people and processes instead of enterprise software to bridge the gaps between systems. Start with people and processes, and if that panacea software comes along, you'll know just what features you'll value in it, having prioritized the reports you value through trial and error ahead of time.

Here are some tips and tricks for sharing dashboards:

- **Avoid inbox overload:** Don't send a new spreadsheet every day or a reminder email for every update. Instead, place the living summary or dashboard somewhere available to all who need access to it, such as an intranet or other shared online workspace. For reporting roll-ups shared among geographically dispersed teams, we like the shared spreadsheets available online via Google Apps for Domains or other hosted shared document services.

- **Archive for safety:** This is critical business data, make sure you archive or otherwise back up previous versions for reference, in case something awful happens to the data or to any of the automated data feeds into it.

- **Include version control / change history functionality:** It's best to see who edited what, when, and maybe then you can even understand why.

- **Control access and make sure the shared space is private and secure:** This data took immense effort to obtain and is valuable, and if it got out to folks outside your company (your competition, for example), you might give away a competitive advantage. Make sure you can control access to the document on an individual level.

Common Data Analysis Pitfalls

Data is great, and more data is even better. But as you refine your goals and focus on the metrics that matter, you want to avoid a couple of analysis pitfalls:

- Trying to monitor too much at once
- Forgetting to consider potentially confounding variables such as time of day, week, month, or year
- Doing much interpretation if the data is faulty or incomplete
- Expecting results to be consistent and stable over time

Analysis Paralysis

We gave many potential key performance indicators (KPIs) to monitor in "What to Measure" in Chapter 3. Make sure you filter your reports to a handful of KPIs to monitor. Avoid watching every little thing about your website.

If you aren't selective, it's easy to get overwhelmed by the number of metrics and slight variations within them. Give yourself and your team the opportunity to concentrate on the essential, by minimizing your reporting and analysis burden.

Twitchiness

Web data varies: hour by hour, day by day, month by month, and season by season. It's best to look at a handful metrics on a meaningful timescale. Don't jump to action in response to every mini-blip in your numbers.

If your web server has been flaky, then looking at your website performance on a daily or even hourly basis is necessary. Otherwise, you might want to filter out some of the hourly or daily noise by aggregating performance to a weekly level before you take action.

Also, set your "decision thresholds" in advance of watching the numbers. A good way to stay honest is to expect that you vet differences in performance against a statistical threshold (for example, such as a confidence interval test). Do this before declaring this year's numbers up over last year's or your email initiative better than your colleague George's direct mail campaign. Take sample size considerations into account!

Neglecting Seasonality

Almost every business has some kind of seasonality or predictable fluctuation in interest and activity. Retail websites may see a lot of demand ahead of the December holidays in the United States. Real estate, apartment rentals, education, and childcare websites have strong trends centered around the school year. Most websites have some kind of day-of-week and time-of-day pattern; for instance, many business-to-business (B2B) and business-to-consumer B2C websites have lower traffic on weekends and weekday evenings.

So, when comparing and interpreting trends, be careful to remove extraneous variables, such as day of week or time of year. And watch your fiscal year patterns. Quarters may have different number of days and weeks when compared to each other and a different number of weekends year over year.

For this reason, we like to compare year-over-year over similar periods: the same day of the week, or the same number of weeks. This gets rid of potentially confounding patterns in the data, such as a variation in the number of Sundays, which is typically not interesting to an analysis!

Believing the Data (If It's Too Good to Be True, It's Wrong)

A good rule of thumb is that when the data is telling you something strange, your tracking is probably off. In the past, we've gone from moments of surprised jubilation when we see a landing page with a 95% conversion rate to consternation when we've discovered that the AdWords conversion-tracking scripts were placed on the landing page, not the thank you page, therefore defining every visitor as a conversion.

Conversely, when things flat-line in your web analytics, after you make sure your web server is intact and serving up your website to visitors, the next place you should check is whether your tracking codes were deleted accidentally.

Watch for sharp changes in your metrics; they usually signal data-quality issues rather than wildly successful or wildly unsuccessful initiatives. A little redundancy in your tracking systems is the key to noticing and repairing tracking goofs.

For example, when you're counting your paid search lead conversions in three places (your web analytics, the AdWords and MSN adCenter interfaces, and in your CRM), you'll be in a good position to repair your dashboard if one tracking mechanism suddenly goes awry.

Not Considering Phone Calls

For businesses for whom a ringing phone is a sign of health, you need to track the phone calls generated by online sales engine activities to fully measure them. In some cases, businesses may get as many as three phone calls for every web form submission, meaning that 75% of your responses to an initiative may be invisible in your website analytics.

Avoid drawing inferences from incomplete data. Track the influence of your initiatives on phone calls.

Not Following Your Lead to a Sale

Marketing channels that drive large numbers of leads that are rejected by your sales team are just noise in the system, diverting your team from higher-value activities. It's better to drive fewer better leads than a high number of junk leads.

You cannot evaluate marketing activities by website visits, web form leads, and phone calls alone. You must measure your efforts against qualified leads for your sales team rather than raw lead counts, and it's even better to measure yourself against sales revenues directly. For this reason, all the tables in this chapter include columns for revenue data, and we *insist* that you pull marketing data into your CRM for analysis. See "Web to Lead to CRM Analysis: Close That Loop!" in Chapter 3.

Proving ROI

When it comes time to evaluate past activities and plan for new initiatives, you have to pin everything to the bottom line (for example, the revenue gained) and compare it to costs or the investment made. Only then can the returns be evaluated. It's an open question whether the cost of Your Online Sales Engine should be drawn from profit or whether it should be considered part of the total costs of operation.

The formula is

$$ROI = (Profit\ from\ activity\ A) / (Cost\ of\ activity\ A)$$

In your business, the profit calculation may be its own unique equation, taking the sale price, customer-retention rate, and cost of materials and service to the customer into account.

What to Consider When Calculating ROI

It might sound trivial, but calculating ROI means quantifying your investment. Because the online sales engine spans marketing, sales, and operations, your investments might take some sleuthing to uncover. Table 9.5 holds some thought-starters for associated costs for different channels.

Table 9.5 Sample Costs for Initiatives

Channel or Initiative	Sample Costs
Organic search	SEO vendor fee Content generation Call center time to answer inquiries
Paid search	Ad spend Call center time to answer inquiries Paid search vendor fee Landing page design and development Creative costs for design and implementation of any display network banner ads
Direct visitors	Brand-awareness marketing Referral Link-building budget Content-sharing or syndication services PR budget or online services for PR syndication
Paid directories	Vendor or listing fees Call center time to answer inquiries
Promotions	Third-party fees (such as Groupon)

Channel or Initiative	Sample Costs
Direct mail	Content generation Production (design, printing, mailing, service fees)
Email	Content generation List purchases Design or implementation
Data acquired from:	Finance or Department Budgets

Do You Consider Internal or "Soft" Costs?

In teams that combine internal staff and external agency support, the external costs will be clearer than the internal ones. You, the client, will receive itemized invoices from agency partners and vendors, but internal costs may hide under the radar. Here are the costs that may be tricky to quantify or hard to categorize:

- **Process management costs**
  - Time spent by internal team managing or coordinating agency efforts
  - Time spent monitoring the metrics, ensuring data quality, and ensuring adherence to process
  - Investment in training and process development

- **Content-generation costs**
  - Time spent by nonmarketing folks supporting marketing activities (includes being a subject matter expert interviewed for web copy, or even web copy creation if delegated)

- **Technology costs**
  - Web hosting, uptime monitoring systems, backup systems
  - IT team time spent in maintenance, monitoring, and supporting the website

- **Sales costs**
  - Time spent by sales or marketing to process and nurture raw leads
  - Time spent pursuing qualified leads

In our experience, many companies omit internal time from ROI calculations, doing the calculations over external agency costs and fees. Perhaps these teams assume that internal team support costs are fixed, operational costs. Arguments can be made in either direction.

Whatever your choice, make sure all involved in reporting and vetting the numbers use the same definitions and criteria; otherwise, you will find yourself mired in a swamp of data that looks analogous but is not!

Calculate Lifetime Value

A critical factor that influences ROI is retention rate. Do people cancel the initial contract? Do they continue a support or maintenance subscription? Do they purchase additional items from you? If so, you may want to take lifetime value into account, because the cost to gain the customer might be spread over more than just the first sale.

Calculating ROI: An Example

Then, sum these costs to figure your investment. Table 9.6 shows sample ROI calculations for TropiCo, with investments in different activities, small investments in website optimization for organic search, a relatively larger investment in paid search, link building to generate referrals, and a direct mail pilot program.

In this simple example, the profit on sales is always 10%, regardless of volume. Here we see that paid search made the company the most profit, yet had a lower ROI than investing in organic search.

Table 9.6 Sample ROI Table on a Handful of Initiatives, Accounting for the Investments Made, in Particular Marketing Channels and Their Return in Sales and Profit

Channel	Investment ($)	Sales ($)	Profit on Sales ($)	ROI (Profit/ Investment)
Organic search	30,000	1,000,000	100,000	3.3
Paid search	300,000	4,800,000	480,000	1.6
Referral	15,000	270,000	27,000	1.8
Direct mail	8,000	60,000	6,000	0.8
Data acquired from	Finance or department budgets	CRM or order- fulfillment system	Finance	You

When ROI Doesn't Matter

Sometimes, an initiative is critical regardless of its ROI. You might not track ROI if your effort is considered by your company as so basic to being in your market it is a "cost of entry" activity or critical to reputation or brand management.

Here are some example activities that may not need ROI support:

- Being seen on your competitor's brand names in paid search.

- Monitoring online conversations about your brand to prevent damage to your reputation or retain customers rather than gain new leads. It's hard to quantify what losses you might have incurred through inaction.

- Sponsoring a high-visibility trade show.

How to Set Projections for Future Performance

After you get your data, share it with your team, and then work with them to create goals for your future initiatives. This review and planning step is where key feedback from the online sales engine feeds additional metrics-driven growth.

Having real data on past performance or pilot projects is critical to projecting future performance. We typically take past trends into account and then project changes in performance, based on factors such as changing budget for paid search spend, new initiatives in organic visibility, updated website or landing page improvements to get on conversion rate improvements, and more.

How to Set Projections for Future Performance

After you get your data, share it with your team, and then work with them to create goals for your future initiatives. This review and planning step is where key feedback from the online sales engine feeds additional metrics-driven growth.

Having real data on past performance or pilot projects is critical to projecting future performance. We generally take past trends into account and then project changes in performance, based on factors such as changing budget for paid search spend, new initiatives in organic visibility, updated website or landing page improvements to get on conversion rate improvements, and more.

Projecting Return on Paid Search Optimization

In "Extending Your Reach with Paid Search Advertising" in Chapter 8, "It's All About Visibility," we discussed best practices for your campaigns. Landing page improvements were covered in "Optimizing Your Landing Pages" in Chapter 6, "Putting It All Together and Selling Online."

Now we cover projecting the effect of improvements after you've gathered some initial benchmark data. Table 9.7 shows some the effect of sample paid search optimization activities and how they will influence your sales metrics.

Table 9.7 Sample Projection Considerations for Paid Search Optimization

	Paid Search Optimization Activity		
Metric	Increase paid search ad spend in existing search engine (for example, increase spend within AdWords)	Increase paid search spend in a novel search engine (expand to adCenter)	Usability improvements to landing pages
Web traffic	Increase traffic. How much? Likely with diminishing returns. Leads are not entirely proportional to ad spend, as shown in Figures 9.3 and 9.4.	Increase traffic. How much? Could be proportional to ad spend, because you may be able to snag similar or lower costs-per-lead in the new engine.	Indirect effect. By increasing conversion rates, your costs per lead will decrease and your paid search budget will get you more leads.
Conversion rate	No effect, unless higher-cost key-phrases converted better or worse than previous set.	No effect, unless visitors are of lower quality.	Increase conversions. How much? Depends on the severity of the impediment you're removing.
Leads	More leads, with diminishing gains, as above.	More leads, proportional to increases in traffic.	More leads through increases in visits and conversion rates.
Sales	More sales, with diminishing gains.	More sales, if quality is equal.	More sales, if quality is equal.
Retention	Unaffected, if quality is equal.	Unaffected.	Unaffected.

Because of the influence of your bids in paid search, you might not be able to project proportional increases in lead counts with increases in ad spend. The bids can work as a step function of subsequent plateaus, with certain bids and certain keyphrases providing you with certain costs per lead, as shown in Figure 9.1.

Eventually, your team will saturate the demand for those keyphrases, and you will not be able to allocate more budget for those bids and keyphrases to gain more traffic. To get more traffic, your team will have to bid on higher cost per lead bids or terms, which will drive up your average cost per lead across the account.

In Figure 9.1, the gray line shows the cost per lead for additional leads as the budget increases. This cost jumps from $10 to $15, then to $20, and to $30. The average cost per lead for the account, shown in black, is the average across the leads gained at the different prices.

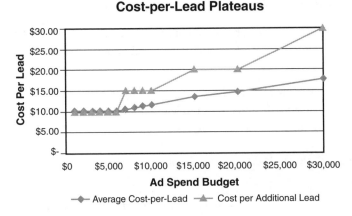

Figure 9.1 *Sample cost-per-lead plateaus in paid search.*

Taking these increases in cost per lead into account, the actual lead count (gray line in Figure 9.2) will be less than the best-case projection of unlimited leads at the best price (black line in Figure 9.2). You will still get additional leads, but a higher cost per lead, so your count will increase more slowly than your spend.

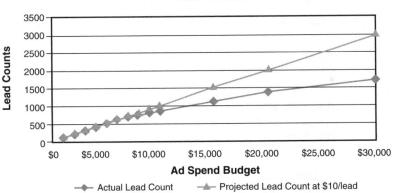

Figure 9.2 *The cost-per-lead plateaus illustrated in Figure 9.1 will cause a flattening of gains in leads even as ad spend budgets are increased.*

If you will also be doing some landing page or conversion rate optimization activities on your website, you may be able to project increases in conversion rates that will get you leads at a lower cost per lead.

Projecting Return on Organic Search Optimization

We covered optimizing for organic visibility in "Writing Web Content for Users and Spiders" and "Increase Your Findability via Local Search and Link Building" in Chapter 8.

To justify expenditures on these activities, you might need to calculate the effect. Table 9.8 shows some the effect of sample organic search optimization activities and how they can influence your sales metrics.

Table 9.8 Sample Projection Considerations for Organic Search Optimization

	Organic Visibility Optimization Activity		
Metric	Increase visibility in local searches through "hCard formats" on location pages.	Increase visibility in image searches.	Blog to increase visibility on target keyphrases.
Web traffic	Increase traffic. How much? Proportional to demand (ascertained by keyword search estimation tools).	Increase traffic. How much? Proportional to demand (ascertained by keyword search estimation tools).	Increase traffic. How much? Proportional to demand (ascertained by keyword search estimation tools).
Conversion rate	Perhaps a slight increase, given location-based searchers are late in the buying decision process.	No effect, unless visitors are less relevant to target audience.	No effect, unless visitors are less relevant to target audience.
Leads	More leads, proportional to increases in traffic and increase in conversion rate	More leads, proportional to increases in traffic.	More leads, proportional to traffic increase.
Sales	More sales, proportional to lead increase.	More sales, if quality is equal.	More sales, if quality is equal.
Retention	Unaffected, if quality is equal.	Unaffected.	Unaffected.

Projecting Return on Conversion Rate Optimization

Improving your website for its visitors will pay off across many, if not all, marketing channels. For more implementation and process details, see the section "Improving User Experience and Conversion Rates" in Chapter 7.

Table 9.9 shows the effect of conversion rate optimization and usability improvements and how they cut across all marketing channels and sales metrics.

Table 9.9 Sample Projection Considerations for Conversion Rate Optimization Activities

	Conversion Rate Optimization Activity	
Metric	Increase visibility of calls to action on informational pages	Improve website search results on an e-commerce website
Web traffic	No effect	No effect
Conversion rate	Increase across all marketing channels (paid search organic search, referral, and so on)	Improved
Leads	More leads, proportional to increase in conversion rate	Not applicable
Sales	More sales, proportional to lead increase	More visitors find products of interest. Visitors may also purchase more per visit
Retention	Unaffected, if quality is equal	Unaffected

The Beauty and Danger of Pilot Tests: Your Mileage May Vary

Pilot tests are a great way to explore new ideas with smaller projects. Example pilot tests might include training a small group of local store owners to start and maintain their Facebook pages to determine Facebook's influence on lead generation or customer retention. Or, you might run a pilot call-tracking initiative for a subset of your marketing initiatives, websites, or locations if you have a local presence.

These pilot tests can help your team scope what it might take to roll out a new procedure across your entire organization. Data from these initiatives can help to build the business case for a larger effort.

Yet, pilot tests by their nature include only a subset of tactics, phone calls, web visitors, or outcomes. And for that reason, their results might not hold true when the process or tactic is extended. Your results, in terms of efficacy of the new process or ROI, may vary when you "really" do it.

Promising pilots may turn to fizzled initiatives depending on a few factors:

- **Cherry-picking your pilot group:** If you roll out your Facebook test to the small group most clamoring to try it, their ardor and commitment may not be typical, and they might invest more and see a greater return than the nonpilot group.

- **Small sample sizes:** Avoid this by running a pilot long enough to pass statistical tests, such as t-tests or confidence intervals on differences between groups. Note that even statistically supported inferences are overturned with the addition of more data.

- **Confounding factors:** If you run a pilot in your time of peak customer demand, you might not see equivalent results during your quiet period.

By all means, do a pilot. Just don't project the results to be exactly the same for all times and under all circumstances. Your pilot predicts performance of a larger effort with similar characteristics as the pilot, a similar time frame or seasonality, similar enthusiasm of the participants, and so on.

Boardroom-Ready Reporting

No matter how high a position you have in your company, you are accountable to someone: your board, the CEO, or your team. With that in mind, it's worthwhile to plan how you will share the highlights from Your Online Sales Engine implementation process with them.

Provide Context for the Numbers

Numbers are great, but they're not fulfilling in themselves. They must be interpreted and made into actionable next steps. Review trends in the numbers, taking into account specific explanatory factors for variance, or stasis. Pull in market-level trends using things such as the Google AdWords keyword tool or Google Insights for Search to show changes in demand for your services.

Sometimes the answer lies outside your own data. For instance, economic factors may drive dips in performance. Figure 9.3 shows a decline in market-level interest in dog- and puppy-training services in the period 2004 to 2011.

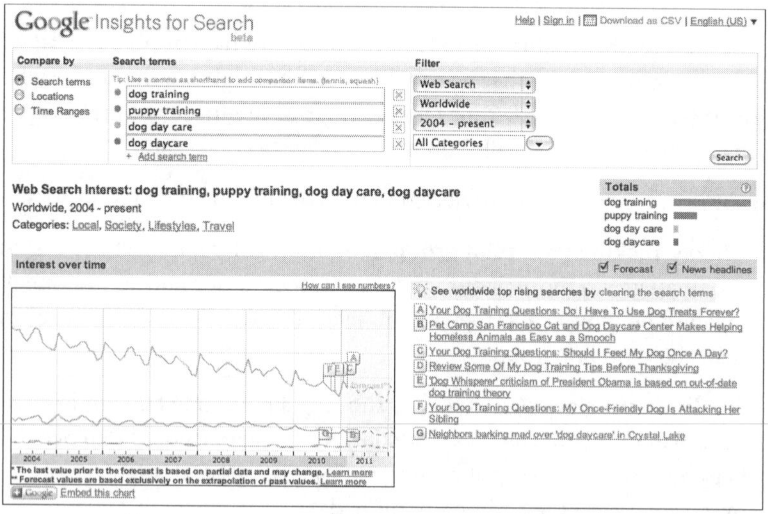

Figure 9.3 *Decline in traffic on dog and puppy training and daycare terms.*

What Is a Good Value?

Is a 2% conversion rate good? Bad? Well, it depends. Is it better than it was last year? Worse? Did the conversion rate stay the same after a sizable investment in new landing page design? Do you calculate that getting the next 0.1% growth will cost $10 or $10,000,000?

Is a $270 cost per lead good? Not if the eventual sale made the company less than the cost of acquiring the customer.

We are typically asked by clients for benchmark values for comparison within an industry. They need to know whether their conversion rate of website visitors to leads is more, less, or similar to their competition.

Unfortunately, without some corporate espionage (which we do not advise), this is impossible to know. This data is held quite close to the vest. Industry professional societies or networking groups may provide you with some informal intelligence, but we'd question the value of comparing yourself against the competition.

The Best Benchmark Is Your Own

Instead of getting distracted with where your competitors stand, you need to compare your marketing efforts against your prior history. Are you improving? Stagnant? Compared to what? Where are the opportunities for growth?

Comparing Against Prior Performance   We love "same time previous year" comparisons, because looking over the same period (a week, four week period, or quarter) alongside a previous year helps to smooth out some of the predictable fluctuations in your web volume and lead numbers that happen, due to seasonality.

Comparing Against Your Goals   Use your goals to create projections for future performance.

Projections keep us honest. In planning cycles, we pause to budget for our activities and project returns, either in ROI or in the number of leads, sales, or other business-critical metrics. The clearest way to show progress is to show progress against a goal.

Figure 9.4 shows the actual performance (filled bar) against the performance forecast (open bar) for web form leads. The 100% mark at the top of graph is the projection for the entire fiscal year, and the open bar shows the forecast for the part of the fiscal year that had completed as of the report.

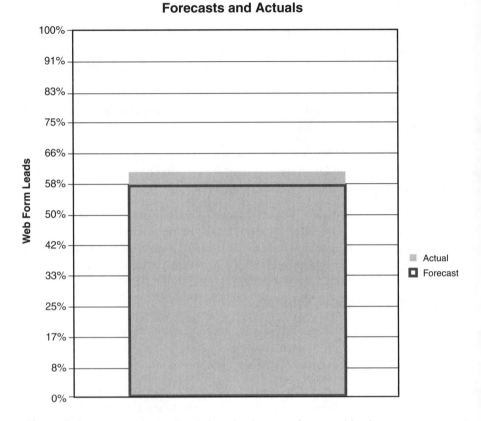

Figure 9.4 *A graph of actual web form leads versus forecasted leads.*

Boardroom Reporting Best Practices

The right balance of visual presentation, prose summary, and tabular data will vary for different audiences. It will depend on their interest and learning style, and it will depend on how the information is best presented.

Reporting best practices include

- Speak to the key concerns of your audience. This likely includes ROI and schedule to realize the return.

- Connect your metrics and your narrative with strategic initiatives and overarching themes.

- Explain your metrics them with appropriate context.

- Focus on quantitative results, explanations for variance, and actionable next steps.

Avoid implementation details (avoid details like "we then got the cost per click down to $0.33 through eliminating several nonperforming keyphrases").

- Invest extra time to whittle your narrative down to the minimum. A short executive summary may get you farther than a long and insightful analysis.

Graph your data. In many cases, a picture substitutes for a paragraph.

Summary

Here's how to bridge traditional divisions between marketing and sales data to see Your Online Sales Engine from your marketing planning, through your web analytics, to your lead nurturing and sales, in your CRM:

- Focus on a handful of KPIs critical to your business.
  - Monitor the systems that generate your metrics to prevent critical data gaps.
  - Gather these from across the enterprise, regardless of source system.
- Commit to a regular reporting cycle to
  - Share your progress.
  - Keep your goals top of mind.
  - Revisit your goals and projections as your understanding matures.
- Make decisions thoughtfully.
  - Define in advance what your decision threshold will be, and back it up with a little statistical analysis.
- Examine ROI on your initiatives, and use your own past performance and carefully interpreted and carefully planned pilot projects to make projections whenever possible.

Gather data on your goals and performance. With a common dashboard measuring your progress against your goals, you'll have the information you need to make informed decisions about both the website and Internet marketing. Interpret the data cautiously, and when you decide to take action make a compelling case for change to your larger team.

Just as you have to consider the audience for your website, you need to consider the needs of your team and the needs of your stakeholders when sharing insights and next steps gleaned from Your Online Sales Engine dashboard.

10

Special Considerations for International Organizations

Companies with a global presence have all the challenges any company does with establishing connections across Your Online Sales Engine potentially multiplied by the number of countries and global field marketing offices involved in the process. Be fearless in the face of organizational complexity, because making these connections will pay off!

Going Global in the New World Order

If you sit in the United States reading this book, you might not be well positioned to understand the global marketplace, because you are most likely not fluent in languages other than English. However, because of population patterns and Internet usage worldwide, many if not most of your potential customers may be sitting outside the borders of the United States, probably searching for your products in languages other than English.

According to comScore, Internet usage is higher in the Asia-Pacific region than in Europe and North America, as shown in Figure 10.1, so pursuing an English-only U.S.-centric strategy is limiting yourself to only a portion of the available market.

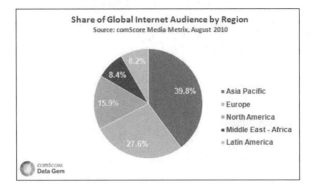

Figure 10.1 *Share of Global Internet Audience by Region from ComScoreDataMine.com.*

The Return of the Silo Problem

Of course, doing business internationally has its share of legal setup, which is outside the scope of our discussion here. Instead, we discuss the online sales engine for companies that already have websites and marketing teams focused globally.

A key issue in a globalized company is coordination across country and language barriers and between teams located in disparate global offices that conform to different business hours and communications protocols. Many information silos can emerge or hide in a global and multilingual company.

Triage for International Disorientation

As you likely can predict after reading this book's other chapters, our approach is to urge you to unify your systems and processes to expand Your Online Sales Engine across all relevant markets and websites.

The "Basic Mechanics" sections of this chapter may very well feel like a list of "well, duh" tasks. If you are an old hand at international projects, feel free to skim. It is pretty tactical, and some or most of the recommendations will seem obvious when you read them.

Yet, we've seen sophisticated and smart folks and large companies make minor or major gaffes in these activities, so it might do you good to read through this summary of mechanics and best practices. At worst, you will experience a little *Schadenfreude*. At best, you might head off a similar glitch at your company.

The Impact of Language, Culture, and Transparency

All the "basic" recommendations later in this chapter are more about the configuration and organization of your campaigns. The key to a successful international online sales engine is of course relevant, localized, and consistent content both on your website and in your campaigns.

We devoted an entire chapter to speaking the language of your customer, and it is true again for global marketing. You need to speak the language of your customer—including their dialect—to effectively market. Otherwise, your website, landing pages, and your materials will sound... well, foreign and wrong.

You need to translate your website content, translate your landing pages, translate your target keyphrases for search engine optimization (SEO) and for paid search efforts, and translate any giveaways such as whitepapers to the native language and then localize to the right dialect for your intended audience.

As in Figure 10.2, a direct translation can often be incorrect, particularly with short phrases that must stand on their own. Don't be tempted to run even your short paid search keyword ads through Google Translator and simply go with that.

Working with Translators and Localization Experts

In today's world, most professional translators and localization experts use computers to do a rough machine translation of the text. Then the human (who has knowledge of both languages) does the manual cleanup, based on cultural and linguistic differences between the two texts.

To accommodate the subtle nuances between target cultures and language, a localization expert takes over, to tweak the translation and do the final cleanup. This needs to be a human, and preferably a native speaker of the target culture and language.

Figure 10.2 *A translated menu that's less than appetizing! Shared by Like the Grand Canyon on Flickr www.flickr.com/photos/like_the_grand_canyon/.*

There's a difference between the Spanish used in Spain, Puerto Rico, Mexico, and countries in South America; a difference between French in France and Quebec; and a difference between the German spoken and written in Germany, Austria, or Switzerland. A localization expert captures the essence of these linguistic specialties appropriately, for your website.

To get a better quality translation (and help to reduce the number of issues that come up during translation), you can do a little preparatory work to smooth the way:

1. First, clean up your English text and make it ready for translation. Use an approach such as "controlled English" and edit the text to get it ready (remove contractions, idioms, metaphors, and so on).

2. Create a glossary to help the translation team.

3. Give the team some leeway to create a better, more culturally appropriate translation.

About Controlled English

The trend among many international organizations is to move toward "controlled English" in documents to be translated. Using controlled English in a document requires that you

- Restrict the core vocabulary. (You might want to make exceptions to this rule, to accommodate your target keywords for SEO.)

- Use a limited range of simple sentence structures.

- Apply it to commercial and technical information, such as operating instructions and simple descriptive writing.

- Simplify as much as possible, whenever you are presenting complex information.

Controlled English is not particularly well suited for theoretical discussions, abstract analyses, or creative writing (all of which are atypical to corporate websites). The advantage of using a writing style like this is that it controls the text quality, accuracy, and consistency between the original English text and its translated counterparts.

Controlled English: An Example   Table 10.1 illustrates several sentences that have had controlled English applied; compare the original text with the edited version to get a feeling for the writing style. Active writing, simpler phrases, and clear verbs are part of the controlled English writing style.

The editing process eliminates passive voice, indirect references or vague adjectives (such as *they*, *main*, or *whole*) complex sentence structures, and nonstandard verbs (*pay out*, *lock up*, *power down*, *reboot*).

Table 10.1 Before and After Sentences, When Editing Using Controlled English

Before	After
Four phase power **is provided by** four generators.	Four generators **supply the** four-phase electrical power.
They are the **main source of power** for the **main** DC Bus and the **whole handheld tool appliance system**.	**These generators** are the **primary power source** for the **primary** DC Bus and the **handheld appliance**.
Three of the generators **are driven by** separate motors and one generator **is driven by** a separate backup power unit.	Three separate motors **operate** three of the generators. A backup power unit **operates** one generator.
The operator **pays out** the cable for the generator.	The operator **releases and controls** the cable for the generator.
If the handheld tool system **locks up, power it down** and **reboot** it.	If the handheld appliance **stops working and displays ***?, push the Off button. Wait for 30 seconds. Then push the On button to start it.**

Additional Methods   There are other competing schools of thought similar to controlled English, namely ASD Simplified Technical English, Basic English, Global English, Plain English, and Globish.

Some people prefer Global English because it can feel more like the original text when comparing it side by side. Global English is characterized by a set of specific (complex) sentence structures to *avoid* as opposed to a set of (simple) sentence structures to *apply*.

Don't get too hung up on which one to pick; they are all making a step in the right direction and can help you prepare your English text for translation by simplifying it.

Preparing Your Website for Translation and Localization

Work through your existing website content and follow these tips, before you send your text out to be translated, to avoid (costly) headaches:

- Use clear, concise controlled English, suitable for online presentation.
- Avoid noun phrases and multiple modifiers (no more than three nouns in a row).
- Avoid gerund phrases ("ing" verbs), which often have no equivalent in other languages.
- Avoid ambiguous direct and indirect objects.
- Avoid metaphors, analogies, and similes.
- Use active voice.
- Keep sentences short (15 to 25 words).
- Put statements in positive form.
- Avoid contractions.
- Avoid unnecessary words.
- Be consistent.
- Avoid too many polysyllabic words.
- Write for eighth grade reading level.
- Avoid idioms and slang.
- Avoid neologisms (newly developed words not yet part of the language).
- Avoid humor.
- Use standard symbols.
- Define acronyms and abbreviations.
- Remove cultural bias.

WORLD-READY ENGLISH

In addition to controlled English, which is a useful method for handling English text before translation, there is another concept known as *world-ready English*. This writing style seeks to eliminate the differences between British English and American English, effectively blurring the line (so that someone from Great Britain cannot identify the text as being from the United States and vice versa).

How is this done? By avoiding or working around terminology and phrases that identify the text as distinctly American or distinctly British.

For example, a British website might state "Whilst speaking to customers, we..." and the American version would be "While speaking to customers, we..." The world-ready version of this sentence would begin, "During customer evaluations, we..." thereby avoiding the whilst/while gap.

World-ready English is a convenient tool for those instances when you are not translating a document but you expect non-native English speakers around the world to be reading it. (Many countries emphasize British English in schools, so some uniquely American phrases could be confusing.)

Create a Glossary

It's helpful for your translation team to have a glossary of the English terms you use on your website. Perhaps you use multiple terms as synonyms, to boost your search engine rankings as part of your search engine optimization efforts.

But a translator (either human or machine) has no way of knowing that those two terms are identical. When two different terms are used, it is generally assumed that they have two different meanings. So you need to spell this out (that the terms are synonymous, for example), to avoid creating confusion during translation.

Deliver the glossary as soon as possible to your translation and localization team. This lets them identify terminology issues early on, clarify terminology, and expedite the translation process. In addition, you want to invest in keyphrase research in your target countries to choose the best fit translated terms both in terms of meaning and in terms of search volume.

Accept Cultural Differences

Don't be surprised when you receive a translated version of your website that is not an exact match to your English original. A good translation is *not a word-for-word match*. Cultural differences abound and need to be taken into account during translation.

For example, French instructions for using computers are much more indirect than in English. The French find the imperative voice ("Fill in your name and address, then download the whitepaper.") bossy, rude, and annoying.

Similar cultural differences exist for other European languages, and can be even more pronounced in Asian and Middle Eastern languages. (For example, a Japanese business document typically does not begin with an Executive Overview section, but instead a brief explanation of why the author has chosen to write the document.)

Case Study: Spidering to Keep All Localized Websites Up-to-Date

With the right technology partners, you can set up quite sophisticated systems to keep a set of international domains concurrent. One global company works with Translations.com to translate and host over 20 localized versions of its website. The foundation of the set of web properties is the English-language website, and it is updated regularly to reflect new products, offers, and content.

Translations.com keeps the localized websites in sync with the English website by spidering the English-language website periodically. This identifies changes that need to be reflected in all of the other language versions of the website. Translations.com translates the new copy and then provides translated drafts to the in-country marketing offices for review before the updates are published.

Basic Mechanics for a Global Metrics-Driven Practice

The critical gaps that exist between marketing and sales systems and processes are only amplified in global companies, because responsibilities might be divided between marketing and sales offices across the globe.

After you and your leadership define your sales engine goals, the trick is to

- Implement the tracking across many websites with different, country-specific top-level domains.

- Unify and standardize the sales force automation (SFA) or customer relationship management (CRM) interface and processes.

- Share reporting on opportunities and sales to feed back into the process.

This is an immense infrastructure project and will require the collaboration of teams across the globe. But without a common process and common goals, your company won't really have a global strategy or global reporting, but a jumble of local or regional approaches and practices instead.

Use a Single Website Analytics Program Globally

Website analytics programs may measure the same things slightly differently. When we have two different analytics programs running on the same website, the metrics vary in minor ways.

Using different analytics programs even to report the same metrics for different domains (say, using Yahoo! Web Analytics for the Japanese website and using Google Analytics for the U.S. website) may lead to confusion. Standardize within the same program across all your websites, and give yourself a common dashboard from which to review your websites and common definitions of metrics.

Set Your Web Analytics to Track Across Top-Level Domains

Your website will likely be set up to let visitors hop to the right country-specific top level domain. If they, by chance, arrive on the .com website, they may be able to jump to the Portuguese-language .br website from a pull-down menu or a country flag in the upper-right corner of the website.

Because you will encourage visitors to hop between domains, you should use a single analytics profile that spans all your website properties. This way, someone that moves from one of your domains to another (say example.com to example.co.uk to see your prices in British pounds rather than U.S. dollars) doesn't look like a visitor who left one domain and then arrived as a new visitor on another.

Aggregate the Analytics Profile

If you treat your country-specific websites as entirely separate websites, you inadvertently inflate your visits and visitor numbers and decrease your conversion rates. Instead, you want your country-specific websites to aggregate their analytics so that a visitor can be represented more accurately as having visited to multiple properties inside the same website constellation.

Within Google Analytics, it requires using the same web analytics profile number (i.e. UA-XXXXX-XX) on all your websites. Deploying the same Google Analytics snippet across all your websites is a snap to do if all of the websites share a common template.

Manual Aggregation of Analytics

But, the procedure is the same, but more manual, if your websites do not share a common template. In that case, you just have to make sure you deploy the same analytics tracking snippet across all your websites on all their pages.

After this is complete, you can then look at the performance of individual country websites by using advanced segments or by creating filtered profiles showing individual country-specific domains. Search on "cross domain tracking" in your website analytics program to learn how to bridge your websites into a summary profile.

Unify Your CRM or SFA Process

Similar to the reasons for unifying your web analytics into one platform across all of your top level domains, if you want to measure incoming leads across the globe, you will want to use a common CRM or SFA system. Otherwise, you won't have a common dashboard to measure the outcomes of your global marketing activities.

The challenges to unifying your CRM or SFA include the following:

- Standardizing address formats across widely varying conventions.

- Character set issues. The database may need to accept accent marks not used in English, Cyrillic characters, Japanese Hiragana, Thai script, Devanagari... and the list goes on. Unicode is typically the best choice for storing data that spans several languages and character sets.

- The need to follow different privacy and marketing guidelines in different jurisdictions.

- The need to reinforce or create standard processes for local sales teams located all over the globe.

- Training to help your team get the most from your CRM. Otherwise you run the risk of garbage in-garbage out.

Going with an SFA or CRM vendor that has built-in support for global character sets, currencies, and experience managing global data is a wise choice. If you are using Salesforce.com, David Taber's *Salesforce.com Secrets of Success* has many best practices and process design and alignment overviews.

Talk to Each Other!

Of course, no amount of process rigor and infrastructure investment can substitute for agreement and good feeling between colleagues, and this comes through meeting each other in person periodically and relatively frequent communications via conference calls, web meetings, email, and IM.

Of course, each of these methods of communication has its challenges in a world with different languages and social customs around interactions, but they are necessary elements to bind your team together.

Best Practices for Global Team Communications

Good global team management is basically regular old project management: useful meetings, clear goals, and "information radiators" for formal and informal knowledge and status sharing.

Tips for better international meetings include the following:

- **Have a regular schedule of meetings with clear agendas:** You might have an annual in-person meeting with monthly web conferences.

- **As always, revisit your goals and speak to progress made against them:** Nothing creates alignment like consistency of process, clarity of expectations, and repetition of what's important.

- **Speak clearly and slowly:** Sometimes the speed with which American English is spoken can be intimidating.

   One company holds a monthly conference call between the Korean, German, Indian, Chinese, and American quality management teams. The call is conducted in English, and although English is understood and spoken by all on the line, there is rarely any discussion or questions for the Americans. The explanation: The Americans talk so fast that others simply are intimidated to interact with them.

- **Consider the time:** Consider rotating the time of the meeting for conference calls so that everyone on the team across the globe gets to meet at times most suited to their time zone.

Tips to foster clear communication include the following:

- **Make a place for asynchronous, informal status communications:** If adopted widely, these virtual water coolers or status boards can take some noise out of email inboxes. Options include

   - 37Signals's Campfire, http://campfirenow.com/

   - Harvest's Co-Op, http://coopapp.com/

   - Yammer, www.yammer.com

   - Salesforce's Chatter, www.salesforce.com/chatter/whatischatter/

- **Avoid local dialect and nonstandard English:** Many people will have learned British English in school, so phrases like *y'all* might not be understood.

Basic Mechanics for Global Organic Search Visibility

If you following best practices on your English-language, U.S.-based .com website to be found by folks looking for answers by search, you should have a great start on organic visibility for international searchers. All the same principles apply:

- **Don't get in your own way by hiding important content** in inaccessible web technologies (see "Watch Your Web Technologies" and "Avoid using Multimedia for Critical and Unique SEO Content" in Chapter 8 "It's All About Visibility").

- **Label things appropriately** so that they can be found on your website, including image and media files (see "Take Advantage of Universal Search: Tag Your Media Files with Target Keywords" in Chapter 8).

- **Build meaningful inlinks** to your website to demonstrate your company's credibility (see "Link-Building Fundamentals" in Chapter 8).

Most likely, you'll need the help of your team on the ground in each of your target countries to identify the sources of valuable inlinks, to create content in the target language, and to prioritize which keyphrases are most valuable to target in your labeling.

The only additional wrinkles for international SEO include the greater variety of search engines out there. Your team will need to do its homework ahead to ensure you're targeting the right search engine and make sure you use the appropriate web address to maximize your visibility.

Focus on the Correct Search Engine

If you want your website to be found, pay attention to where people go to search. In most of the world, Google is the top search engine. Google is king in the Americas and much of Europe and the Middle East, but a distant second or third to other search engines in the five countries listed in Table 10.2.

Table 10.2 Five Countries Where Google Is Not the Dominant Search Engine

Region	Top Search Engine	Second Search Engine
Russia	Yandex	Google
China	Baidu	Google
Japan	Yahoo!	Google
South Korea	Naver	Daum
Taiwan	Yahoo!	Google

Review the top search engines in key countries and follow suggestions for targeting your content to be found there.

Optimization Outside of Google

Although Google is still very dominant in many countries across the world, there are some places, notably where other character sets are more prevalent, where local search engines outrank Google. If you're interested in marketing in one of those countries, look at them to see how search engine optimization differs from Google (or Yahoo! U.S.).

Yandex (Russia)   Of the three non-Yahoo! search engines, optimizing for Yandex is the most similar to optimizing for Google. Yandex is said to be "Google-like" in its use of inlinks and page content to rank websites, but has a deeper understanding of Russian grammar and vocabulary that, so far, gives it an edge over Google there.

Baidu (China)   Although Chinese has many important regional dialects, Baidu operates in simplified and traditional Chinese. Baidu is influenced by such things as whether it is a Chinese top-level domain (see below) and whether your website is hosted in mainland China. Baidu places more emphasis on metadata than Google does.

Naver (South Korea)   Naver is less than an index of the entire Internet in Korean language than a guide to user content within the Naver network of social media websites and user-generated content.

The Naver results page pioneered mixing social, video, image, and website listings that Google adopted as "universal search." For that reason, Naver depends less on the traditional sources of SEO strength for Google (inlinks, content relevance, and consistent labeling).

Daum (South Korea)   Like Naver, Daum is more a guide to user-generated content within its forums than a classic index. It has a popular and sometimes controversial forum, called Agora, where people discuss news, politics, and pop culture. Similar to Naver, SEO requires more effort in social media mentions.

Yahoo! (Taiwan)   Although Yahoo! has merged with MSN/Bing globally, the roll-out of Bing powering Yahoo! search results had only started at the time of this writing. Yahoo! organic search results in Taiwan will be populated by Bing as it is in the United States and Canada.

Yahoo! (Japan)   Interestingly, Yahoo! Japan did not merge with MSN/Bing as Yahoo! did elsewhere, so Yahoo! in Japan will have searches populated by Google rather than by Bing. So, in Japan, you can use the same optimization practices you use for Google, because Yahoo! Japan results will be Google results.

But, this is all changing rapidly, and there's a fair bit of misinformation available, so keep an eye on the current state if you're focused on Taiwan and Japan.

Search Engine Popularity Fluctuates   Search engine popularity is relatively dynamic, as Google surpassed Seznam in the Czech Republic only recently. You want to check for the most recent statistics for your target markets!

Tune Your Social Strategy to the Right Channel

Although Google is close to dominating the international search engine landscape, the international social media landscape is more diverse. Therefore, your social media strategy should not focus on only one website, such as Twitter or Facebook.

Instead, consider where your target audience may go. Brazilians like Google's Orkut best, and Russians prefer Vkontakte to Facebook. In China, Qzone has beaten Facebook for market share.

Over the past few quarters, Facebook has overtaken some homegrown social networks, so it is worth checking for the most up-to-date statistics before committing to a particular website in a global social media visibility strategy.

Mind Your Website Top-Level Domains

Use country-specific top-level domains (TLDs) for best organic search visibility in your target countries. The list of TLDs is managed by the Internet Assigned Numbers Authority (IANA).

So, our mythical TropiCo company should use www.example.com for the United States (and www.example.br for Brazil rather than www.example.com/brazil or br.example.com).

If your research indicates you're targeting Google, you can use Google Webmaster Tools to set international targeting for your websites.

If you cannot use the appropriate TLD and you must fudge things a little by using a subdomain or subdirectory, *and* you are also targeting Google in that country, you can give Google a little help to find you by setting your geographic targeting in your Google Webmaster Tools account (see Figure 10.3).

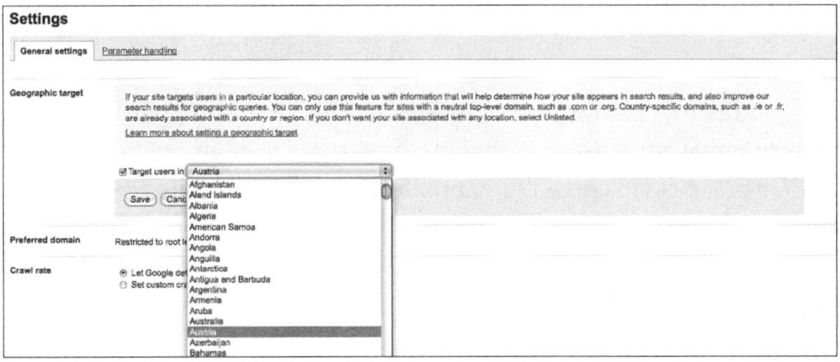

Figure 10.3 *Setting your geographic target in Google Webmaster Tools.*

Basic Mechanics for Global Paid Search Configuration

Deploy your paid search in the most popular search engine for the country you're targeting (see Table 10.1 countries where Google is not the main engine). Only *after* you are getting all the leads you can for your budget (and to get additional leads you would have to pay more per lead) should you even consider going to the second search engine.

See "Projecting Return on Paid Search Optimization" in Chapter 9, "Running the Feedback Loop," for the logic behind this recommendation.

Create Regional Campaigns

After you've decided which search engines to target, you want to set up your campaigns specifically for each region. Even if your research tells you that all your paid search needs to be done in Google AdWords, you still want to break up your campaigns to target specific geographies and specific languages. Setting them up this way will help you track budgets and track your success at the regional level instead of averaging over everything.

Advertising in China

If you're going to focus on China, you need to set up an account with Baidu PPC Phoenix Nest, also known as Baidu PPC Search Marketing Pro. Account setup will be tricky for an English-language marketer because the user interface to manage paid search on the Baidu platform is available only in Chinese.

Your best bet here will be a local partner in China, or a relationship with a company or individual who is fluent in Chinese and familiar with Baidu's interface.

Advertising in Russia

If you focus on Russia, you want to set up your account with Yandex Direct, Yandex's paid search platform. Yandex Direct offers English-language online help materials to guide advertisers. Although the materials are in English, a successful Russian-language campaign will require fluent Russian to write ads and manage and optimize keyphrases.

Advertising in South Korea

Naver offers a mix of paid search options interspersed in its long and scrolling results page, rich with multimedia and social media information. Paid search on Naver used to include a section powered by Yahoo!'s search marketing engine, Overture, but as of 2011 it eliminated this relationship. Daum currently uses Overture for some paid search ads, although some believe it will follow Naver and also end its relationship with Yahoo!

English-language information about paid search in Naver and Daum is quite limited. Your best bet here is a local partner in Korea, or a partner local to you who is fluent in Korean and savvy in these search engines.

Advertising on Yahoo! for Japan and Taiwan

For the two countries that have Yahoo! as their top search engine, Japan and Taiwan, you need to pursue different strategies. For Yahoo! Taiwan, when it switches over to having its results fed by Bing, you can use the MSN adCenter interface. For Yahoo! Japan, when it switches over to having its results fed by Google, you can use Google AdWords.

Set Geographic Targets

You can set geographic targets in AdWords and other paid search platforms. Figure 10.4 shows the geographic targeting dialog for in the Google AdWords web interface, allowing you to pick bundles of countries or choose individual countries.

Use the Right Language

You need to focus on the appropriate language in your keyphrases, ad text, and landing pages. You also need to configure your paid search account to focus on appropriate languages. These are separate actions.

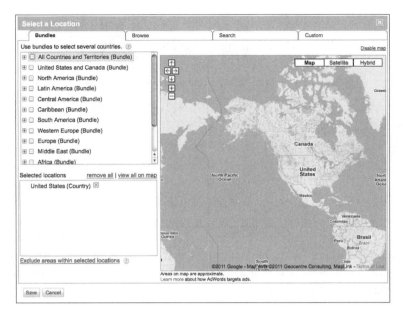

Figure 10.4 *Location targeting dialog in the Google AdWords web interface.*

Translate Your Keyphrases, Ads, and Landing Pages

Sometimes you get lucky, and because of the nature of the product, people will choose to search in English for it across the globe. We see this sometimes for scientific and technical products. More typically, though, especially with business-to-consumer (B2C) products, running English search terms in countries with other native languages is not going to be productive for you.

Table 10.3 shows competing examples, drawn from two companies both advertising in Japan. In Example 1, the English language paid search has much more limited visibility compared to the Japanese language keyphrases and ads; it garnered fewer impressions and saw disproportionately fewer clicks.

In Example 2, however, the English phrases have higher visibility and a higher clickthrough rate. One thing that might explain the difference for Example 2 is that both English language and Japanese search terms are available for an ad campaign running in Japan. The Japanese terms are translations of the English terms, done by native Japanese speakers in Japan.

In both cases, in Table 10.3, the total impressions and clicks across the English-language and the Japanese-language campaigns is higher for having both languages available. So, it's worth doing the translation and also testing English language terms if that is appropriate for your audience.

Table 10.3 Impressions (Ads Seen), Clicks (Ads Clicked) and Clickthrough Rate for Two AdWords Paid Search Campaigns in Japan

Campaign	Language of Keyphrases and Ads	Impressions	Clicks	Clickthrough Rate
Example 1	English	57,115	212	0.37%
Example 1	Japanese	280,911	1,455	0.52%
Example 2	English	75,138	798	1.06%
Example 2	Japanese	49,776	305	0.61%

Don't forget that landing pages typically contain a focal image that might need to be "translated," as well. For example, the landing page for an appliance store displaying products typically sold in North America would look very odd to someone from Europe, where the washing machines, dryers, and refrigerators are all considerably smaller. Here's another situation where a little A/B testing up front can save a campaign.

Configure the Language for Paid Search

Choose the appropriate language to display your geotargeted campaigns, as shown in Figure 10.5. We've seen folks frustrated because their German-language paid search ads were getting no visibility in Germany because their German terms were restricted to matching English phrases.

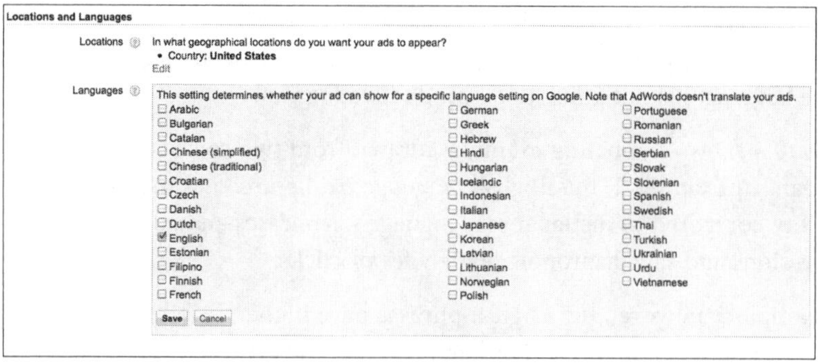

Figure 10.5 *Set your location and language for ad groups in the Google AdWords interface.*

Working with Time Zones

Watch your time zones, too! We've also seen a business-to-business (B2B) company showing ads in Australia based on the business day in the United States. This settings glitch had the ads showing in Melbourne from 1:00 a.m. to 9:00 a.m., almost exactly backward from when they should have been visible!

We typically do not restrict timing on showing ads, but if you do, be careful about time zones! Figure 10.6 shows the Google AdWords dialog for restricting the time and day of week for ad display.

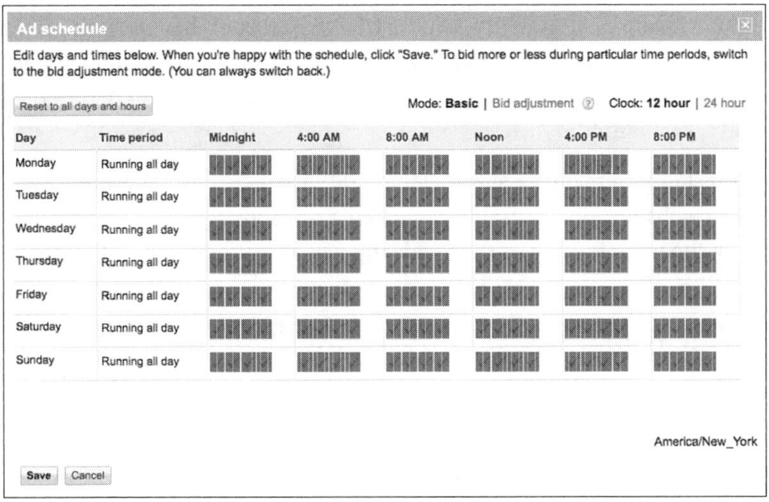

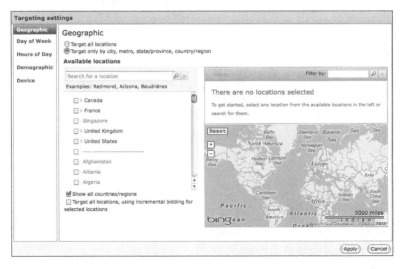

Figure 10.6 *Time-of-day configuration in Google AdWords web interface. Note the time zone in the lower right.*

There are similar dialogs in the MSN adCenter interface for setting location targeting and time of day, as shown in Figure 10.7.

Figure 10.7 *The targeting settings dialog in the MSN adCenter paid search platform.*

Basic Mechanics for Global Usability

You might very well wonder whether anything in this world could ever be defined as "globally usable." (Even a simple tool such as the fork is not globally usable, at least not without some training.)

Perhaps one day, globally usable will be the standard for typical website development. But today, global usability is more of a stretch goal than something realistically attainable, particularly with budgetary constraints in place. Still, you can take some measures to do the best you can today (and hopefully, do a better job at it than your competition).

What you should remember about global usability is that one size does *not* fit all. To make a website globally usable, you need to customize at the local level. Changing the website copy to the local language is just one step in the process.

Before You Translate: Character Set Issues

Make sure your content management system (CMS) can display the character sets required for the languages you intend to display.

In the code for each HTML page in your website should be a single line defining the character set used on the page. This information can be included on the page in the page template, or through the .htaacess file, or set individually on a page by page basis, depending on your CMS configuration.

When this specification is omitted, the visitor's browser may default to a standard character set, which might not map well to the content on the page and provide a bad user experience and potentially hide your content from search. Make sure you have things set up well so that your translated pages render seamlessly.

Tip

In addition, make sure that your browser has the right fonts available to render pages in other languages, just so you can see what's on the page! Your browser should do a pretty good job out of the box, but if you are seeing nonsense characters on pages in another language, look for a language pack for your browser or your computer to bridge the gap.

Working with Forms

User interface elements, such as those on a basic contact form, need to be adjusted to handle international addresses:

- Many countries format the street name before the street number (Main Street 123, not 123 Main Street).

- ZIP (or postal) codes often precede the city name, and can include alphabetic characters as well as numbers.

- Remember to include a drop-down list to select the country.

- Phone numbers might include country codes (preceded by a plus sign), and have other unusual punctuation conventions (comma, period, or underscore), that vary from North American standards. Other countries often have longer phone numbers (more digits), as well.

The bottom line is that you should loosen your data-checking constraints on addresses, to allow website visitors to actually complete a form and become a new prospect. Another option is to create multiple forms with different data checking rules for different countries and address formats.

Working with Other Data

Here are some additional data guidelines to increase the usability of your website content:

- Date formats also vary by country (days often precede the month, for example). Even when a date is used in a sentence, the format varies from the American English standard.

- Be aware that most of the world uses the metric system for units of measurement.

- Provide temperatures in both Fahrenheit and Celsius.

- Currency conversion should be addressed.

- Electrical standards also vary (110 volt versus 220 volt).

If you have a product that works with multiple standards, explicitly state that to avoid ambiguity. It won't affect your North American customers, and someone overseas won't buy your product unless they're sure it will work in their country.

A Note for E-Commerce Websites

Do not forget that website visitors living in other countries need different payment options on an e-commerce website. One of our authors lives in Germany and has had countless experiences where an e-commerce website's shopping cart cannot accommodate a credit card with a foreign billing address (even when shipping within the United States).

It's important to note, as well, that the online shopping economy of many countries simply doesn't work with credit cards. You'll exclude website visitors, and therefore sales, if you require a credit card in some countries. (For example, in Germany only 5% of the population has a Visa or MasterCard, and only "touristy" restaurants accept them... yet you can pay at any restaurant using your ATM bank card instead.)

Consider accepting other payment methods besides the standard credit cards. An international wire transfer, which seems daunting to a U.S. customer, is standard fare throughout Europe when shopping online. (Many people bank online, so it's a simple matter of opening a new window to complete the transaction separately at your bank.)

 Tip

Take a look at what eBay, PayPal, and Amazon do in your target countries. What payment types do they accept and how do they handle shopping cart checkouts? This is a good way to get an idea of what online payment methods are typical in a target country.

Making It Usable

The real goal is to create a website targeted to a country, matching the website visitor's cultural characteristics. (Language is just a start.) This means going beyond getting the simple things right, like avoiding offensive graphics.

More important, the website must work in the way that business is done in that country. It should look as much as possible like a website native to that country, for the best results. When you meet an overseas website visitor's expectations, the likelihood of a successful online interaction increases.

The inherent problem with striving for global usability is that there is not one way to design a website that is most usable to every culture, worldwide. You need to examine your target markets, your expected growth in those foreign markets, and weigh the cultural differences against your sales goals to identify how far you're willing to go to meet cultural expectations with your website.

Conduct Testing Locally

Ideally, with a sky-is-the-limit budget, you would conduct usability testing locally, in each of your target countries, to create a set of websites that each appeared culturally appropriate to its target audience.

Consider that you'll need to get around the language barrier to local usability testing, somehow. Do you speak (or understand) other languages? Can you recruit usability test participants that speak some English so that you can understand what is happening while you watch behind the one-way mirror?

Another option to test locally while reducing costs is to have staff in your overseas offices conduct the usability testing, even though they are not trained in usability practices. This often eliminates the language barrier, although the test results may not be as accurate or presented as well as a usability specialist might have done.

Of course, there is more than one way to conduct usability testing. We've outlined several methods in "Qualitative User Analysis: Observations, Usability Tests" in Chapter 7, "Making Websites That Work."

Conduct Testing Remotely

One often-preferred method of conducting usability testing in foreign markets is to use remote testing, which can be more attractive economically than in-person testing in another country.

Remote testing involves using a desktop sharing tool such as WebEx to see the test participant run through a prototype of your website, and you can use an audio link or the telephone in conjunction with it.

The upside is that costs are reduced, the downside is that you can't observe participants working through the test, only their onscreen actions, so you have very little visual feedback. Another potential downside is that you may need to be in your office at extremely strange hours to accommodate the time difference in your target market.

Something Is Better Than Nothing

Clearly, there are pros and cons for applying any of these methods to achieve global usability. But it is better to attempt a more usable website for each of your target audiences than simply to ignore your foreign markets and design a website interface solely for North America.

It might feel overwhelming to realize that you have market share in multiple countries and must test in each and every one. Don't panic. Start slowly, but *do* start. Choose a target country in each of the main areas of the world (one in Europe, one in Africa, one in Asia, and so on).

Or if you can choose just one country due to budget constraints, then do so. You'll learn so much from that first test that it's well worth the effort.

Summary

The path to international Internet marketing success is exactly the same as the path for any other marketing success: setting goals, tracking metrics, speaking to your customer, and making a website that works for your local audience. Yet, the complexity of translating content, obtaining data from business units and offices across the globe, and brokering agreement on standard lead management process adds to the challenge.

Be undaunted; good data and success lie in wait for those who brave the thickets of data gathering and content creation across many field offices and many websites.

Confirm you've handled the international basics as well as worked through the language and translation issues:

- The key to global success is translated, localized, relevant content.

- Simplify and standardize your writing to prepare for translation.

- Create a glossary for often used terms. Research the SEO value of alternative translations.

- Build a process to keep your websites up-to-date.

- Create and maintain one unified global dashboard for your web analytics and CRM reporting.

   Choose or build your CMS to accommodate the variation in addresses and currency necessary to your markets.

- Focus on the right search engines in your target markets for search engine optimization and paid search. At the time of this writing, the top engine was Google except within Russia, China, South Korea, Japan, and Taiwan.

   For paid search, use the correct language, geography, and time zone settings to ensure your campaigns are visible.

- Make sure your forms and shopping cart checkout work in your target countries.

- Invest in diversifying your user research to include an international audience. Test in as many locations as you can.

Appendix

TropiCo's State of the Web Report

Our mythical company, TropiCo, made some progress with their online sales engine in the past year and created a corporate "State of the Web" report to share with other business units and shareholders.

This report was prepared for two of TropiCo's Tropical Business Groups divisions: the Pineapple Company and the Passionfruit Company. The report reviews the past year, compares the data from the previous year, and examines why the successes occurred. It also includes a section on how the team plans for move forward from here.

Table of Contents

Executive Summary

Part I. The Year in Review: The Data

General Traffic Trends

Geographic Distribution

Traffic Sources

Quarterly Leads Trends

Part II. How It Happened

Paid Search (Setup, Management, and Expansion)

Search Engine Optimization

Usability

Local Search

Referral Media

Strategy, Analysis, and Reporting

Part III. Looking Forward to 2012

Localize the Online User Experience

Engagement: Move Online Strategy Toward Interactive Brand Experience

Maintain Momentum from FY 2011

Executive Summary

The past year, 2011, was a year of significant change in the online presence for both of TropiCo's Tropical Business Group brands, the Pineapple Company and the Passionfruit Company. This report is a brief summary of changes that occurred, their causes, and recommendations for fiscal year (FY) 2012. This report is divided into three separate sections: Parts I, II, and III.

About Part I

Part I, "The Year in Review: The Data," summarizes the year's trends. There are four major highlights:

- Search engine traffic to the Passionfruit Company and Pineapple Company websites increased almost 60% in FY 2011.

- The year 2011 saw tremendous overall growth in both total website visitors and leads.

- We increased the diversity of marketing channels and the kinds of visitors who came to the websites by adding local search to the activities.

- A test market study revealed that presumably three out of four people who contact a Passionfruit Company or a Pineapple Company smoothie bar after visiting the website do so by picking up the phone and calling.

About Part II

Part II, "How It Happened," reviews the budget and how we used it to make a significant impact. There were three major areas of focus:

- **Paid search:** We leveraged past successes by implementing a systemwide paid search campaign for the Pineapple Company and expanding paid search for the Passionfruit Company.

- **Increased visibility:** We moved toward reducing dependence on paid search by implementing search engine optimization (SEO) strategies to improve the organic visibility of the websites.

- **Analytics:** In FY 2011, we performed visitor behavior analyses to assess whether visitors to the Pineapple Company and the Passionfruit Company websites were getting the most possible out of their visit. We began to "close the loop" and link website visits with phone calls.

About Part III

Part III, "Looking Forward to 2012," describes how we will continue to grow the online presence of the Passionfruit Company and the Pineapple Company brands in the coming fiscal year.

Part I. The Year in Review: The Data

This section provides a high-level overview of the major trends and traffic observed in FY 2011. As much as possible, we compare the data to FY 2010 and make comparisons between the two brands.

General Traffic Trends

An increasing number of Americans are using search engines to find what they need online. Paid search campaigns are continuously optimized to take advantage of the increase in traffic. Additional steps have been taken to ensure that visitors who reach the websites are more likely to turn into leads.

In contrast to the increase in search engine traffic, we experienced a drop in other marketing channel efforts, such as referrals and direct traffic in FY 2011. We suspect that visitors are relying on Google as their "bookmark" engine, often typing in a keyphrase that got them to the website in the past, instead of trying to remember or spell the name of the company or service.

This is a huge shift in user patterns, and shows that the value of other sources, such as referrals, may decrease in the coming years.

It is important to note, however, that the decrease in direct traffic is not an indication that offline brand awareness is any less important. Based on our analysis, people who might have typed "pineapplecompany.com" directly into their browser are now instead typing it into their search engine. Therefore, offline brand awareness continues to be an important part of TropiCo's Tropical Business Group marketing strategy.

The increase in daily traffic was reflected in both the Pineapple Company and the Passionfruit Company's website traffic. Figure A.1 shows that the average number of daily visitors increased 23% for the Passionfruit Company and almost 100% for the Pineapple Company between FY 2010 and FY 2011.

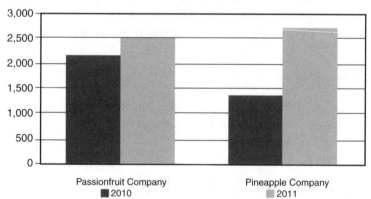

Figure A.1 *Average visitors per day by brand.*

Geographic Distribution

Almost all geographies were winners in FY 2011 growth, but large regional markets saw significant increases in traffic as both the Passionfruit Company and the Pineapple Company increased their online presence in these very competitive areas.

Figure A.2 shows how much of an increase the Passionfruit Company saw in its three largest regional markets; for the Pineapple Company, there was a similarly large increase in the Michigan, Ohio, Pennsylvania, Florida, and Illinois markets.

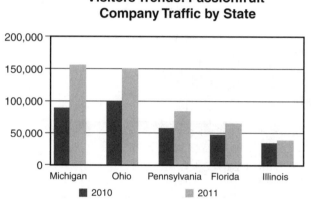

Figure A.2 *Passionfruit Company traffic by state for FY 2010 and FY 2011.*

Traffic Sources

Not all market channels increased equally in FY 2011, especially for the Pineapple Company. Figures A.3 and A.4 show large increases in both organic search and paid search traffic for the Passionfruit Company and the Pineapple Company web-sites, while direct (bookmarked) referral (traffic from other websites) and paid directory (Internet Yellow Pages) traffic remained stable or dropped off.

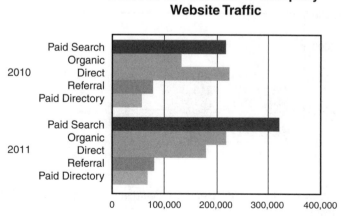

Figure A.3 *Sources of Passionfruit Company website traffic.*

Given that the Pineapple Company launched a paid search strategy in FY 2011 beyond just the few isolated markets in FY 2010, the brand saw a huge increase in paid search, going from very minimal website traffic to nearly 300,000 visitors.

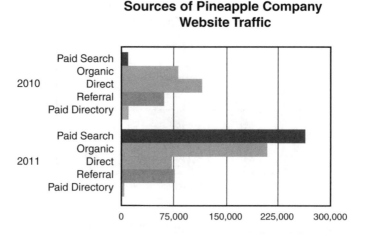

Figure A.4 *Sources of Pineapple Company website traffic.*

Quarterly Leads Trends

While website traffic increased in FY 2011, lead generation increased even more. Figure A.5 shows the increase in leads for each quarter as compared to FY 2010. In FY 2011, the two combined brands increased the number of leads generated in FY 2010 by more than 45%.

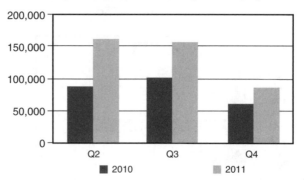

Figure A.5 *Leads by quarter for the Passionfruit Company and the Pineapple Company, combined by fiscal year.*

Part II. How It Happened

The results we've reported were a direct consequence of the activities planned for at the beginning of FY 2011. Broadly speaking, our activities fell into these categories:

- **Paid search:** We launched paid search campaigns for the Pineapple Company beyond those in minimal isolated markets. We leveraged past successes for the Passionfruit Company by expanding paid search beyond Google, to Yahoo! and Bing. Landing pages, which highlight regional information, were implemented for the Passionfruit Company's paid search campaigns in a variety of test geographies.

- **Search engine optimization and usability:** We moved toward reducing dependence on paid search by implementing SEO strategies to improve the organic visibility of the websites. We took advantage of local search opportunities, and tested referral media strategies to harness the power of opinion leaders, creating buzz and increasing traffic to the websites.

- **Strategy, analysis, and reporting:** In FY 2011, we ensured that our efforts were working properly through careful data testing and measurement, including detailed monthly reporting. We wanted to make sure that website visitors were getting the most possible from their website visit, and were being "led" to contact a smoothie bar. Finally, for the Passionfruit Company, we also started to close the loop between marketing efforts and orders with a pilot program, tracking online visitors and phone calls.

- **Local search:** All local search listings for the Pineapple Company and the Passionfruit Company smoothie bars were updated on Google and Yahoo! to be accurate and reflect the current brand language.

- **Referral media:** At the beginning of FY 2011, a strategy was explored to link from restaurant and smoothie bar online directories to generate traffic to the Pineapple Company and Passionfruit Company websites.

- **Expenditures:** Table A.1 and Figure A.6 show the activities and dollar expenditures for FY 2011 for both the Pineapple Company and the Passionfruit Company brands, organized by activity.

Table A.1 Actual Budget Summary for Pineapple Company and Passionfruit Company Brands

Category	Pineapple Company	Passionfruit Company
Paid Search Advertising, including Setup and Management	$350,000	$525,000
Search Engine Optimization	$55,000	$82,500
Usability	$35,000	$52,500
Local Search	$10,000	$15,000
Referral Media	$35,000	$52,500
Strategy, Analysis, and Reporting	$15,000	$22,500
Total FY 2011 Budget	**$500,000**	**$750,000**

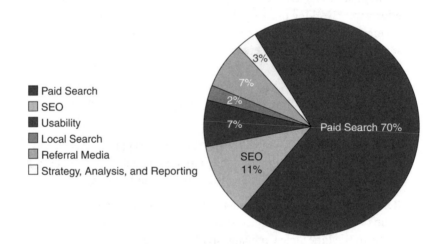

- Paid Search
- SEO
- Usability
- Local Search
- Referral Media
- Strategy, Analysis, and Reporting

3%
7%
2%
7%
Paid Search 70%
SEO 11%

Figure A.6 *Proportion of the Passionfruit Company budget spent for each activity in FY 2011. The Pineapple Company has a similar proportion for each activity.*

The next sections of this report describe in detail how each strategy was implemented and highlight the key outcomes.

Paid Search (Setup, Management, and Expansion)

In terms of both budget effort and results, paid search was the cornerstone of the FY 2011 effort for Pineapple Company and Passionfruit Company.

Strategies

Our key strategies for paid search were to

- Improve customer qualification.

- Launch the Pineapple Company campaigns systemwide, expanding from minimal isolated markets. Expand both the Pineapple Company and the Passionfruit Company campaigns into additional search engines, increasing reach and reducing the cost per conversion.

- Develop regional landing pages to increase conversion rates.

Implementation

Customer qualification was achieved through optimizing keyphrases and managing ad copy. A series of careful, tactical management efforts included improved targeting and conversion rates for individual keyphrases. We also made continual adjustments of bids for keywords that were too expensive for the value they created. Ad copy was optimized through A/B testing.

Expanding into additional search markets was an initiative started in Q1 FY 2011. Expansion included Yahoo! and Bing, as well as the Content Network for the Passionfruit Company. At the beginning of FY 2011, Google AdWords made up 100% of all paid search engine traffic.

By the end of 2011, the ratio for both Pineapple Company and Passionfruit Company was

- 77% Google AdWords

- 23% Yahoo!/Bing

These distributions are also a reflection of the actual market share of each engine. Google AdWords reflects an enormous proportion of overall search engine traffic, with Yahoo! and Bing a distant second. Bing continues to be relatively minimal. The diversification among these search engines has resulted in increased reach and a lower overall cost per conversion as Yahoo! and Bing are less expensive.

At the beginning of Q4 FY 2011, we developed regional landing pages for paid search traffic in five selected pilot markets (Michigan, Ohio, Pennsylvania, Illinois, and Florida) to assess whether regional content on landing pages would improve conversion rates.

Outcomes

The FY 2011 paid search strategy was very successful. Table A.2 highlights major paid search optimization results for Passionfruit Company comparing FY 2010 to FY 2011. As the table demonstrates, leads and lead-conversion rates increased in FY 2011, while the cost per conversion went down.

Table A.2 Comparison of Paid Search Efforts for Passionfruit Company Brand in FY 2010 and FY 2011

Period	Leads	Lead-Conversion Rate	Cost per Lead
2011	15,000	1.75%	$35.00
2010	1,155	1.05%	$61.00

The Pineapple Company did not have a substantial paid search campaign before FY 2011, making a year-to-year comparison not possible. Figure A.7 shows how the cost per lead decreased across the fiscal year as the campaign was optimized. The cost per lead did not exceed $40 after December 2010. Monthly leads increased over the course of the year, but are also affected by seasonality.

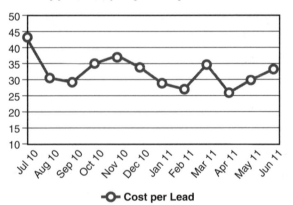

Pineapple Company Cost per Lead - FY 2011

Figure A.7 *Cost per lead for FY 2011.*

The effort to carefully manage keyphrases and ad copy improved conversion rates from FY 2010, as well. Figure A.8 shows the results for each marketing channel between the two years. Conversion rates across different market channels did not improve nearly as dramatically as conversion rates for paid search.

Paid search showed the greatest improvement in overall conversion rate, although organic search and direct traffic (visitors who are aware of a brand) represent the highest conversion rates.

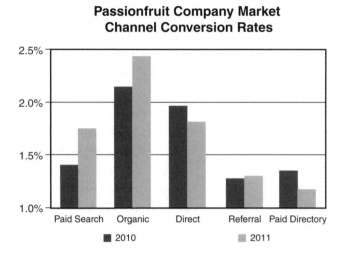

Passionfruit Company Market Channel Conversion Rates

Figure A.8 *Passionfruit Company market channel conversion rates across fiscal year. Pineapple Company has similar distributions.*

Generally, conversion rates for organic search will be higher, but as the Passionfruit Company and Pineapple Company start to experience higher organic visibility on keywords less directly associated with their name, this number may drop. We predict that conversion rates for paid search will continue to improve in FY 2012.

Table A.3 shows how expanding into additional markets reduced the overall cost of paid search by using more efficient but less visited search engines like Yahoo! and Bing.

Table A.3 Cost per Lead by Brand and Search Engine, FY 2011

Category	Pineapple Company	Passionfruit Company
Google AdWords	$57.00	$42.00
MSN AdCenter (Yahoo! and Bing)	$39.50	$32.50

As Table A.3 shows, the Pineapple Company has a higher overall cost per lead when compared to Passionfruit Company. The Passionfruit Company and Pineapple Company do not have identical strategies as their budgets differ.

The Passionfruit Company budget affords us the opportunity to emphasize "exposure" as part of the goal of the campaign, with website traffic seen as an opportunity to develop and cultivate brand. Therefore, we accept higher cost per clicks to generate traffic that may not convert right away as long as the time spent on the website is significant.

In addition, the Passionfruit Company smoothie bars have a denser presence than the Pineapple Company in some of the very competitive markets.

Fruit smoothie paid search costs in Metropolitan Philadelphia and Southern Florida are more than 40% higher than the national average for the same keywords, which means that the Passionfruit Company smoothie bars are paying significantly more per click in those markets.

The preliminary results of the Passionfruit Company regional landing page test are encouraging. To date, the regional landing pages have generated 81 conversions at a conversion rate of 3.26%. The nonregional landing pages have generated 24 conversions at a conversion rate of 2.45%.

Additional data is required to provide conclusive results, but the data to date is very promising. If the +.81% conversion rate difference continues, this effort could increase total leads for FY 2012 by as much as 30% for the same paid search traffic.

Search Engine Optimization

As powerful as paid search is for online marketing, paid search traffic encompasses approximately 20% of all online search engine traffic. The other 80% is organic search traffic. A key goal in FY 2011 was to identify ways to improve the visibility of the Passionfruit Company and Pineapple Company websites for people using organic search as their primary information gathering tool.

Strategies

Organic search improvements are made through a series of small, tactical improvements that can make a large impact on overall visibility. Generally these decisions revolve around two major goals:

- Increasing the amount of content in general
- Careful selection of targeted keyphrases to use in the website content

A key goal of these activities is to create visibility for non-brand name keywords in organic search. For the Passionfruit Company and Pineapple Company, our research found that people looking for smoothie bars used keywords such as

- Smoothie
- Daiquiris
- Fruit bar

Implementation

In some cases, these are not keywords that Passionfruit Company or Pineapple

Company would use to describe themselves, but analysis showed overwhelmingly that these are the keywords used by customers to find smoothie bars provided by the Pineapple Company or the Passionfruit Company. When people reach the website using these keywords, they can get a strong sense of the Passionfruit Company and Pineapple Company brands.

After identifying the most strategic targeted keyphrases for the Passionfruit Company and Pineapple Company, we increased the website's visibility of these keywords with these recommendations:

- Changes to page titles and tags

- Introduction of inline link text to emphasize essential keyphrases

- Changes to the technical infrastructure of the website to expose local copy (particularly smoothie bar location data in search results)

- Bringing the newsletter content forward within the website, thus improving organic visibility

Implementation of these modifications has begun for both websites and we anticipate a launch of these revisions early in FY 2012. We expect a solid impact on the visibility of the Pineapple Company and Passionfruit Company websites for these nonbranded organic search keywords.

Usability

As important as traffic is to a website, the key measure of its success is how many visitors take action. A major goal of our FY 2011 efforts was to identify ways to improve the Passionfruit Company and Pineapple Company websites so that visitors could more easily get the information they need and then contact a smoothie bar.

Subtle changes to usability can have big effects. If a change improves conversion rates by even half a %, for example, it could increase the number of leads for the Passionfruit Company by nearly 300 leads per month.

Strategies

We analyzed 1 year of web server logfiles with the goal of developing strategies to improve the overall conversion rate. As a result of our analysis, we recommended

- Changes to page copy (including changes to layout for easier online reading and skimming)

- Richer interlinking of internal pages to clarify which topics are covered on which pages (sometimes called improving the "information scent")

- Improvements to the locate-a-smoothie bar process

Implementation

These changes are scheduled for completion early in FY 2012 for both the Passionfruit Company and Pineapple Company websites.

Strategy, Analysis, and Reporting

The essence of the Internet marketing strategy revolves around measuring effects, testing theories, and taking action after we learn something valuable. All the previously described activities in this report include *some* reporting and analysis component, but two analytical questions emerged during the fiscal year.

These questions were:

- Will the introduction of local franchise websites have a negative impact on sales or leads, relative to the same visitors using the corporate website?

- How many people who come to one of the brands' websites make contact through a phone call?

Local Franchisee Versus Corporate Website

In early Q2 2011, TropiCo's Tropical Business Group introduced a program that allowed the Passionfruit Company franchises to set up websites that would allow them to post information for their individual smoothie bars. TropiCo's Tropical Business Group also agreed to link the corporate website's "locate a smoothie bar" results to the local websites. A major question about the project was whether the local websites would have a positive or negative impact on conversion rates.

Using a sophisticated Google Analytics configuration, we were able to track visitor traffic that started on the main corporate website and then was redirected to a local website during a website search. The analytics configuration was completed in Q4 2011.

By June, we had two major findings:

- Visitors using paid search almost never went to a local website but instead completed the contact form on the corporate website.

- Conversion rates for local websites were about as good or slightly higher than for the corporate website.

To date, 125 conversions have been tracked. The majority of traffic was to websites for smoothie bars that have recently opened. Now that they are open, we will be able to identify a clear set of patterns and trends, but our tentative conclusion is that local websites will not have a significant positive or negative impact on conversion rates.

Close the Loop Test

A key question that we set out to answer at the beginning of 2011 was "how many phone calls are we getting as a result of website traffic?" In Q3 2011, we set up a test deployment of a phone call tracking mechanism to assess numbers of conversions through phone calls, as opposed to web form submissions.

The test included 24 Passionfruit Company corporate smoothie bars in Southern Florida. Five months of data have been collected for pilot smoothie bars.

As Tables A.4 and A.5 show, results suggest that call volume in Southern Florida is extremely high when compared to people using contact forms across Florida as a whole. Table A.4 contains call data for the Passionfruit Company for Southern Florida, while Table A.5 contains target markets and directories for both companies across Florida.

Table A.4 Total Calls and Average Minutes per Call Across 24 Southern Florida Passionfruit Company Smoothie Bars, January to June 2011

Southern FL Calls	Average Minutes per Call
5,650	1.95

Table A.5 Total Visits, Conversions, and Conversion Rate for All Passionfruit Company Smoothie Bars in Florida, January to June 2011

FL Website Visits	Conversion Rate	Total Conversions
74,000	2.42%	2,100

This data suggests that phone calls resulting from website visits may make up more than 75% of all potential website leads. Although the exact value can't be calculated, leads generated by phone calls could mean that return on investment (ROI) for online marketing efforts is two to three times higher than current estimates.

In addition, 5 months of data confirm that if we can extrapolate the Southern Florida calls to a national level, the Passionfruit Company smoothie bars may be receiving over 9,100 calls per month!

The pilot study found striking differences in the average call length across different smoothie bars, which suggests either differences in markets or different phone call processes.

Local Search

Local search is a kind of organic search that people use when looking for services in a specific location. It is a rapidly growing segment of search; searches with geographic modifiers made up over 80% of all organic keyphrases used to find the Passionfruit Company website in FY 2011.

We found that optimization of the websites for local search could have a real impact on traffic to the Passionfruit Company and Pineapple Company websites.

Strategies

The local search listing project was largely an implementation and maintenance effort carried over from FY 2010.

Implementation

In Q1 FY 2011, we submitted or updated listings on Yahoo! and Google for the Passionfruit Company and the Pineapple Company. In Q2 FY 2011, we optimized the listings using keyphrases identified in the search engine optimization assessment.

Throughout the year, we continued to

- Monitor reviews making sure that reviews were accurate, and then contested any as necessary

- Ensure the accuracy of listings

- Analyze traffic from local listings

Outcomes

Total traffic from local searches increased 83% to about 1,000 visitors per month in FY 2011 for the Passionfruit Company and Pineapple Company combined. This traffic represents high quality visits: Total conversions from local search increased over 117% in the same time period.

Maps.google.com visits increased 320%, with conversions up nearly 600%. Local.yahoo.com visits increased 55%, with conversions increasing 85%.

Although traffic from websites like Google maps was about 1 % of total traffic, there were two very promising trends in local search. First, the trends increased steadily over the year, which shows an increased interest in local search as a strategy by users.

Second, the effort to improve local search had a positive overall effect on nonbrand organic search. Organic search of nonbranded search keywords increased more than

170% in FY 2011, which was nearly three times the amount that overall organic search increased. The majority of these increases were from low-traffic, local searches, such as "smoothie bar in Pompano Beach" or "smoothie Columbus OH."

Referral Media

Links coming from other referring websites into the Passionfruit Company and the Pineapple Company websites help to raise the organic visibility in the search engines.

Strategies

A strategy implemented at the beginning of FY 2011 was the use of linking from other websites to generate qualified traffic to the Pineapple Company and the Passionfruit Company websites.

Implementation

Listings were implemented on directories for both the Passionfruit Company and the Pineapple Company in three test markets for each brand. Referring websites were chosen based on

- High overall traffic
- Topical relevance
- Geographic relevance

Table A.6 shows the markets and directories selected for each brand at the beginning of this pilot project.

Table A.6 Target Markets and Directories for the Pineapple Company and Passionfruit Company Brands

Brand	Target Markets	Target Directories
Passionfruit Company	Atlanta, GA Philadelphia, PA Minneapolis, MN	SmoothiesRUS.com Craigslist.com Frozenfruit.com
Pineapple Company	Atlanta, GA Miami, FL Cincinnati, OH	SmoothiesRUS.com Craigslist.com Frozenfruit.com

Outcomes

The managing editor for each target market was contacted resulting in the smoothie bar locations, as well as branded-specified text being listed in their restaurant and smoothie bar section. Most listings were in place by mid-September.

Traffic generated from this test was extremely low. The pilot is ongoing, but it appears that it will be much less cost-effective and powerful than other marketing channels.

Based on our findings, in early Q3 FY 2011 we reallocated 60% of the original budget to search engine optimization and usability projects.

Part III. Looking Forward to 2012

While our efforts in FY 2011 have been effective, we believe there are even more opportunities for improvement and growth. Our projected FY 2012 efforts fall into these categories:

- Localizing the online user experience
- Increasing engagement (develop an interactive brand experience)
- Maintaining momentum built from FY 2011 efforts

Localize the Online User Experience

To bring the online user experience to the local level for customers, we will expand efforts in two key areas:

- **Local search:** Given the success of local search efforts, we plan to continue to maintain local listings and measure their impact on the traffic to the Pineapple Company and Passionfruit Company websites.

- **Landing pages:** Pending final analysis of the Passionfruit Company results, we recommend that localized landing pages be rolled out across the Pineapple Company websites for all geographies.

  Planned implementation includes development of a dynamic tool to synchronize landing pages with smoothie bar databases, and include interactive maps on landing pages using the Google Maps application programming interface (API).

Engagement: Move Online Strategy Toward Interactive Brand Experience

To increase the level of engagement for website visitors, we plan to expand activity into more engaging social media:

- Enter brands within popular online communities (such as MySpace, Facebook, and Twitter)

- Monitor online blogs, comments, and conversations

Maintain Momentum from FY 2011

To maintain the momentum we gained from FY 2011 and continue building on those efforts, we will address these three key areas:

- **Paid search:** Given the success of the paid search campaigns in FY 2011, we recommend that TropiCo's Tropical Business Group continue optimization at similar spend levels for the Pineapple Company and the Passionfruit Company.

- **Close the loop:** We suggest rolling out a phone call tracking system for the entire Pineapple Company brand that allows detailed, specific tracking of calls. Calls should be tracked from the initial search through to the point where a caller makes an appointment to visit a smoothie bar. This kind of information can help inform paid search and organic search efforts, with the goal of finding the most efficient keyphrases, keywords, and trends in online search.

  The call-tracking system will also be useful in improving the quality of how calls are handled by the individual smoothie bars and how this initial contact can ensure that a caller is more likely to become enrolled.

- **SEO and usability:** We recommend that TropiCo's Tropical Business Group assess the effectiveness of the FY 2011 SEO and usability recommendations. The assessment will identify additional actions that we can take to improve the organic visibility and usability of both websites (scheduled for Q3 FY 2012).

Index

Numbers

37Signal Campfire, 249
37Signal Highrise, 85
301 redirects, 172-173
404 error pages, 163-164

A

A/B testing, 158
accepting cultural differences, 245-246
Accuri Cytometers website, 164-165
ad copy, 209-210
ad groups, 209
advantages of Internet marketing, 3-4
advertising
    in China, 253
    display advertising, 212-214
    in Japan, 254

paid search advertising, 5-6, 10-11, 205-212
    ad copy, 209-210
    ad groups, 209
    common pitfalls, 211-212
    keyword research, 208
    managing, 206-207, 211
    quality scores, 210-211
    search engines as paid search vendors, 206
    in Russia, 254
    in South Korea, 254
AdWords Quality Scores, 210-211
aggregating analytics profile, 247-248
alignment, 127
Alterian SM2, 165
analysis paralysis, 224
analytics. *See* web analytics
annual website maintenance tasks, 167

Applicor, 85
assessing keywords, 111-112
attention analysis, 151-152
attributing leads
    explained, 88
    first-click attribution model, 89
    hybrid approach, 90
    last-click attribution model, 88-89
audience
    company staff, 96
    current customers, 96
    gathering feedback from, 105
    identifying, 94, 97
    job candidates, 96
    listening to, 97-98
    potential customers, 94-96
    speaking your audience's language
        case study: Tutor Time, 113-114

keyword research,
109-110
word market analysis,
110-113
watching, 97-100
website personas
adapting websites to per-
sonas' needs, 105-107
case study: persona-
driven redesign,
107-109
developing, 100-102
sample personas,
102-105
audiences
share of global Internet
audience by region, 240
targeting, 214
automated attention analysis,
151-152

B

Baidu, 251
blogs
best practices, 186
blogging for SEO benefit,
185-186
hosting, 187
boardroom reporting, 234
best practices, 237
comparing against goals,
235-236
comparing against prior
performance, 235
defining good value, 235
providing context for numbers, 234
budgeting, 13
budgeting websites, 173
business analysis, defining
KPIs (key performance indicators) with, 55-56
buying process, 7-8

C

calculating
lifetime value, 228
projected ROI, 65-67
projecting return on con-
version rate optimiza-
tion, 232-233
projecting return on paid
search optimization,
229-232
ROI, 226-228
call to action, 137
call to action methods, 83
call tracking, 82-84, 225
calls to action, 153-154
Campfire, 249
canonical URLs, 197-199
capturing lead sources, 61-62
character sets, 258
Chatter, 249
childcare provider case
study, 17
China, advertising in, 253
choosing keywords, 112-113
clarity, 137
click analytics, 81
ClickTale.com, 156
closing the loop, 38-39
capturing lead sources,
61-62
case study: reviewing customer conversion data in
Salesforce, 63
explained, 60
impact of Internet marking
on sales, 60-61
moving lead data into
CRM, 62
TropiCo case study, 277
CMS (content management
system), 8
Co-Op, 249

cognitive walkthroughs, 155
communication
global team communica-
tions, 248-249
speaking your audience's
language
case study: Tutor Time,
113-114
keyword research,
109-110
word market analysis,
110-113
communications. *See* boardroom reporting
company staff as audience, 96
comparing against
goals, 235-236
prior performance, 235
consent forms, 160
contact methods
case study: landing pages
with custom 800 num-
bers, 60
live chat, 49
mailto links, 47
online contact forms, 48
telephone contacts, 48
content, 12
content management system
(CMS), 8
content performance,
tracking, 79
content team, 169
context, providing for
numbers, 234
contextual ads, 214
contrast, 127
controlled English, 242-243
conversion funnels, 45, 80
conversion rate optimization,
projecting return on, 232-233
conversion rates, improving,
148-149

critical measurements,
determining
conversion funnel, 45
e-commerce businesses, 47
influences on leads and
revenue, 44-45
lead-generation
businesses, 46
CRM (customer relationship
management) systems, 8, 84
explained, 84-85
follow up, 86-87
lead attribution
explained, 88
*first-click attribution
model, 89*
hybrid approach, 90
*last-click attribution
model, 88-89*
lead management case
study, 90-91
lead nurturing, 87
lead scoring, 87
moving lead data into, 62
required input, 85-86
Salesforce.com, 84-85
unifying, 248-249
Crowther, Carla (fictional website persona), 104-105
cultural differences, accepting,
245-246
current customers, 96
custom 800 numbers, 60
custom call to action
methods, 83
customer conversion data,
reviewing in Salesforce, 63
customer relationship management systems. *See* CRM
systems
customer-driven online sales
engine process
increasing visibility, 38
revisiting metrics, 38-39

customers
current customers, 96
designing for, 7
potential customers, 94-96

D

daily website maintenance
tasks, 165
dashboards (web analytics), 73
content performance
data, 79
dashboard assembly, 223
demographic data, 74-76
goal monitoring, 79
traffic source data, 76-78
when to use, 81
data analysis pitfalls, 223. *See
also* web analytics
analysis paralysis, 224
believing data, 225
neglecting seasonality, 224
not considering
phone calls, 225
not following leads to
sale, 225
twitchiness, 224
Daum, 251
decision making, integrating
KPIs (key performance indicators) into, 58-59, 64
defining KPIs (key performance indicators), 55-56
demographic data, 74-76
designing websites. *See* website
design
developing website personas,
100-102
display advertising, 212-214
distractions, reducing, 137

E

e-commerce businesses, 47
e-commerce conversion
rate, 148

e-commerce websites, adapting
for global usability, 259-260
Eloqua, 85
email mailto links, 47
employees as audience, 96
English
controlled English, 242-243
Global English, 244
world-ready English, 245
errors, Page Not Found,
164-165
executive summary (TropiCo
State of the Web report),
264-265
Extensible Markup Language
(XML), 195

F

Facebook, 204-205
feedback, gathering from
audience, 105
files
logfile analysis
sample logfile, 72, 81
*W3C extended logfile
format, 71-72*
robots.txt, 194-195
sitemap.xml, 195-197
firewalls, content hidden
by, 196
first-click lead attribution
model, 89
following web conventions,
149-150
forms
adapting for international
addresses, 258-259
form analytics, 156
online contact forms, 48
optimization, 150-151
frames, 192-193

G

geographic distribution,
  TropiCo State of the Web
  report, 266-267
geographic targets, 254
Global English, 244
global markets, moving
  into, 16
global metrics-driven
  practice, 246
global organic search visibility
    search engines, 250-252
    website top-level
      domains, 252
global paid search
  configuration, 253
    geographic targets, 254
    language issues, 254-256
    regional campaigns,
      253-254
global team communications,
  248-249
global usability
    challenges, 260
    character set issues, 258
    e-commerce websites,
      259-260
    forms, 258-259
    importance of, 261
    local testing, 260-261
    remote testing, 261
    website content, 259
glossaries, 245
goals
    comparing against, 235-236
    maturing
      case study: Happy
        Puppy, 218-219
      case study: TropiCo,
        219-220
    monitoring, 79

Google, 250
    Google AdWords, 65, 111
    Google Analytics, 65, 73
    Google Webmaster Tools,
      152, 197
granularity of landing pages,
  138-139
graphic design, 127-128
graphic designers, 169

H

Happy Puppy case study,
  14-15, 218-219
Harvest Co-Op, 249
Heisenberg uncertainty
  principle, 218
hero shots, 135-136
high-level information architecture, 128-130
Highrise, 85
hosting blogs, 187
hybrid approach to lead
  attribution, 90

I

IA. See information architecture, 118
identifying audience, 94, 97
improving
    conversion rates, 148-149
    user experience. See user
      experience, improving
information architecture
    case study: McKinley.com,
      119-121
    completing, 126
    explained, 118-119
    high-level information
      architecture, 128-130
    information architecture
      process, 120-122

    keyword analysis, 128
    navigation structure, 124
    page layout, 125
    page templates, 131-133
    personas, 128
    research, 122
    scenarios and paths,
      123-124
    testing, 126-127
    website mission, 133
    website skeleton/wireframe,
      122-123
Information Architecture for the
  World Wide Web: Designing
  Large-Scale Web Sites
  (Morville and Rosenfeld), 119
Ingstone, Keith, 153
inlinks, 12
integrating KPIs (key performance indicators) into business
  decision making, 58-59, 64
internal/"soft" costs, 227-228
international organizations
    case study: spidering to
      keep localized websites
      up-to-date
        global metrics-driven
          practice, 246
        web analytics, 247-248
    global organic search
      visibility
        search engines, 250-252
        website top-level
          domains, 252
    global paid search
      configuration
        geographic targets, 254
        language issues, 254-256
        regional campaigns,
          253-254
    global team communica-
      tions, 248-249

global usability
  challenges, 260
  character set issues, 258
  e-commerce websites,
    259-260
  forms, 258-259
  importance of, 261
  local testing, 260-261
  remote testing, 261
  website content, 259
language issues
  accepting cultural differ-
    ences, 245-246
  controlled English,
    242-243
  creating glossaries, 245
  Global English, 244
  preparing websites for
    translation and local-
    ization, 244
  translators and localiza-
    tion experts, 241-242
  world-ready English, 245
share of global Internet
  audience by region, 240
silo issues, 240
time zones, 256-257
triage for international disorientation, 240-241
unifying CRM or SFA
  process, 248-249
Internet research, impact on
  internet sales, 2-3

J-K

Japan, advertising in, 254
job candidates, 96
KarmaCRM, 85
key performance indicators.
  See KPIs
keyphrase rank, 51-52

keywords, 9-10, 190-191
  assessing, 111-112
  choosing, 112-113
  keyword analysis, 128
  keyword tools, 111
  researching, 109-110, 208
KPIs (key performance
  indicators)
  defining, 55-56
  definition of, 44
  integrating into business
    decision making, 58-59
  KPI reporting on leads and
    sales, 64
  paid search KPIs
    paid-search traffic and
      on-site outcomes, 53-54
    secondary paid search
      metrics, 54-55
  quantity versus quality,
    64-65
  SEO KPIs, 50
    off-site metrics, 51-52
    on-site metrics, 51
    secondary SEO metrics,
      52-53
Krug, Steve, 161

L

landing pages
  custom 800 numbers, 60
  designing, 133-134
    call to action, 137
    clarity, 137
    clear copy, 135
    design cycle, 138
    granularity, 138-139
    hero shots, 135-136
    offers, 137
    reinforcing offer, 134
  maintaining, 139-140
  optimizing, 140-144
  user research, 142-143

language issues, 241
  accepting cultural differ-
    ences, 245-246
  character set issues, 258
  controlled English, 242-243
  creating glossaries, 245
  Global English, 244
  global paid search configu-
    ration, 254-256
  preparing websites for
    translation and localiza-
    tion, 244
  speaking your audience's
    language
    case study: Tutor Time,
      113-114
    keyword research,
      109-110
    word market analysis,
      110-113
  translators and localization
    experts, 241-242
  world-ready English, 245
last-click lead attribution
  model, 88-89
lead-generation businesses, 46
lead-generation conversion
  funnel, 80
leads, 225
  attribution
    explained, 88
    first-click attribution
      model, 89
    hybrid approach, 90
    last-click attribution
      model, 88-89
  capturing lead sources,
    61-62
  influences on, 44-45
  lead generation conversion
    rate, 148
  lead management case
    study, 90-91
  moving lead data into
    CRM, 62

nurturing, 87
scoring, 87
TropiCo State of the Web report, 268
lifetime value, 228
link building, 200-201
listening to audience, 97-98
live chat, 49
local business listings, 202-203
local search, TropiCo case study, 278-279
local testing, 260-261
localization issues, 241-246
logfile analysis
  sample logfile, 72, 81
  W3C extended logfile format, 71-72

M

mailto links, 47
maintaining websites, 162
  annual tasks, 167
  monthly tasks, 166
  quarterly tasks, 166-167
  SEO (search engine optimization), 167, 173-174
  weekly/daily tasks, 165
managing paid search advertising, 206-207, 211
manufacturing company case study, 16-17
marketing metrics, 169, 221-222
Marketo, 85
maturing goals
  case study: Happy Puppy, 218-219
  case study: TropiCo, 219-220
McKinley.com, 119-121
media files
  tagging with keywords, 190-191

when to use, 191-192
metadata, 188-189
metrics, 5
  case study: landing pages with custom 800 numbers, 60
  closing the loop, 38-39
    capturing lead sources, 61-62
    case study: reviewing customer conversion data in Salesforce, 63
    explained, 60
    impact of Internet marking on sales, 60-61
    moving lead data into CRM, 62
  contact methods
    live chat, 49
    mailto links, 47
    online contact forms, 48
    telephone contacts, 48
  critical measurements, determining
    conversion funnel, 45
    e-commerce businesses, 47
    influences on leads and revenue, 44-45
    lead-generation businesses, 46
  explained, 43-44
  global metrics-driven practice, 246
  KPIs (key performance indicators)
    defining, 55-56
    definition of, 44
    integrating into business decision making, 58-59
    KPI reporting on leads and sales, 64
    paid search KPIs, 53-55

quantity versus quality, 64-65
    SEO KPIs, 50-53
  marketing metrics, 221-222
  projected ROI, calculating, 65-67
  sales metrics, 222
  what to measure, 49-50
  when to measure, 56-58
microsites, 194
minimizing visitor wait time, 152
moderating tests, 160-161
monitoring goals, 79
monthly website maintenance tasks, 166
Morville, Peter, 119
multimedia
  tagging with keywords, 190-191
  when to use, 191-192

N

Naver, 251
navigation stress test, 153
navigation structure, 124
NetSuite, 85
NetVibes, 165
The Non-Designers Design Book (Williams), 127
nurturing leads, 87

O

off-site metrics, 51-52
Omniture SiteCatalyst, 73
on-site metrics, 51
online contact forms, 48
online reviews, 203-204
online sales engine, 5-7
  customer-driven process
    increasing visibility, 38
    revisiting metrics, 38-39

ROI-driven implementation process, 39-40
online visibility. *See* visibility
optimizing
  forms, 150-151
  landing pages, 140-144
  SEO (search engine optimization). *See* SEO (search engine optimization)
organic search. *See* SEO (search engine optimization)
organizational silos, removing, 8

P

page layout, 125
Page Not Found errors, tracking, 164-165
page templates, 131-133
page-level SEO (search engine optimization), 181-185
paid search advertising, 5-6, 10-11, 205-212
  ad copy, 209-210
  ad groups, 209
  common pitfalls, 211-212
  keyword research, 208
  KPIs (key performance indicators)
    paid search traffic and on-site outcomes, 53-54
    secondary paid search metrics, 54-55
  managing, 206-207, 211
  quality scores, 210-211
  search engines as paid search vendors, 206
  TropiCo case study, 270-274
paths to website content, 105-107, 123

pay per click (PPC), 6
personas, 128
  adapting websites to personas' needs, 105-107
  case study: persona-driven redesign, 107-109
  developing, 100-102
  sample personas, 102-105
phone calls, tracking, 82-84
pilot tests, 233-234
planning websites
  annual tasks, 167
  monthly tasks, 166
  planning for failure, 162-165
  quarterly tasks, 166-167
  SEO (search engine optimization), 167, 173-174
  tracking Page Not Found errors, 164-165
  weekly/daily tasks, 165
Plex, 85
potential customers, 94-96
PPC (pay per click), 6
prelaunch checklist (websites), 171-172
prior performance, comparing against, 235
project goals. *See* goals
project managers, 169
projected ROI, calculating, 65-67
  projecting return on conversion rate optimization, 232-233
  projecting return on paid search optimization, 229-232
proximity, 127
puppy accessories interview questions, 98

Q

quality scores, 210-211
quantitative user research
  A/B testing, 158
  form analytics, 156
quarterly website maintenance tasks, 166-167

R

radian6, 165
reading level, 154
recruiting test participants, 160
redesigning websites
  301 redirects, 172-173
  budgeting, 173
  prelaunch checklist, 171-172
  project roles, 168-171
referral media, TropiCo case study, 279-280
regional campaigns, 253-254
relaunching websites
  301 redirects, 172-173
  budgeting, 173
  prelaunch checklist, 171-172
  project roles, 168-171
remote testing, 261
removing organizational silos, 8
repetition, 127
reporting. *See* boardroom reporting
research, user research
  A/B testing, 158
  form analytics, 156
  surveys, 155-156
researching keywords, 109-110
retargeted ads, 214
return on investment. *See* ROI
revenue, influences on, 44-45

reviews, online reviews, 203-204

rewarding test participants, 160

robots.txt file, 194-195

Rocket Surgery Made Easy: The Do-It-Yourself Guide to Finding and Fixing Usability Problems (Krug), 161

ROI (return on investment), 226

    calculating, 226-228

    internal/"soft" costs, 227-228

    lifetime value, 228

    projected ROI

        projecting return on conversion rate optimization, 232-233

        projecting return on paid search optimization, 229-232

    when to track, 228-229

ROI-driven implementation process, 39-40

Rosenfeld, Louis, 119

Russia, advertising in, 254

S

sales

    impact of Internet marketing on, 60-61

    impact of Internet research on, 2-3

sales force automation (SFA), 84. *See also* CRM systems

sales metrics, 222

Salesforce.com, 63, 84-85

Salesforce.com: Secrets of Success (Taber), 84, 248

SAP, 85

scenarios, 123-124

scoring leads, 87

script-based tracking, 71

search engine optimization. *See* SEO

search engine results pages (SERPs), 179-181

search engines, 206, 250-252

seasonality, 224

secondary paid search metrics, 54-55

secondary SEO metrics, 52-53

SEO (search engine optimization), 6, 167, 173-174

    blogging for SEO benefit, 185-187

    canonical URLs, 197-199

    content hidden by firewalls, 196

    frames, 192-193

    global organic search visibility

        search engines, 250-252

        website top-level domains, 252

    global paid search configuration

        geographic targets, 254

        language issues, 254-256

        regional campaigns, 253-254

    KPIs (key performance indicators), 50

        off-site metrics, 51-52

        on-site metrics, 51

        secondary SEO metrics, 52-53

    link building, 200-201

    media files, 190-192

    metadata, 188-189

    microsites, 194

    page-level SEO, 181-185

    projecting return on

        organic search optimization, 232

        paid search optimization, 229-231

    robots.txt file, 194-195

    search engine results pages (SERPs), 179-181

    sitemaps, 195-197

    TropiCo case study, 274-275

    web technologies and, 190

    widgets, 193

SERPs (search engine results pages), 179-181

SFA (sales force automation), 84, 248-249. *See also* CRM systems

silos

    analyzing data from multiple silos, 221

    issues with international organizations, 240

    removing, 8

SilverPop, 85

Site Performance tool, 152

sitemap.xml file, 195-197

sitemaps, 195-197

size of websites, 11

small business safety, 12-13

social media, 38, 204-205

"soft" costs, 227-228

software company case study, 17-18

South Korea, advertising in, 254

speaking your audience's language

    case study: Tutor Time, 113-114

    keyword research, 109-110

    word market analysis, 110-113

spidering to keep localized websites up-to-date, 246

Stackhouse, Paul (fictional website persona), 102-103

State of the Web report (TropiCo), 263

    Executive Summary, 264-265

    Part I. The Year in Review

        general traffic trends, 265-266

geographic distribution, 266-267

quarterly leads trends, 268

traffic sources, 267-268

Part II. How It Happened, 269-270

local search, 278-279

paid search, 270-274

referral media, 279-280

search engine optimization, 274-275

strategy, analysis, and reporting, 276-277

usability, 275-276

Part III. Looking Forward to 2012, 280-281

table of contents, 264

success story case studies

childcare provider increases web conversions, 17

major software company grows sales, 17-18

manufacturing company improves sales, 16-17

moving into new global markets, 16

surveys, 155-156

T

Taber, David, 84, 248

technical team, 169

telephone contacts, 48, 60

templates, 131-133

testers, 169

testing

A/B testing, 158

global usability

local testing, 260-261

remote testing, 261

information architecture, 126-127

pilot tests, 233-234

usability testing, 158-159

acting on results, 161

moderating tests, 160-161

recruiting and rewards, 160

user research techniques, 159

time zones, 256-257

TLDs (top-level domains), 252

top-level domains (TLDs), 252

tracking

content performance, 79

demographic data, 74-76

Page Not Found errors, 164-165

phone calls, 82-84, 225

traffic sources, 76-78

traffic sources

tracking, 76-78

TropiCo case study, 267-268

traffic trends, TropiCo case study, 265-266

translation, preparing websites for, 244, 258

translators, 241-242

Trellian Keyword Discovery, 111

triage for international disorientation, 240-241

TropiCo

goals, maturing, 219-220

State of the Web report, 263

Executive Summary, 264-265

Part I. The Year in Review, 265-268

Part II. How It Happened, 269-270

local search, 278-279

paid search, 270-274

referral media, 279-280

search engine optimization, 274-275

strategy, analysis, and reporting, 276-277

usability, 275-276

Part III. Looking Forward to 2012, 280-281

table of contents, 264

TropiCo case study, 15

Tutor Time case study, 113-114

twitchiness, 224

Twitter, 204-205

U

unifying CRM or SFA process, 248-249

Urchin, 73

URLs, canonical, 197-199

usability testing, 158-159

acting on results, 161

moderating tests, 160-161

recruiting and rewards, 160

TropiCo case study, 275-276

user research techniques, 159

user experience, improving, 148-149

best practices

attention analysis, 151-152

calls to action, 153-154

cognitive walk-throughs, 155

form optimization, 150-151

reading level, 154

visitor wait time, 152

web conventions, 149-150

usability testing, 158-159

acting on results, 161

moderating tests, 160-161

recruiting and
    rewards, 160
user research
    techniques, 159
user research
    A/B testing, 158
    form analytics, 156
    surveys, 155-156
    UX checklist, 161-162
user research
    A/B testing, 158
    for landing pages, 142-143
    form analytics, 156
    surveys, 155-156
user research techniques, 159
user researchers, 168
UX checklist, 161-162
UX designers, 168

V

value, 235
visibility, 38, 178
    display advertising, 38,
        212-214
    local business listings,
        202-203
    online reviews, 203-204
    paid search advertising,
        5-6, 10-11, 205-212
        ad copy, 209-210
        ad groups, 209
        common pitfalls,
            211-212
        keyword research, 208
        managing, 206-207, 211
        quality scores, 210-211
        search engines as paid
            search vendors, 206
    search engine results pages
        (SERPs), 179-181
    SEO (search engine opti-
        mization), 6
        blogging for SEO benefit,
            185-187

canonical URLs, 197-199
content hidden by fire-
    walls, 196
frames, 192-193
link building, 200-201
media files, 190-192
metadata, 188-189
microsites, 194
page-level SEO, 181-185
robots.txt file, 194-195
search engine results
    pages (SERPs), 179-181
sitemaps, 195-197
web technologies
    and, 190
widgets, 193
social media, 38, 204-205
web spiders, 178-179
visitor wait time,
    minimizing, 152
visitors. See web visitors

W

W3C extended logfile format,
    71-72
wait time, minimizing, 152
watching audience, 97-100
web analytics
    aggregating analytics pro-
        file, 247-248
    click analytics, 81
    data analysis pitfalls, 223
        analysis paralysis, 224
        believing data, 225
        neglecting seasonality, 224
        not considering phone
            calls, 225
        not following leads to
            sale, 225
        twitchiness, 224
    data from multiple silos, 221
    demographic data, 74-76
    explained, 70

for international organiza-
    tions, 247-248
logfile analysis
    sample logfile, 72
    W3C extended logfile
        format, 71-72
    when to use, 81
marketing metrics, 221-222
sales metrics, 222
script-based tracking, 71
TropiCo case study,
    276-277
web analytics dash-
    boards, 73
    content performance
        data, 79
    dashboard assembly, 223
    demographic data, 74-76
    goal monitoring, 79
    traffic source data, 76-78
    when to use, 81
web conventions, 149-150
web spiders, 178-179, 194-195
web visitors
    gathering demographic
        data about, 74-76
    traffic sources, 76-78
website audience. See audience
website budgets, 13
website content
    adapting for global
        usability, 259
    paths to, 105-107
website design, 12-13
    content, 12
    graphic design, 127-128
    information architecture
        case study:
            McKinley.com, 119-121
        completing, 126
        explained, 118-119
        high-level information
            architecture, 128-130

information architecture process, 120-122

keyword analysis, 128

navigation structure, 124

page layout, 125

page templates, 131-133

personas, 128

research, 122

scenarios and paths, 123-124

testing, 126-127

website mission, 133

website skeleton/wireframe, 122-123

landing pages

designing, 133-138

granularity, 138-139

maintaining, 139-140

optimizing, 140-144

user research, 142-143

planning and maintenance

annual tasks, 167

monthly tasks, 166

planning for failure, 162-165

quarterly tasks, 166-167

tracking Page Not Found errors, 164-165

weekly/daily tasks, 165

SEO (search engine optimization), 167, 173-174

size, 11

user experience. *See* user experience, improving

website redesign/relaunch, 168

301 redirects, 172-173

budgeting, 173

prelaunch checklist, 171-172

project roles, 168-171

website metrics. *See* metrics

website mission, 133

website personas

adapting websites to personas' needs, 105-107

case study: persona-driven redesign, 107-109

developing, 100-102

sample personas, 102-105

website prelaunch checklist, 171-172

website skeleton, developing, 122-123

website top-level domains, 252

website visibility. *See* visibility

weekly website maintenance tasks, 165

widgets, 193

Williams, Robin, 127

wireframe, developing, 122-123

word market analysis, 110-113

WordPress, 12

WordStream, 111

WordTracker, 111

world-ready English, 245

X-Y-Z

XML (Extensible Markup Language), 195

Yahoo!, 251-252

Yahoo! Web Analytics, 73-74

Yammer, 249

Yandex, 251

year in review (TropiCo State of the Web report), 265

general traffic trends, 265-266

geographic distribution, 266-267

quarterly leads trends, 268

traffic sources, 267-268

QUEPUBLISHING.COM
Your Publisher for Home & Office Computing

Quepublishing.com includes all your favorite—and some new—Que series and authors to help you learn about computers and technology for the home, office, and business.

Looking for tips and tricks, video tutorials, articles and interviews, podcasts, and resources to make your life easier? Visit **quepublishing.com**.

- **Read the latest articles and sample chapters** by Que's expert authors

- **Free podcasts** provide information on the hottest tech topics

- **Register your Que products** and receive updates, supplemental content, and a coupon to be used on your next purchase

- **Check out promotions and special offers** available from Que and our retail partners

- **Join the site** and receive members-only offers and benefits

QUE NEWSLETTER
quepublishing.com/newsletter

 twitter.com/
quepublishing

 facebook.com/
quepublishing

 youtube.com/
quepublishing

 quepublishing.com/
rss

 Que Publishing is a publishing imprint of Pearson

FREE Online Edition

Your purchase of **Internet Marketing Start to Finish** includes access to a free online edition for 45 days through the Safari Books Online subscription service. Nearly every Que book is available online through Safari Books Online, along with more than 5,000 other technical books and videos from publishers such as Addison-Wesley Professional, Cisco Press, Exam Cram, IBM Press, O'Reilly, Prentice Hall, and Sams.

SAFARI BOOKS ONLINE allows you to search for a specific answer, cut and paste code, download chapters, and stay current with emerging technologies.

Activate your FREE Online Edition at
www.informit.com/safarifree

> **STEP 1:** Enter the coupon code: XXMRUWA

> **STEP 2:** New Safari users, complete the brief registration form. Safari subscribers, just log in.

If you have difficulty registering on Safari or accessing the online edition, please e-mail customer-service@safaribooksonline.com

2408262